RESISTING JIM CROW:
THE AUTOBIOGRAPHY OF
DR. JOHN A. MCFALL

Dr. John A. McFall, circa 1940s when he wrote this autobiography

Resisting Jim Crow

The Autobiography of Dr. John A. McFall

Edited by Lahnice McFall Hollister

KITTAWAH PRESS LLC
KITTAWAHPRESS.COM
SIMPSONVILLE, SC

Editorial and design services provided by
Modern Memoirs, Inc.
www.modernmemoirs.com

Lauren Nivens Creative
www.lnivens.myportfolio.com

Cover design: Karen Powell
www.powelldesign.com

ISBN: 978-1-7376813-1-1
LCCN: 2021918547

To Mother

Whatever she commanded was complied with,
whether I liked it or not,
and so whatever I am is due largely to her.

Dr. John A. McFall

CONTENTS

FOREWORD

Publishing the autobiography of Dr. John A. McFall, the brother of my much-loved grandfather, Paul McFall, is not ancestor worship. It is published by necessity given the lack of African American voices within history books.

John McFall was born in Charleston, South Carolina in 1878—the year after the disputed gubernatorial election that marked the end of Reconstruction in the state. He was the first of eleven children born to a Black couple and was among the first generation born in freedom in South Carolina. By the time he reached manhood, African American men were being disenfranchised and all Black people were essentially designated second-class citizens. He tasked himself with resisting the Jim Crow laws that were crippling the political and economic strides women and men of African descent had made in the first decade after Emancipation. He died in 1954—two months after the Supreme Court issued its landmark decision in the *Brown v. Board of Education* school desegregation case on May 17th of that year. This volume contains Dr. McFall's never-before-published manuscript in which he eloquently reports on events between those milestones.

Much has been written about the cruelties and the violence in the Jim Crow South. Dr. McFall's first-person account provides "bricks" and "mortar" to assemble a more comprehensive view of this nation's past. He makes this history personal by offering his account of how legalized racial segregation was infused into a Southern city. He tells about growing up in a tightly knit family, playing on Charleston streets and waterways, and attending Charleston schools. As a future pharmacist working his way through college in Philadelphia, John was told that his color barred him from jobs for which he was qualified.

Upon earning a Doctor of Pharmacy degree from the Philadelphia College of Pharmacy and returning home, he encountered similar challenges faced by other Black Charlestonians. Being intelligent and law-abiding were not enough. He was male and he was over twenty-one.

But he was not white.

Therefore, he was not entitled to even the common courtesy of being called Mister or Doctor by any white person, whether man, woman, or child. Dr. McFall met adversity head-on. He insisted on this courtesy for himself and others in the Black community as he navigated the color line and the white power structure. His defeats and victories provide insight into Black agency occurring in Charleston and other urban areas with imbedded, state-sponsored segregation.

I transcribed this manuscript from a digitized copy of the microfilm preserved in the John W. Work III Papers at the Special Collections and Archives of the John Hope and Aurelia E. Franklin Library at Fisk University. That media was at times hard to read and to navigate. This version was created by retyping the entire manuscript. Capitalization, punctuation and spellings were edited for consistency. Illegible text and transcription comments are bracketed [ ]. Headings, a table of contents, an index, and photos were also added. Otherwise, Dr. McFall's original text is unchanged. Researchers are encouraged to consult the files at Fisk.

Dr. John A. McFall's civic activity is also recognized in the following books:

> Baker, R. Scott. *Paradoxes of Desegregation: African American Struggles for Educational Equity in Charleston, South Carolina, 1926-1972*. University of South Carolina Press, 2006.

> Drago, Edmund. *Initiative, Paternalism, and Race Relations: Charleston's Avery Normal Institute*. University of Georgia Press, 1990.

Lau, Peter F. *Democracy Rising: South Carolina and the Fight for Black Equality Since 1865.* University Press of Kentucky, 2015.

Morna Lahnice McFall Hollister
Simpsonville, South Carolina
June 2021

PREFACE BY JOHN A. MCFALL

My children have often expressed the wish that I would write the story of my life and its experiences, both personal and public, and to record therewith something about the life and civic activities of the Negro group in Charleston during my time. In compliance with their wish, I give them this narrative. None of it is for publication, as it is written solely with a desire of giving them pleasure, information and perhaps a clearer understanding of the reasons behind some of my acts, especially those concerned with the Charleston Mutual Savings Bank. In recounting these events, I have relied entirely upon memory as I have no other records to draw upon, which makes me mindful of what has often been said of memory—that it is fickle and cannot be relied upon. Perhaps there is some truth in that statement, since time, in its ever-changing cycles, may minimize or may exaggerate the importance of earlier events. This possibility has been kept in mind, and so I have sought to avoid mere conjecture whenever or wherever supporting evidence was lacking. Instead of presenting merely a chronicle of passing events, I have endeavored to associate them with the environmental surroundings of their time, especially the economic, political, social and religious ones—a good bit of which I knew from personal experience and some that were a part of the customs, traditions and mode of life that were prevalent during my early life.

I use this pattern because I believe that it alone can give a clear picture of the advancements that had taken place within the Negro group in Charleston during the first twenty-five years following the emancipation, and also to present a later picture that had its beginning depiction in the rising flow of

Tillmanism[1] which enveloped Charleston in 1895 and which, with the support of the United States Supreme Court decisions, deprived the Negroes of their political rights, fostered ill will between the races and ultimately succeeded in seriously impairing the Negroes' economic status.

1 An agrarian movement led by Governor Ben Tillman (1890–1918) characterized by white supremacy and violence against Black people.

Early Years

I was born fifteen years after Lincoln signed the Emancipation Proclamation, from ancestry which fades into the usages and customs of slavery. We have a photograph of my great-grandfather, on Father's side, "Ancestor" we named him. And from him down to my grandchildren are six generations who bear or have borne the name McFall. On Mother's side there is the recollection of my great-grandmother and the more intimate grandmother who never spoke about the days of her enslavement, but who was brave enough to leave her rural home in upper South Carolina and move away to begin life anew, bringing with her, her mother and her children, Mary Ann, Henry, Paul, Lizzie and Charlotte. Perhaps she was also accompanied by other relatives for when she ultimately reached Charleston, after living a while near Summerville, in the Bacons Bridge area, there around a number of "cousins" whose relationship is more or less vague. Among them being Cousin Mary Ann Green, Cousin Bella and even more remote than them was one who gave rise to a "brass ankle"[2] clan at Bacons Bridge.

Grandmother McFall's ancestry is likewise hidden in the annals of the slave regime of a plantation on the Sampit River

---

2   In Dr. McFall's time, a tri-racial group of people with European, African, and Native American ancestry.

near Georgetown and in the myth like stories that my father would tell about the old plantation. There was one that described a huge iron cauldron in which [illegible] food was cooked for the slave children on the plantation and that its size was such that more than a hundred children could be fed from it. And another about the family cemetery in which were interred all of the dead, both black and white, with its central walkway, at the head of which the old patriarch was buried, and that facing him to the right were the graves of his children with tombstones designating them, "my white son—or daughter, and to the left, tombstones designating "Colored son—or daughter." Perhaps it was more than mere myth, for Grandmother McFall, whose maiden name was Henrietta Alston, had been carefully reared and could read and write. She was a devoted Bible student and when she came to Charleston brought with her, her Bible, which is now in my possession. It is a copy of the sixth edition of the Bible published by the English College at Rhemes in 1582, revised and printed according to the clementine edition by James Reilly at Dublin in 1794. When I was nine years of age she presented me with a copy of *Pilgrim's Progress* and a year later with a copy of *Millennium Dawn* an esoteric work that predicted the end of time, much of which she read and explained to me but none of which I understood or cared for. Her photograph taken on glass sometime during the 1840s show her to be a rather striking personality, [illegible] poise and beauty. I do not know the year of her marriage to Grandfather Joseph McFall but it must have been about that time as her oldest son, John Allen, after whom I was named, enlisted and served in the U.S. Navy during the Civil War.

Grandfather McFall had several brothers, one named Guy settled in Charleston and there was one who went to Savannah, Georgia. The others have been lost to memory in the general dispersion that followed the Civil War.

Grandfather and Grandmother McFall had six sons, John Allen, Thomas Alston, Cornelius, Joseph, Barney and Edward.

Grandfather McFall was a painter by trade and followed that vocation during his life. His eldest son, John Allen went to Philadelphia after the Civil War and settled there. Cornelius became a barber and resided in Charleston. Joseph was a cotton sampler but on the death of the cotton business in Charleston found employment as a waiter. Barney was a tinner and sheet metal worker but died in the early 1890s. Edward, the youngest of them was a painter and paper hanger whose adventures defy depiction. He roamed far and wide in these United States and ultimately came home to die. And thereby hangs a tale, for Edward was once a dependable worker but in his early youth he went to Philadelphia and there acquired fame as a freak bicycle rider by establishing a time record for speed on a bicycle over a railroad trestle bridge near Darby, Pennsylvania, for which he received several trophy cups. He returned to Charleston but having lost his zest for work, soon converted his trophies and several of Grandmother McFall's antique heirlooms into cash that he could live the life of Riley, or that of a philanderer.

It was his fortune, whether good or ill no one knows, to have been passing the Old Bethel Church graveyard one night when a pistol shot rang out. Edward investigated and saw a man and a woman run from the cemetery and enter a building nearby. He entered the cemetery and found the corpse of a man lying there and near it a woman's handkerchief which he appropriated. A few days later a Pinkerton detective contacted him and took him to a local hotel. After staying there a couple of days Edward disappeared from Charleston, going to Jacksonville, Florida. An anxious but much richer man, leaving behind him an unsolved murder that remains a mystery to this day.[3]

From Jacksonville he went to New York and married a girl by the name of Martha Cox who owned two lots in Astoria,

---

3 "Still Hidden in Mystery: Little Light Shed on the Pinckney Killing," *The [Charleston] Evening Post*, 7 May, 1899, p.8. col. 2–3.

Long Island near where the Williamsburg Bridge now at [illegible]. About a year later he showed up. Martha had found solace [illegible] from Charleston with whom he resided until the horrendous earthquake and fled where he went and established himself as a plumber and pipe fitter. Shortly thereafter his [illegible] him there and life progressed smoothly until he found new charms with new friends for whom he abandoned his racial identity and also his "cousin." He and his newly acquired friends moved to the state of Washington to engage in farming. While there he learned about the proposal to build the Williamsburg Bridge. His thoughts immediately returned to Martha and her two lots and created visions of wealth in which he could share if he could find Martha. Ultimately, he found her in Philadelphia and sought a reconciliation but it seems that during the years of his absence that Martha was unable to pay the annual taxes on the lots and so they had been sold at tax sale. Edward now was in somewhat of a dilemma for it seems that his newfound friends, the Coffeys, had financed his trip to the East and now were seriously and insistently demanding information about the progress of the sale. [Illegible] Martha's lots he had promised them a share of the profits. In the meanwhile, his abandoned "cousin" was trailing him with frequent letters demanding the return to her domicile. Martha though willing to be reconciled refrained from that until he could give her a plausible excuse for his long absence.

He sought refuge from his dilemma by coming to Charleston purportedly with $3,000.00 which no one ever saw, to while away the time until New York lots could be sold. One night he suffered a heart attack and died. I was called to the house to consult about his funeral arrangements. One of my uncles had gone through his wallet and counted $107.06 and said a portion of the expense could be paid with that. I looked across at [four lines illegible]. Internment save what was defrayed by his worldly goods to the extent of $7.00. We are not a superstitious family, but on the day of Edward's funeral, the horses in one of the carriages in which my sisters Laura, Ella, Thomasina and Lizzie were riding, ran away, tearing through Mill Street into Rutledge Avenue and there collided with a telephone wire pole, breaking it in two the [upper] portion of which fell across the top of the carriage, but being upheld by the wires only laid there. The horses had broken loose from the carriage leaving it a wreck [with the] fainting hysterical girls inside. It was many months before Ella recovered from the shock. And though as I have said, we were not superstitious, yet the facial expression on each of us evidenced the unspoken thought that Edward was still causing trouble.

Charleston from the Old Order to the New: Reconstruction to Jim Crow

The environment in which my parents, their relatives and neighbors lived during the two decades immediately following the emancipation was one in which the old order, that of the slave system, was being translated into a new order, one in which personal freedom [and the] rights of citizenship pertained. It should be remembered that the status of the American Negro was not clearly defined until the amendments that endowed him with the rights of citizenship were enacted. Until then he was merely the flotsam and jetsam on the waves of American life. Now that his status had been established there followed the herculean task of attaining the standards of American citizenship. It was one in which progress was necessarily slow since so much was involved in the process. The customs of slavery had to be erased from the minds of both the Negro and the whites, and this required time since the traditions that slavery had impressed upon the Negro during his two-hundred-and-fifty years of bondage could not be erased in the twinkling of an eye. With the whites it was a far simpler process for it was largely only an economic problem, the transition from a system of slave labor to one of free competitive labor. But to the ex-slave it involved many more problems, for in addition to the erasure of the slave complex and the earning of a livelihood under competitive methods, was the establishment and maintenance of a home and the firmer establishment of the family institution. Though the latter had had some degree of acquiescence under the slave regime, it operated solely within the exigencies of slavery, the right to sell a chattel. And so separation of slave families were frequent. There was also the mixed family—where the female slave became the mother of children by her owner.

At the time of emancipation a majority of the Negroes in Charleston were enmeshed in the toils of these situations and also that of being nameless individuals for as slaves were merely human chattel, designated as my "slave ---" without benefit of surname. This however was but a minor obstacle for the ex-slave simply took the name that appealed to him, though usually it was that of the owner of the plantation on which he formerly lived.

Since the "family institution" allowed slaves had a financial value in proportion to the fecundity of the "family," it was often a directed relationship in which the slaves had no choice and so in large measure is the responsibility for many of the later separations that occurred among these so-called families. Despite these handicaps the Charleston ex-slave quickly adapted their lives to purer marital relationship with benediction from the church.

Their religious affiliations had long been established, for the white church had ordained such. Education however was limited. Among the former free Negroes it was common and many slaves could read and write but the vast majority could not. By 1867 a number of public and mission schools were in operation under the direction of teaching corps that were diligent and conscientious in their efforts to instruct the ex-slaves.

There was however in the meanwhile a temporary halt given to the Negroes' march of progress, for shortly after Lincoln's assassination, his successor in office, President Andrew Johnson issued a proclamation appointing Benjamin F. Perry Provisional Governor for South Carolina and directed him to call a convention of white voters, as provided for in an earlier proclamation, and have that convention amend the constitution of the state and elect its usual officers and representatives to the Congress. The amended constitution as adopted included those sections known as the "black code" with [which] virtually re-enslaved all Negroes, both former freemen and ex-slaves. For it restricted Negro labor to agricultural pursuits and barred them from other vocations except upon payment of high annual license fees, from all of which whites were exempted. It also prevented the migration into the state of Negroes who could essay the role of educators or leaders, except when a bond of not less than $1,000.00 was posted with a county official as a guarantee for good behavior or against becoming a public charge, with the right to the authorities to administer punishment by imprisonment or by lash and deportation from the state should their conduct or activities be deemed reprehensible by the authorities.

The viciousness and intent of this legislation provoked Congress for if allowed to stand it would have contradicted in entirety the victory of the Union armies and make meaningless the Emancipation Proclamation. Congress retaliated by the enactment of the second Reconstruction Bill and the appointment of a Military Governor for the state. This was quickly followed by enactments of the amendments to the federal Constitution which gave the Negro the unrestricted rights of citizenship.

Under the military governorship an election was held for the purpose of electing members to a Constitutional convention. This convention was duly convened. Its membership comprised Negroes, poor whites, whites with Republican party fealty and some ex-Confederates and resulted in the drafting of a new constitution for the state under which all of its people, Negroes and whites alike, shared equally in its rights, privileges and benefits.

It provided for a public system of education, not merely that of elementary training but also for higher education of Negroes and whites together at the University of South Carolina.

The public school system in Charleston provided separate schools for Negroes and for whites. The Shaw Memorial Society of Boston erected the Shaw Memorial School on Mary Street as a memorial to Col. Robert S. Shaw, the gallant commander of the 54th Massachusetts regiment, which had fought so gallantly at the battle of Fort Wagner on Morris Island, across the bay from Charleston. In its agreement with the City Board of School Commissioners, the Society exacted that at least two of the teachers employed at Shaw be Negroes and that the school be supported by public funds. A second school, the Morris Street School, previously used by whites was also set apart for Negroes. These schools had a combined accommodation for 1,000 pupils and were in operation in 1868.

Their families, with the exception of two Negro teachers at Shaw School consisted of whites and under the guidance and direction of Mr. Henry P. Archer, a gentleman of extremely high qualities both as an educator and as a friend to mankind, made splendid progress. Many of the white teachers were from prominent local families and gave faithful service, and I may add from personal knowledge, taught with a degree of kindness and patience that could not be excelled.

The initiation of the educational program and the exercise of governmental authority by the new Republican party provoked a silent revolution among the ex-slave owners and resulted in the organization of the Ku Klux Klan, a secret organization that had as its main objective the intimidation and killing of Negroes who sought to exercise the rights of freemen and the rights inherently theirs under the Constitution.

The Klan was especially active in the upper part of the state. My grandmother who resided in the Yorkville area for some time after emancipation had personal knowledge of some of their activities and told me of several incidents. The white robes they wore and also draped their horses with, she said, was donned for the purpose of having the ex-slaves believe that the wearers were the ghosts of ex-Confederate soldiers, who had returned to take vengeance on the Negroes, hoping thus to instill in them a fear of the supernatural.

Negroes who accepted positions of leadership were singled out for killing. She told of a raid that was made on a little settlement near her home. It was known as "Free Issue Town" where a few free Negroes had their homes before emancipation. A meeting was planned at a church there but one of its members, who was employed by an old white physician in Yorkville, was told by her employer to remain at home and not attend that meeting. Reasoning that raid on "Free Issue Town" was imminent, she got word to the members of the church that such might happen. The Negroes prepared themselves for the attack and laid an ambush by a bridge over which the Klan had to pass, and when the Klan arrived they opened fire, killing several of the raiders. The Klan, she said, always carried their dead away and buried them secretly at night that the Negroes would remain in ignorance of their death.

I have seen it authoritatively stated that the Klan killed over eight-hundred Negroes in South Carolina during its activities. The federal government sent a troop of cavalry to the Yorkville section under command of Captain Custer, the same who died in Sitting Bull's massacre, to put down the Klan. My grandmother knew him well for she was his laundress. She described the results of one raid, in which she said the troops brought the captured Klansmen in tied to their horse tails.

Though Madodo never told it, I always felt that her reason for moving from Yorkville was her fear of the Klan.

The success of the Klan in instilling fear and intimidation among the ex-slaves is beyond doubt for in addition to the killing of more than eight hundred Negroes they destroyed hundreds of homes and barns. Their greatest success however was in checking a movement that had begun in 1865 among ex-Confederates to migrate en masse to Brazil, where one or two had already gone. A temporary halt to the movement followed Wade Hampton's[4] plea that it be postponed for a while. After which it was forgotten.

The desire to leave South Carolina was also prevalent among Negroes. But with them, it was back to Africa. The land of their birth where remoteness from the whites would give personal safety if nothing more. Several had previously gone to Liberia at the expense of the African Colonization Society and though little was known in South Carolina about the success of the enterprise it held an attraction for many. Several groups left Charleston for Monrovia but many returned preferring the hardships and difficulties of life in America to those they found in Liberia. The last group of emigrants to leave Charleston sailed on the *Azor.*

The apparent certainty that removal of federal troops from the state would bring an end to the Republican administration gave birth to a new idea, the establishment of a "black state." This idea was proposed by "Daddy" Cain, a minister of the A.M.E. Church, who insisted that so long as the whites were able to dominate the Negroes, so long would injustice and strife continue. He wanted to have South Carolina a solidly black state to which the Negroes from elsewhere in the United States could settle and there work out their destiny.

All ideas for migration or for the establishment of a "black state" were forgotten when Wade Hampton's appeal for the formation of a coalition government got a response from many Negroes some of whom were political leaders of influence. For there were many who realized that the severe criticism that had been directed against the "bond ring" would not permit that party to continue in power should Grant withdraw the federal

---

4   Wade Hampton, a South Carolina politician and leader of the Redeemers who restored white rule.

troops. For it was only through the presence of those troops that ballot box stuffing and other forms of election fraud by the white Democrats could be controlled.

A majority of Charleston Negroes continued their allegiance to the Republican party because that party had brought them emancipation and had also erased the "black code" from the statute books of the state, a smaller though forceful group allied themselves with the Democratic party and wore the "red shirt" of Hampton. Such as these derived the sobriquet "Democrat" to their names, and as such were considered fair game for taunts of small boys. One in particular whom I remember was "Democrat" Jenkins, whose children were always fit subjects for abuse by other children.

The effort to deprive the Negroes of Charleston County of political power did not go unchallenged for it provoked two riots: in both of which the Negroes assumed the offensive. One occurred at Cainhoy, a small village on the Wando River in which some whites were killed. The second, known as the Broad Street riot had its origin in charges of election fraud. Tension ran high and but for the individual bravery of Lieut. Fordham, a Colored officer of the police force, who singly went among the rioters and persuaded them to disperse and so prevented what might otherwise have resulted in bloodshed.

The balance of political power returned to the whites in Charleston County, though the adjacent counties, Beaufort and Georgetown remained predominantly Republican.

The Democratic party retained the membership of Negroes, many of whom shared in minor appointment and positions of trust. The last election of a Negro on the Democratic ticket in Charleston was that of Mr. George H. Heares, who was elected to the state legislature just prior to the ascendancy of Ben Tillman. In municipal elections everyone who was registered voted as they chose.

During the ascendancy of the Democratic party, the Republicans maintained their party organization and continued its power on the National Committee and at the nominating conventions of the party and in return received and distributed its share of political "plums." Of the Negroes who so shared was Dr. Bozeman who held the position of Postmaster for Charleston. Nearly half of the personnel at the post office were Negroes. The highest ranking of whom was Mr. J.B. Mushington in the money order department. Several clerks were appointed at the Custom House among them were Mr. R.G. Purvis who had previously served as Adjutant General for the State and Mr. J.W. Bennett, who subsequently became a bishop in the A.M.E. Church.

The economic status of the Negro had rapidly become a satisfactory one within ten years after the emancipation. Many of them had engaged in business and found a ready patronage from whites. In the meat business, the Negro butchers, among whom may be named the Gaillards, the Stokiens, the Grants, Trescott and several others of lesser note had almost a monopoly of that field and occupied most of the stalls in both the downtown and uptown public markets. The wholesale retail fish business was largely dominated by C.C. Leslie and Thad Marshall. The first Negro druggist to establish in Charleston was Dr. Dingle who opened his store on King Street near Spring during the1880s . Small grocery stores, fruit shops and wood dealers were numerous. Two small cigar factories were in operation, one on Calhoun Street opposite the green and the other at corner of King and Woolfe Streets by the Borings. One Negro by the name of McNeil operated a jewelry store on Calhoun Street where the Buist School now stands. Several operated livery stables among whom were "Democrat" Stephney Riley, Jason Brown, Richard Jones and the Mazycks.

Shoemaking, the actual making of shoes and boots by hand, was largely done by Negroes, the more prominent shops were Dacosters on Meeting Street and Houstons on Society Street.

Tailoring, both merchant and general, was largely participated in, the largest merchant tailor was James Parks who conducted his store on King Street north of Ann. Mr. Parks carried an extensive line of woolens and gave employment to a number of tailors. Among the other tailors with establishments were Mr. Sanders, Mr. Elliot, the Logans and one or two others whose names I have forgotten. These stores and also white tailoring establishments gave employment to many tailors and female vest makers. Negro women were extensively engaged at dressmaking—several employed three to four "hands."

In the construction trades the majority of workers were Negroes, carpenters, brick masons, plasterers, painters and roofers and as such were indiscriminately employed by white contractors. A number of Negro contractors carried on extensive businesses, chief among them were Preston, Harrison, Alston, Lewis and Hollings.

The lumber mills, door sash and blind factories, the rice mills and its cooper shops, Pregnall's shipyard, Riley's iron foundry and the fertilizer mills on the outskirts of the city were manned mostly [by] Negroes.

Mr. Isaac Greener was acid maker at the Ashepoo and had sole charge of its chambers. Mr. Freeman was engineer of the Tryall, a stern wheel tug, and had charge of the transportation of phosphate rock for that company, bringing it from the mine to the washers.

A number of other crafts were followed, there was Glover's Harness and Saddlery Shop, Purchell's Monument and Stone Yard. Parker's tin and sheet metal shops and in addition to these, a number of smaller establishments that carried on horse shoeing, blacksmithing, wheel wright and wagon building, tinning and roofing. Two printing establishments were operated one by James Chisolm and the other by Thorne. During the 1880s, the press foreman for the *News and Courier* was Negro, Mr. Jackie Walker, who was highly commended in an editorial in that paper for sticking to his presses during the night of Charleston's memorable earthquake, that the morning's issue of the paper would appear.

Several Negroes were engaged in coastwise shipping and operated as owner-captains of two masted schooners. Practically all of the rice crop from the plantations of South Carolina were hauled by them to the Charleston mills. The following owned and operated boats, Capt. Harleston, Capt. Graddick and Capt. Black.

Peter Hall owned and operated the only "water boat" in the harbor, bringing fresh river water from the Edisto river and selling it to steamers.

One weekly newspaper was published by Negroes. I have forgotten its name but it was edited by Mr. Robert Smith, who was subsequently forced by political pressure to abandon the project. Mr. Smith later moved to Fort Worth, Texas where he established the Farmers co-operative bank, an institution that is still in existence.

The explanation for this wide diversity of vocational ability and the acceptance of the Negro in the industrial field lies in the fact that for more than a century before the emancipation slaves and free Negroes were trained and used in these varied occupations and at the beginning of the Civil War at least fifty percent of the construction and productive work in Charleston was performed by them. When the war ended many of the white mechanics had disappeared and so there was greater opportunity for work to the Negro who remained.

In addition to that, the apprenticeship system was in vogue and it was traditional that every boy or girl should acquire proficiency at some trade.

In personal service, as barbers, there was but one white in the entire city. These shops followed the pre-war custom of being either shops for whites or shops for Negroes. And strange to say in the field of undertaking, the burying of Negro dead was largely monopolized by a white man, Livingston, who conducted his establishment on Wentworth Street near King. Most of the midwives were Negroes, several of whom were employed solely by whites.

A number of Negroes were employed in white establishments and by white firms. Practically all of the cotton brokers employed Negro samplers and in some instances Negro buyers. Mr. William Birnie was perhaps the most prominent of them.

The Dowie and Moise Company wholesale and retail druggists, that operated where the Geer Drug Co. now is, employed Mr. William Elfe as one of its manufacturing druggist. Mr. Elfe was subsequently my tutor when I apprenticed at Dr. McClennan's pharmacy. I have in my possession Mr. Elfe's private formulary book which he compiled in 1863 and believe it to be the oldest formulary compiled by an American Negro. Mr. William Meyers was employed for many years at O'Neill's shoe store on King Street as a clerk. Another Negro, Mr. Boyden was employed as a clerk by the Welch and Eason Grocery Co. The patronage at all of these stores was principally white and so excludes as an implied reason for their employment an attraction for Negro patronage.

Randall George who lived on Spring Street is perhaps the first Negro pioneer in the field of industrial production. By lease and by purchase he acquired large holdings of pine forest lands and established and successfully operated turpentine and resin stills. At his death, about 1890 he left a very substantial fortune.

Another unique enterprise operated by Negroes was the Noisette farms. The Noisettes, two brothers, were not farmers but highly skilled horticulturists who had gained international fame for a specie of roses they had developed and to a lesser extent for a variety of tomato they had produced, one similar to the present "acme" variety. They held extensive land holdings in the upper western portion of the city and also operated a floral stall in the downtown market.

But by far the most interesting and from a standpoint of racial collaboration, the most instructive, was the Pilot's Association, whose membership had the sole right to pilot ocean going ships into and from Charleston Harbor. Its membership consisted of both Negroes and whites. Each member held a United States pilot license. They were the sole arbiters as to who could exercise the duties of a pilot at the port of Charleston as well as the only ones who could train apprentices in that work. Life among the pilots was an extremely democratic one for when on station they lived, slept and ate together. Each took his turn in bringing in a ship and as pilot was in supreme command of the vessel until it either dropped anchor in the harbor or was tied to a dock. The Association would allow no ship captain to express a choice of pilot and would brook no lack of courtesy nor disrespect to the one they appointed. Negroes comprised about one-third of the members and all held the nautical title of Captain, for it was with that authority that they functioned. Several of them I knew, especially the two Capts. Jenkins, Capt. Moore and Capt. Escridge.

Until the emancipation only free Negroes could own property. At the end of 1860, the free Negroes of Charleston paid taxes on over $800,000.00 of real and personal property. A few of them were slave owners and as did the whites, suffered financial loss through the liberation of their slaves and from other causes incident to the war but on the whole still able to carry on for most of their real property remained intact.

As the economic readjustment progressed, many ex-slaves began to purchase lots on the outskirts of the city and to erect small homes thereon. Many others bought small farms on the adjacent islands, James Island, John's Island and Edisto and some of them like the Fludds and Stevens on John's Island, the Thornes and Becketts on Edisto and the Richardsons, Browns and Blacks on James Island soon extended their holdings into large acreages.

Across the Ashley River in St. Andrews Parish a small number of Negroes established and incorporated the first all Negro town in Charleston county, the town of Maryville.

A summary of so varied a program in which industry, thrift and home ownership are combined reveals the existence of a healthy economic environment in which the Negroes of Charleston dwelt. During the early post-war period it suffered but one shock, the suspension of the Freedmen's bank, which fortunately though the total loss was large, was so widely distributed throughout the South that it produced only a small loss to individual depositors.

The city boasted a Negro Militia, the origin, function or reason for existence of which, I do not know. Conjecture would grant that it was deemed advisable to create a legally armed and supervised soldiery for the protection of the community, and which, it may be inferred was its Negro community since the whites did likewise. In all probability the Negro militia antedates the white militia who probably were not organized until after Hampton's rise to power. The Negro militia consisted of two regiments of infantry and included one company of cavalrymen who were more or less picturesquely mounted. Several of the infantry companies had armories, some owned by the company and some only rented quarters.

The Carolina Light Infantry had the most pretentious armory, the building on Chalmers Street, later owned by the Good Samaritans. Each company wore a distinctive uniform and were armed with U.S. Army Springfield rifles. My father was a member of the Douglass Light Infantry. Some of the other companies I can recall were the Attucks, the Sumter and the Carolinas. Colonel Robinson, who in private life conducted an upholstery and cabinet repair shop was the commanding officer when the Negro militia was disbanded during the Tillman regime.

The religious life of the Negro followed that of the pre-Civil War period and included many of its trends and patterns, especially those that led towards racial separation and to a lesser extent, the retention of white ministers by Negro congregations.

The majority of Charleston Negroes in pre-war days were members of the Methodist, Baptist and Presbyterian Churches where emotional expression found greater opportunity than it did in churches with more formal rituals. And also because those churches granted them the privileges of becoming, leaders, deacons and in some instances "local" preachers. The minority number of the Negroes were connected with the Catholic, Episcopal and Congregational churches. Free Negroes of mixed blood were mostly affiliated with the Episcopal and Catholic churches, though quite a number held membership in other denominations, especially the Methodist. Free Negroes of unmixed blood ("free bona fide Blacks") were predominantly of the Methodist persuasion.

The post-emancipation trend was towards voluntary separation from white churches and the election of Negro ministers, except in the Catholic church where the priests are appointed by the Bishop, the Episcopal churches where it was the choice of the congregations and in one Methodist Church, Centenary.

A majority of the Negro Methodists organized themselves into the African Methodist Church of South Carolina by founding Emanuel Church, the "mother church" and shortly thereafter two others, Morris Brown and Mt. Zion. Others of the original Methodist group organized and affiliated themselves with the Methodist Episcopal Church (North), with Old Bethel, Centenary and Wesley. They also established Baker Seminary with quarters on East Bay, as a training school for its ministers and which became the nucleus from which Claflin University was founded.

The Presbyterian Church Board of Missions sponsored the continued operation of Zion Church and established Wallingford Church and its annex mission school.

The Episcopal church continued the operation of Calvary Mission on Beaufain Street and the mission at the corner of Elizabeth and Chapel Streets where the congregation that later incorporated St. Mark's Church then worshipped. When St. Mark's Church building at the corner of Warren and Thomas Streets was completed a few years later, the congregation acquired the rights of a parish and moved to its new building.

The Baptists organized the Morris Street Baptist Church from out of which there later emerged Memorial and Salem Churches.

The Catholic church continued to concentrate its Negro members at St. Peter's on Wentworth Street though a number of its Negro communicants worshiped at St. Patrick's. The Catholic Church did not then forbid intermarriage of whites and Negroes for one such marriage was performed there, that of Mr. and Mrs. Malone who resided on Radcliffe Street, across from the church, where the Condon driveway now enters. Mrs. Malone was a friend of my mother.

The Congregational church was the last white church in Charleston in which the membership separated. For it was not until 1868 when a majority of its Negro members requested that demits of membership be issued them and the privilege to establish a separate church be granted. Their applications were received and discussed at a regular meeting of the church, the old Circular, and the same were ordered, granted. The meeting adopted resolutions attesting the keen and high regard in which the Church held their Colored members and since the request to separate was voluntary one from the petitioners that it was granted. The white congregation more over gave financial aid towards the purchase of the lot on Pitt Street where the proposed church was erected. Several of the Colored members who did not join with the petitioners continued their membership and worship at the white church until their death.

The general attitude of Negroes towards religious obser-
vances during the 1880s was almost puritanical in its response.
Civil law forbad stores and drinking places from opening on the
Sabbath. Only drug stores were exempted and these could only
sell medicines for the sick. Window displays in stores had to be
hidden behind drawn curtains. The only recreation permitted
was a promenade walk, usually down to ["The Battery"][5] and
back. Church services began with early morning prayer meetings and followed by a series of sermons and meetings extending through the day until 10 o'clock at night. Policemen were
stationed near churches to maintain order and to prohibit
horse-drawn vehicles from going faster than a slow walk. For in
those days it was a misdemeanor to disturb public worship by
any outside noise that could be heard within the church.

The Negro church, especially the larger ones, did not restrict
their activities to only spiritual affairs but allowed use of their
auditoriums for lectures, concerts and public meetings and so
the cultural and informational standards of the community
were elevated. It was at a church lecture at Mt. Zion that I heard
Frederick Douglass speak and at a concert at Morris Street Baptist Church that I heard Flora Batson sing.

In times of stress and tension, it was to the church that the
Negroes turned for guidance. Once when a prominent Negro,
Stephney Riley was murdered and rioting was feared, a meeting was called at Morris Brown Church and the people were
calmed when they were assured that vindication of the murder
would not be given except [if] it was supported by true evidence.
And again at the same church a few years later, when clouds
of oppression first showed on the horizon, when a public mass
meeting expressed its fears, that the apparent trend to deprive
the Negro of adequate educational facilities, of economic

---

5   The Battery is a landmark in Charleston consisting of a seawall and
    promenade.

freedom and of full political rights unless checked would mean the re-enslavement of the race, and gave origin to the first unified effort by Negroes to stem the rising tide of Negro oppression.

A new addition to the social life of the Charleston Negro was the formation of fraternal secret societies, the Masons, the Odd Fellows and the Good Samaritans and later the Pythians and several others of purely local origin and membership. Among the early Masons was Mr. C.C. Leslie, who while a seaman on a Confederate blockade runner, was initiated into the order in Scotland. Mr. Wm. Birnie and several others who had been initiated in the West Indies on return to Charleston joined in the organization of the first lodge. I have in my possession one of the original aprons of the Royal Arch Chapter. Most of the furniture now used by the Prince Hall Royal Arch chapter of Charleston is the original furniture of the first chapter.

The fraternal organizations did much to inculcate and stimulate ideals for living. Especially so did the Odd Fellows and the Samaritans who created juvenile departments in which children were enrolled and there taught the tenets of good behaviour, industry and parliamentary usages and debate. Which subsequently proved its value when an otherwise illiterate person would be soon taking part in debate or presiding at a church meeting with ability and decorum. Unfortunately a few years later when he had acquired a little more education and some sophistication, these juvenile lodges were considered "monkey shines" by the lowly and so were allowed to disappear. Strange to say however, that fifty years later when the whites established the "Boy Scouts" with similar objectives to those of the old juvenile lodges, that Negroes begged the privilege of partaking of the very things they had previously cast aside.

The social heritage bequeathed the Charleston Negro by his pre-emancipation forbears exercised a decided influence on the social patterns of [this] first generation after the Emancipation. At the beginning of the Civil War there were approximately 3,200 free Negroes in Charleston against a slave population of about 18,000. Many of the free Negroes had lived there for over a century and in addition to having accumulated wealth had maintained schools for the education of their children since 1790. A large number of them were mulattoes and these had organized among themselves "burial" societies in which membership was restricted to those of mixed blood. There were also many free full- blooded Negroes who styled themselves the "bona fide free blacks" who also organized a "burial" society for those were the only organized associations permitted Negroes by law. The oldest of these societies were organized about 1700 and the youngest as late as 1844. Two of these early societies had their cemeteries on Pitt Street near Calhoun Street adjacent to each other. The one to the south is the Brown Fellowship, a name which distinguishes its membership, and to the north the "[illegible]" that was owned and controlled by the "bona fide Blacks."

The societies of more recent date of organization all had their cemeteries in the Magnolia cemetery section, north of the city limits. And from the rosters of several it appears that the "color restrictions" had largely been discarded. Among these more recent societies, are the "Brotherly," the Humane and the Unity and Friendship. The Unity and Friendship Society organized in 1844 is perhaps the only one of the pre-emancipation societies that has maintained an active membership to the present time.

The privileges, prerogatives and attainments acquired by the free Negroes, prior to emancipation had set them apart from the slaves and thus established caste barriers which were more or less fixed. Some of them were slave owners and so to all appearances, were in accord with the institution of slavery. But among them were some who bought slaves, who possessed the physical requirements of the Brown Fellowship Society, emancipated them and welcomed them into their organization, which largely shows that these caste barriers were more or less rigidly fixed. Briefly then the social stratae of early Charleston may be enumerated as: the whites, the free mullatoes, the free Blacks and the slaves. Social intercourse between the first three and the last was restricted and limited by law. Custom fixed the limitations between the whites and free Negroes. While fate, fortune and sustaining power decreed the relationship between the free Negroes, it must be remembered that the free Negro possessed but few legal rights. And so required a "guardian" who held his property for him in trust and who represented him in all matters arising between him and white [people?]. Now many of the free mulattoes had "guardians" who had a more or less close personal relationship with them which was not often so with the free blacks. And so the sustaining power of the guardian, who in all instances were required to be whites, could exercise, influence or make easy the life of his ward. And this generated envy, bitterness and hatred on the one hand and condescension and superciliousness on the other to such an extent that it became a definite part of the heritage of color consciousness then so prevalent and so much a part of the social concept that it had a corrupting influence on race development. So evident it was during the 1880s that it would commonly happen, when a mulatto child would pass a black one on the street that the latter would sneeringly remark, "black is honorable yellow is abominable."

And this was all the more intensified when the membership of St. Mark's Church in 1875 presented its application to the Diocesan Convention of the Protestant Episcopal Church of South Carolina for admission into union with the Convention. The following year the application was acted upon and refused. But the Convention saw to it that the full report with its reasons for refusing admission was published and is in part in these words:

> The members of this congregation with very few exceptions are mulattoes, many of whom were free before the war and were known as a peculiar class in our community, owning slaves themselves and generally avoiding intercourse with those who were entirely

black. Some of this class had established with their former masters and among our white people generally reputations for integrity and civility ------------

The females of this class sometimes held relations with white men which they seemed to consider and respect, very much like, if not truly marriage. The results of such associations are numerous in our streets. It is this class in which miscegenation is seen and which tempts to miscegenation. If miscegenation should be encouraged among us, then this class should be cherished and advanced.

The report evidences within itself symptoms of vicious politics. For its real intent was to extend a new form of propaganda and appeal to Northern whites for their aid towards abolishing the military control under which South Carolina was maintained.

Its effect upon the Negroes was two-fold as it concentrated attention upon St. Mark's which never before had so been singled out and with such effect that seldom would one of darker hue enter its portals. But it did not stop there for the venom it engendered seeped through the community and entered its churches, its schools, its political activities and even into business relationships between individuals. And as time passed and its effects abated, though few knew its origin or how it had been spread, it became a tradition that only time and truth can eradicate.

The relationship between the masses, both Negro and white, when considered from the viewpoint of a newly established order of life was a satisfactory one. Many of the former relationships continued without interruption. Especially that of domestic service, for many of the ex-slaves continued their employment and to dwell in the servant quarters of their ex-owners who now were their employers. Whites whose fortunes had been depleted by the war rented their servant quarters to Negroes.

Segregation was then unknown in Charleston as Negroes lived any and everywhere; enveloped in a spirit of racial tolerance and harmony that largely had its origin and force from those whites who dwelt "south of Broad Street." For they still exercised authority and controlled business life of the city.

In striking contrast with its background of ancient architectural beauty were the alleys and lanes of the section, Stall's Alley, Longitude Lane, Lightwood Alley, Price Alley, Bedon's Alley, Elliott Street and the eastern end of Tradd Street still showing the effects of the bombardment by the "Swamp Angel" teeming with Negro waterfront workers, fishermen and washwomen.

In the upper section of the City dwelt the white bourgeoise, they who never received a bid to the St. Cecelia, and amid them the rest of the rank and file of Charleston Negroes. Many of the whites who occupied the upper section of the city were foreign born, who had recently come to Charleston. Those of Jewish origin were principally along upper King Street where they had their shops, dealing principally in men's ready to wear. The Germans, who were many, concentrated on the grocery business and as a sideline with greater profits a barroom to the rear of their shops. These shops were usually the places where Negroes idled and spent their money for food or for cheap whiskey. Whatever of prejudice the German then felt was usually well concealed, for if openly expressed could drive business away. The Irish dwelt mostly on the eastern side of town, near the Mall ever hostile towards Negroes from other sections of the city but ardent friends to those who lived within their area. To the north of the Irish section was "little Mexico" populated by "brass ankles" who were rapidly becoming "free white and twenty-one."[6]

---

6 An expression used to define the white American ideal, dating back to the 19th century when property ownership was removed as a perquisite for white male enfranchisement. The phrase gained popularity in films produced in the first part of the twentieth century.

Legalized segregation as is now experienced was then unknown to Charleston. Railroad transportation was sold at first-, second- and third-class fares and automatically separated the cultured from the cruder. Streetcar transportation, then the horse-drawn variety made no distinctions. The parks of the city were open to all at all times and were only monopolized on the fourth of July when the Negroes took full possession of the "Battery" and of the Mall where the "tu lu lu" was danced. Heinsohn's ice cream parlor on South Battery made no distinction, neither did Gardner's soda fountain on King Street near Calhoun. The Academy of Music, the city's principal theater, had no restrictions. As a rule all of the small beer parlors served Negroes.

What there was of racial separation was purely voluntary and not by legislative distaste. Custom had established some of what there was, as in barber shops, restaurants and hotels. All else was purely that of personal choice and evidenced itself similarly in both races, by those of like taste resolving themselves into small social groups or even becoming the majority as is often seen in church congregations. In much the same manner the various Negro churches and fraternal societies developed distinctive cultural standards.

Law and order and fire protection were in the city adequate departments in which both Negroes and whites were customers. The Police Department with headquarters at the corner of Meeting and Broad Streets, where the Post Office now is, and an uptown station on King Street and Cannon had about one-third of the personnel Negroes. Lieut. James Fordham appointed in 1874 was the top-ranking Negro officer, and next lower in rank Sargent Brown, a brother of Mr. Jason Brown. The others were patrolmen. It was before the day of the telephone callbox and patrol wagon, so when an arrest was made, the arresting officer had to walk his prisoner to the nearest station. If the prisoner was inebriated and could not walk then he would be parked on [the] sidewalk while the officer went to the station, got a

stretcher and an assistant and carried the prisoner in. Policemen were forbidden by law to strike an inebriate with his club
or hand and it is told of one Negro policeman who arrested a
drunken white man who would not walk and insisted that the
stretcher be brought and dared the officer to strike him as it was
against the law, at which the officer seized him by the shoulders,
brought him to an erect position and said, "I'm not going to hit
you with my club nor strike you with my fist" and then he drew
his head back and butted the drunk on the head and asked "[Is]
you goin'?" at which the drunk replied, "I'll walk." All of which
showed resourcefulness.

The policemen used the barracks in common. No special beats were assigned them and in those they were rotated.
Arrests were made without regard to color and testimony
was never questioned when made by a Negro arresting officer
against a white.

There was one Negro magistrate, Judge Elfe who served for a
number of years with evident satisfaction to the public.

The volunteer Fire Department that served the city prior
to 1882 was a more or less mixed group of firefighters, especially during the Civil War when the bombardment from Morris Island was continuous. In 1873 a group of Negroes who had
been serving with the volunteers organized themselves as Hook
and Ladder Company, Truck No. 3. The company had a comple-
ment of forty men and was officered by Foreman Elfe and Asst.
Foreman George M. Mears. In 1882 on organization of the City
Fire Department on a full- and part-time pay basis, Truck No. 3
was made a part thereof with headquarters on Meeting Street
near Ann. Its personnel consisted of four full-time firemen and
eight on-call men. Former assistant foreman, George M. Mears
was appointed Captain in charge. The company responded to all
fires and established an enviable reputation for its ability and its
faithfulness to duty.

In the professional field of medicine Dr. M.G. Champlin is the dean. Whether he was a slave or freeman I do not know. Dr. Champlin had in turn been office boy, assistant and general factotum to Dr. Ogier and as such served an apprenticeship in medicine under him. As his ability progressed he was placed in charge of the sick slaves sent to Dr. Ogier for treatment and soon acquired a reputation as an able physician. After emancipation, the state legislature by act, granted him the right to practice medicine. I knew Dr. Champlin well, for we were neighbors and once he treated my grandmother for an injury.

The first regular Negro physician to reach Charleston was Dr. Howard, a graduate of Harvard. But shortly after his arrival at Charleston he became inveigled with the idea of migrating to Liberia. Which he did but like many others who went there became dissatisfied and quickly returned to the United States and settled in Philadelphia. Dr. Bozeman who was the next to settle in Charleston did not enter practice but went into politics and for several years served as postmaster at Charleston.

Early during the 1880s, the Negro community planned...

[Missing page]

I find it strange to tell that not until now have I ever given thought to my birth, save merely as a date for chronological record. For it was not until my sixtieth birthday that I was surprised with a "birth-day" party.

But of birth itself and the enigma which surrounds it, many years passed before I gave it more than passing thought. Often did I read Omar Khayyam's quatrain,

> Into this Universe and Why not knowing
> Nor Whence, like Water willy-nilly flowing;
> And out of it, as Wind along the Waste,
> I know not Whither, Willy-nilly blowing.

And the more I read it, the more I contemplate its mysteries for birth and death the coming and passing of life, are mysteries beyond the ken of human minds. We know that it begins in heredity and terminates in posterity and that none is conscious of either the realm from whence it came or where it goes but only knows that the realm is solely the province of the Creator.

We begin existence as an animate organism which holds within its being mental factors which develop into two minds, a conscious and a sub-conscious mind, which through intercommunication produce the faculty of "conscience." Which faculty by virtue of its external experience guides the individual through a life existence in which either good or evil and success or failure ensues. It is conceded that heredity exercises some influence on posterity. But there is no doubt but that the higher values of life come from the environmental experiences in which good example and proper precept predominate.

The process of mental development during the first few years of life does not allow very early conceptions of either time, place, events or persona since the normal requirements for physical growth and maintenance preclude them for being, as it is essential that the individual become more mature and the brain capacity increased before these concepts can be recorded. Hence the concepts of our early years are vague, hazy and indistinct. Such that we may have are usually associated with the maternal contributions of love, warmth and succor. And are the ties which bind the child to its mother and in turn created reciprocal affection.

Charleston of My Youth

My early recollections are limited to those which brought me happiness, pleasure or thrills. Perhaps I also had my fears, but if I did, I suppose I cried and Mother came, and then all was calm and contentment again.

So life grew within me; moulded by pattern laid down by Mother and the environment she grew about me. Whatever she commanded was complied with, whether I liked it or not, and so whatever I am is due largely to her. As I look back through the years, I can more fully appreciate the methods she used in directing my life. Whatever measure of success has come to me, has come because of the training she gave and the aspirations she encouraged.

She was self-sacrificing to an extreme, and through all of it was always happy, smiling or laughing, even under the most trying circumstances. I could not appreciate much of this at the time it occurred but only did so after many years had passed.

She was an indefatigable worker, for in addition to the usual care of the home and the bearing and rearing of eleven children, she found time to make most of our clothing and to sew for others. And in addition to conduct the operation of a little shop in which wood, vegetables and a few other odds and ends were sold, and as a further sideline, personal attention to two or three cows which she kept from which the surplus milk, beyond what we consumed, she sold. The proceeds from these sources together with Father's earnings cared for the home, contributed to our education and bought the home on Palmetto Street.

Somehow or other I find it impossible to describe Mother as she appeared to me during my early years. I have no vivid or accurate conception of how either she or Father looked during their younger years. To me, she then personified a force from which emanated love, comfort and cheer and these to me were ample for all the needs I had.

My earliest recollection of her vividly recalls an occasion on which she took me to the old Irish woman, whose reputation as a healer of eye ailments exceeded that of our early eye specialists, for treatment for an eye condition. The application when used burnt like all fury and that together with a yellow [missing word], which I distinctly remember, produced a cure.

Our folks were simple folks in those days, in the year 1881. We then lived on Woolfe Street. To the rear of our home stood the Rohde Grist Mill and Grain Store with its frontage on King Street. Across the street and opposite to us lived a white family, the [Masons?] in whose home I often strayed and always found a cordial welcome as well as delectable cookies. Next door as dwelled the [illegible] who became lifelong friends of our family. Their son [illegible] who was lame from birth and I were playmates. His grandmother, Mrs. Howard, who resided with them, was one of Charleston's well-known midwives. She not only delivered me but for many years after made frequent visits to our home, each time bringing her little black bag with its calamine powder and [scorched?] linen rags, and on her departure would leave behind another little baby. To me she was mystery personified, for I never could learn how she did it.

Across the street at the corner of King lived the Borings. The[y] conducted a cigar factory and store. One of their boys, Jack, and I were schoolmates at Avery and also friends until his death. Next door to them on King Street was Mrs. Behren's vegetable shop. She was a kindly old Irish lady who would give me fruit and was always nice to me. It was at her place that I first saw a watering hose used. To me it was a wonderful sight, to see the stream of water ascending in an arc and then striking the warm earth to create a vapor of steam and dust.

Our home was shared by my grandmother, whom we all called "Madodo," her mother and her two daughters Lizzie and Charlotte. The former I called "Aunty-ma." Nicknames were rather common in those days. The custom perhaps had its origin in either slavery or earlier African usage. However that may be it became my lot to be renamed "Maussa" by Madodo, an appellation that filled me with disgust and annoyance for many years. My sister Laura enjoyed for an only too brief a period, as I felt, the nickname "Missie" but that soon became taboo, while I, for the next ten years of life was doomed to answer whenever Madodo called for "Maussa." The custom of nicknaming soon disappeared for the Negro group but in its wake was substituted a glamorous and esthetic nomenclature which often belied the characters concealed beneath them.

Madodo's mother, my great-grandmother, seemed to me to be always sitting in her chair. A weird, mysterious person who never petted me nor invited me to her. One day there was a strange stillness in the house and people came and bore her away in a box. I heard them say that she was dead. To me death was then a meaningless phenomena and it was many years later before I could understand the stark tragedy which ends life.

Father was a vague somebody I could not fully understand. He would coddle me but [his] coddling never carried the warmth nor brought the satisfaction that Mother's did. Neither was it as welcomed by me as was what given by the other women in the house for theirs was with an intimacy with which I was familiar. Many years passed before I came to know [him?] intimately, until then it was only Mother.

One day the house was filled with bustle and ado. The "front" room was opened and cleaned. The little "whatnot" with its porcelain ornaments was dusted and returned to its corner. The kitchen emitted delicious odors from cakes that were baking. Everybody was busy. No one gave me attention or seemed aware of my presence. That night people came, strange men and women, until the house was filled by them. Then "Aunty-ma" came downstairs wearing the most wonderful dress I had ever seen. It was made from brocaded satin and was in a beautiful dark garnet color. I later learned that the event was her wedding. I was so enamored with her dress that all else is forgotten. Even Henry Hill whom she married faded from the picture and remained an unknown to me until he cut my hair several years later. He was a barber by trade.

A little later Father moved Mother and me, taking Laura along, to the little cottage that he was buying on F Street. I have no recollection as to how or when we moved; only the realization that we were somewhere else than on Woolfe Street. F Street was then in the remote outskirts of the city and was a part of a small subdivision of small lots on narrow streets for sale to Colored people. There I found adventure. The little cottage with its three rooms and odor of fresh paint and the newness of its construction was something to be explored. I missed my former playmates in Woolfe Street but found a new joy in ransacking the little drawers on Mother's bureau. The loss of my former playmates was quickly compensated by the wider space and newness of the section in which I lived, for it offered an unlimited field for exploration. F Street ended about two hundred feet to the south of our home, at a small farm where strawberries were grown. There I would stray and crawling through the fence bars, pick strawberries and suck them to my heart's content. It was my first experience with growing things. Soon the farmer and I became friends. But since the berries had not been sweetened, I soon tired of them. South of the farm was the cattle lot, where cows and other animals were loaded and unloaded from the railroad cars. From the vantage point and safety of the farm, I could see the herds of cattle as they were driven into the stockades. I could see drovers with their long whips and the men on horseback driving the milling cattle into the pens. The mooing from the cows and the bleats from the calves, with the rising dust and odors would hold me spellbound. At night when all else was stilled and the cars were being loaded, I could hear the tattoo of their hoof beats that would awe me and hold me sleepless for a while and then would lull me into sleep.

To the rear of our home were the Southern Railway tracks. Father, before his marriage, had been a brakeman on the railroad and so enjoyed a fraternity with railroading men, and knew many of the brakemen, engineers, conductors and porters. During the summer months when the Pullmans passed, the porters would throw pieces of ice over our back fence and it was my work to gather them and bring them in to mother. Artificial ice was then an unknown luxury to Charleston. All ice was brought in by ships and stored in "ice houses" until used. It was such a rare luxury that most folks could only enjoy it on Sundays. So we considered ourselves extremely fortunate in the daily enjoyment of a luxury, even though they were scraps that came over the back fence.

Next to the cattle lot was a blacksmith's shop where I would go and watch the sparks fly from the anvil or look on in fascinated wonder when a horse was being shod. But these attractions soon lost their appeal in the greater attraction that arose next door to our home where a two-story house was under construction. I would steal over and watch the carpenters work and gathering up shavings and block ends that fell from their tools would use them as playthings. Father had given me a small pearl-handled pocketknife. It was the one great joy of my life. I would slice the shavings with it and was always trying the keenness of the blade on anything that came handy. There was a well in our yard that supplied us with water. It had a wooden [missing word] that gave safety. But there were cracks between the boards and one day while at the well, my knife fell through a crack and disappeared into its depths. I was heartbroken over the loss. I have lost much during the later years, but never did I suffer a loss more poignant than that of my knife. When I saw it slip between the cracks and disappear into the depths of the well, it seemed as if my world had crumbled. All the joy and pleasure it had brought me disappeared with it and there remained only a yearning to recover it. That yearning became an obsession with me and was so intense that forty years after I took over a mortgage of the property and sought to buy it. But the title had a cloud and could not be perfected so I allowed the property to go to tax sale and forfeited my interest in it. In the meanwhile the cottage had been extended into a two-story building with eight rooms. The well had been closed and all that remained of it was a small portion of its brick coping. The financial loss I sustained was considerable and is only recorded in my "forgotten memories" but I am sure that the loss of my knife shall ever be with me.

Shortly after the completion of the building next door to us, Father sold the cottage. He was then employed at Dr. Baer's wholesale and retail drugstore on Meeting Street near Market. The distance from F Street to there was great, so it became necessary that he live nearer to his workplace. So we moved to Calhoun Street. Our new home was centrally located, on the north side of the street, four doors east of Coming. A white church now occupies its former site. It was a rather large house and sat about forty feet back from the street behind a somewhat nondescript flower garden. A shell walkway bordered with althea trees led from the street to the piazza entrance. The house contained six rooms and two attics. Madodo and her daughter and son, Charlotte and Paul, lived there, and also Mr. William Wigg and his wife, Mrs. Emily Wigg. Mr. Wigg was candy and ice cream maker at Macmillan's Ice Cream Factory. He was a short, chubby jovial man and often brought me candy. In the rear of our yard there was a stable in which a man by the name of Ford kept his horse and furniture-moving dray. Ford lived in a room above the stable. Sometimes he would take me on his dray and ride me for a block, then put me off and caution me to run straight back home.

Next door to us, on the west, resided Dr. Champlin, his sister and her two daughters, the Gadsens. The doctor was a rather unique personage. He was very meticulous in his attire and usually wore a long black frock coat, trousers to match and a high beaver hat. He was lame and always carried a gold-handled black walking stick. In cold weather he never used an overcoat but would drape himself in a large plaid shawl, a style that was then common. Next door to Dr. Champlin lived the Sanders. Mr. Sanders was minister in the Reformed P.E. Church and in addition to his clerical services, operated a tailoring establishment in which he employed three men. His daughter, Miss Ellen, who was then attending Avery Institute, taught me the alphabet and also the first rudiments of the three Rs.

At the corner of Coming Street were the Puckhabers. They were German immigrants and operated a grocery store. It amused me to see them wearing the heavy wooden sabots [a kind of wooden shoe] they had brought from Germany. I called them their "little boats." On the opposite corner was a fruit shop kept by an immigrant Italian. One night shortly after we had moved to Calhoun Street, Mother took me there to see an incandescent electric lamp. Electricity had but recently come to Charleston and was a novelty to be seen. The Edison bulb with its carbon filament emitting a golden yellow light was something to be marveled at for its brilliancy so far exceeded that of the "fish tail" gas lights then commonly used, that it made stores so equipped appear dark and drab.

A couple of doors to the east of us lived the Lubs. They were Germans and operated grist mill and feed store. They were extremely frugal and industrious. They owned the house in which we lived as well as the mill and the residence to the front of it. I would often go into the mill and watch the horses, harnessed to long poles which turned the mill stones, travel continuously the little circle in which they moved. Upstairs above the mill was a loft with huge bins in which the whole and the cracked corn was stored. There I would climb and spend hours rolling about in the corn and sliding over the smooth floor. Sometimes their daughter Katie would join me and we would have a rollicking time.

The Lubs rented the front room of their home to a Colored harness maker by the name of [Glover?]. Sometimes I would go in and watch him at work. His place however was the meeting ground of convivial minded friends who would often send me out to buy Duke cigarettes and would reward me with pennies or with the pictures of actresses that were packed with the cigarettes. When Mother learned of my visits there she sternly forbad me ever going there again.

In the next block, at the corner of St. Philip Street was the Charleston Orphan House, an institution for white orphans. The building was surmounted by a high dome-like structure in which was housed the "alarm bell" which sounded twelve times at noon each day except Sundays. It also announced the location of fires for the information of "callmen" by ringing the box number from which the alarm was sent in. When the bell would ring we would watch it and note the bell clapper movement and the interval that elapsed before we could hear it sound. Why the interval happened was always a question. But in later years it served to clarify some physics for me.

Just below Calhoun Street on St. Philip was a little Jewish synagogue where the Jews held services on Friday evenings at the rise of the evening star and on Saturday mornings. We would congregate near the corner to observe them as they [illegible] and listen to them as they conversed in Yiddish. A group of larger and more venturesome Negro boys would usually be around and would tease the Jews by chanting a little song which went like this,

Had a piece of mutton
Stuck it on a button
Gave it to a curly headed Jew la la.

When the Jews would turn and look the boys would run away.

Calhoun Street was a paved street, with Belgian blocks in the center and cobble stones on the sides. It always intrigued me to watch the large amount of traffic that went by, carriages, wagons, buggies and drays but even more intriguing than these was the Colored jewelry store owner who would ride by on his bicycle. His was not one of the modern versions for they had not arrived then but was one of the early models with a high wheel in front and a small wheel to the rear. He would be attired in the cyclists' dress of the 1880s consisting of black knee breeches, white shirt with ruffled collar and cuffs, black stockings and laced shoes. He would methodically pedal along and always seemed oblivious of the many children who raced along beside him until he dismounted at his shop.

On moonlight nights the Negro militia used Calhoun Street in front of our home for a drill ground. It was an interesting sight to watch them go through their maneuvers and to hear the thud of their guns upon the paving blocks when ordered to "rest arms." Father was a member of the Douglass Light Infantry but I have no recollection of ever seeing him march with his company. His Springfield army rifle was my favorite toy when no one was looking. On one fourth of July he took me to the Douglass' armory on Hassell Street but the happenings there failed to interest me as there were no other children present.

One of the biggest crowds I ever saw gathered on Calhoun was on the day that Stephney Riley's funeral procession passed.

The city was all agog with rumors of rioting about to break loose. But as sometimes happens, the "thrill" of a big funeral quieted the rumors and so everything became calm and peaceful. Stephney Riley was a very prominent Negro and because of his political affiliation became popularly known as "Democrat" Riley. He was an officer in the Negro militia and was prominent in church, fraternal and social organizations. He owned and operated a livery stable on Bull Street near Smith. His patronage came largely from whites. He was a skilled horseman and gave lessons in horseback riding to many of the white ladies of the city. His home was the gathering place for many of the white gentry who spent their evenings there enjoying the hospitality of his wine cellar. One evening when a number of such were gathered there and conviviality ran high, an altercation arose between him and Dr. Bellinger over some apparently trivial affair. At which Dr. Bellinger drew his pistol and shot Riley.

When his death became known excitement ran high. There was general fear of a riot being started by the Negroes. Many whispered rumors were extant as to the actual motive behind the crime and were such that they pictured the murder in an entirely different aspect from that of a drunken brawl. However wiser counsel prevailed and rioting was averted.

The day of the funeral was a virtual holiday for Charleston's Negroes. The streets along which the cortege passed were lined with men, women and children. The excitement of passion soon became one of curiosity. Everybody wanted to see the funeral and soon Zion Church where it was held was filled. An overflow of the crowd collected in the churchyard where they milled around with excitement. A ballad song telling about the murder had been composed by some unknown author and was being whistled and hummed everywhere. It carried several verses and a refrain. I have forgotten the verses but the refrain went like this–

Bellinger shot Riley on the sly
He shot him in the eye
And he made poor Riley die
Bellinger shot Riley on the sly.

The procession came through Calhoun Street. As far as I could see, from in front of our home, the sidewalks were lined with Negroes, many of whom had been standing there for hours awaiting the procession. They were quiet and with the exception of an occasional call to someone at a distance, only a murmured buzz of excitement and anticipation was heard.

As the procession approached the crowd filled to the curb straining necks to obtain a closer view. The excited murmurings which but a moment before had filled the air now quieted and was only broken by an occasional hysterical shriek. I was somewhat frightened by the crowd for I had never before been among so many people. Curiosity however got the better of me and so to get a closer view I squeezed through the crowd and reached the curb.

First came the carriages bearing the pallbearers, then the hearse with its dead. Next followed a soldier, leading Riley's horse, fully harnessed, with Riley's boots tied across the empty saddle. Behind the horse came the "drum corps," consisting of a bass drum, a small drum and a fife, playing over and over again "the dead march." Then followed the carriages with the family and friends and lastly the soldiers, and the end.

No event in a child's life is filled with more anticipation than that of Christmas and Santa Claus. I had passed several Christmases but the one which Santa Claus brought me my first and only velocipede is one that I shall always remember. My velocipede shall always retain its place among the memories I cherish. I am sure that it was not a new velocipede when I received it. However that fact did not minimize its value one iota for to me it was as good as new. It was built of wood and had three wheels, two at the rear and a larger one in front by which it was propelled and steered. The seat was covered with black "oil cloth" and the wheels had sheet iron tires. The pedals are large round wooden spools inserted on an iron axle and fitted into the hub of the front wheel. It had been freshly painted a brilliant red color and how proud was I over it. I never tired of riding it. It took me to new distances and expanded my horizon and brought me in touch with a larger world in which lived people I had never before known.

That winter was an intensely cold one. And one night it snowed. It was my first sight of snow and it was wonderful to see how bright it made everything look. Mother took me out on the upstairs porch and allowed me to take up a handful of it and eat it. But that was as far as I got for she kept me in the house until it was all melted and the cold had moderated.

One day I heard that the city was all agog for Grover Cleveland, the first Democratic president in twenty-three years was coming to Charleston. A big parade was planned, the city was decorated and a public holiday proclaimed. I was in bed sick with a bad cold and sore throat. Madodo took charge of me and dosed me with some vile medicines, chief of which was castor oil and my own urine. My cold and throat grew better and finally I was allowed to get up but not in time to witness the parade nor see the events, I could only hear the music from afar and swallow my disappointment.

Shortly after we came to Calhoun Street Mrs. Howard brought me a second little sister. I can vaguely remember her as a very pretty little olive-skinned baby. I was not deeply interested in sisters since I had one and that one was enough. One day Mother was crying and father was sad and quiet. Then people came to attend the baby's funeral for she was dead. Mother told me that she had gone to heaven. I had been told that those who went to heaven became stars that shined from the heavens and on clear nights we would watch the stars and wonder which was Ellen.

One night the rain fell in torrents and the wind blew harder than I had ever heard it blow before. The trees in our yard bent with the blast until they seemed to touch the earth. It thundered and lightninged and the house shook from the blast until it seemed that it would fall apart. It was my first experience with a hurricane. I was terribly frightened, but not the only one, for fear was in all of us, for hurricanes left death and destruction in their wake. The next morning when it had subsided some, Mother took me to a rear window and pointed to where the Citadel Square Baptist Church was. Its steeple had been blown off and in falling had crashed into a building across the street from it, killing several of its occupants.

The Lubs who kept the grist mill had the contract to supply the city's Old Folks' Home with food. Once a week they made deliveries. Once I was permitted to accompany the driver on a delivery. It was a new experience to me for I had never before been more than three blocks away from home except when with my parents. The Old Folks' Home, a city institution for indigent Negroes was then located in the far northwestern section of the city and abutted the "Potters Field" where pauper dead were buried. To reach it, we drove through Calhoun Street, crossing the bridge which spanned the pond where Ogier Street now is, then out through Rutledge Avenue to a lane, that is now Fishburne Street and through to the Home. It was like entering a fairy land, I had never before seen so many trees. They bordered the lane through which we drove. Their shade and coolness cast a sense of unreality about me. Beyond these trees were large fields of growing fields much larger than the strawberry farm I knew on F Street. It was all a revelation to me and gave me my first glimpse of the great beyond and left me all excited. After the delivery was made, dusk came down and the return drive home in the semidarkness found me half asleep and tired but strange to say not nearly as hungry as I usually was at bedtime.

Life was beginning to have its problems. Many of the things I wished to do did not meet Mother's approval and when I did them brought me punishment. It seemed so much easier to do the things I desired to do than to do the things permitted me. I could not understand why I was not permitted to eat whatever was in the house especially if it was nice and appetizing except when permission to do so was granted or why the things I craved most were denied me. One of my greatest delights was to eat the "brown" sugar we used. That and the condensed milk became temptations that I could not resist. Mother would punish but I would steal. No matter where she hid the little wooden bucket in which they were kept I would find it and gorge myself until fear crept in. Then I would shy away and assume an air of innocence to hide my guilt. One day Mother contrived a new hiding place for the bucket. She suspended it to the kitchen rafters, supposedly beyond my reach. I bided my time and when opportunity [came?] pushed a table beneath it, placed a chair upon the table and so got the bucket. I then enjoyed myself to the utmost after which I returned the bucket to its place and went about my way as if nothing had happened. When Mother went to the bucket and found what had happened she called me and questioned me. Of course I pretended all innocence but that did not prove me guiltless. Until then Mother had always used the orthodox method of punishment. But since that had not curbed my tendencies she, upon the spur of the moment contrived a new method. She took me in the yard, sat me in a chair and tied me there. I could not even move my hands. Then she took the remainder of the condensed milk and smeared my face with it. Within a few minutes every fly in the neighborhood was perched upon my face and since my hands were tied, I could not brush them off. A little later Mother came and untied me. She washed my face and then told me, that if I ever did such again that she would tie me up for a much longer time. I then and there lost my taste for brown sugar and condensed milk but in its place I learned the lesson of property rights, that things did not belong to you until they were given or earned.

In later years I would often tease Mother about her "brutality" in thus punishing me at which she would always laugh. And so it became an incident that caused me to love her even more dearly than I formerly did.

That autumn Mother told me that I was going to school in a few days. She had made me some suits from white linen cloth, a cap and some shirts. These together with a pair of stockings that were dyed in two colors, yellow and red and my brogan shoes with brass toe plates completed my outfit. On cold days I wore a shawl about my shoulders. I was sent to a small private school on Smith Street conducted by Miss Anna Montgomery. It was not far from home and I easily learned the way. To the rear of Miss Montgomery's yard was the (Ogier Street) pond. During our recess periods we would go [to] the pond and make lines with bent pins for hooks and try to catch minnows. I never saw a successful attempt. But one day by leaning too far over the water, I fell in. One of the larger boys, London Johnson, pulled me out and took me to Miss Montgomery. She wiped my face and sent me home with one of the other pupils. When I got there, Mother became very much excited but that quickly passed and in its place came a very hurtful spanking, as she said for trying to fish when I should have been doing what the teacher commanded.

Our church life was in the Baptist church. Father and Mother were then members of the Morris Street Baptist Church where Laura and I attended Sunday school. In 1887 they withdrew their membership and joined with those, who under the leadership of Rev. Robinson founded Memorial Baptist Church. From then on I attended the Sunday school at Memorial. Father became the Superintendent of the sabbath school.

Our residency on Calhoun Street brought many new friends to the family and many new playmates for me. Some of whom remained to be lifelong friends. The Sanders, Miss Darling Plumeau, the Bells, (Hiram Bell family) the Fridies and many others.

It was about this time, that my Uncle Paul decided to leave Charleston and go with the Norden firm, a firm of cotton brokers to New York. Mr. Birnie who had taught him to classify cotton strongly urged him to do so. Paul was a very diligent student and had perfected himself for clerical work and so a few years later when the Nordens retired from "spot" cotton transactions and dealt only in contracts Paul was able to do clerical work and continued with the firm until its dissolution years later.

In the spring of 1886 Grandmother McFall took me with her on a visit to Philadelphia, to see her son, my uncle Allen, after whom I was named. I have no recollections of the journey neither when going or returning. Just why what ordinarily should have been an impressive occasion, my first railroad journey, is forgotten I do not know. Perhaps they were crowded out by the more vivid experiences I found there. When we reached Philadelphia Uncle Allen met us and took us to his home on Emmaline Street. Emmaline Street is one of the smaller streets in South Philadelphia. His home was a small two-story brick dwelling and was similar in type to all of the other houses in the block. It had a high wooden stoop where we would sit in the late afternoons and on occasions sip a delicious hot stew that was peddled to the neighborhood by an old woman who lived across the street from us.

Since we had arrived in Philadelphia sometime prior to summer vacations, I was enrolled at the kindergarten not far from our home. White and Colored children attended the same school. The teachers were white and I have no recollection of any discrimination or unkindness being shown me. I vividly recall that at the noontime lunch of milk and rolls that the teacher was kind and attentive. We sang game songs and did our play dances in groups. I was first given card stitching lessons, in which a perforated piece of cardboard was stitched with colored threads to depict various pet animals and birds. I was later transferred to a group that made clay models of things.

One day Uncle Allen took us to Darby to see a lot that he had bought and on which he planned to build his home. It was a rather large lot and was then planted with vegetables. It was located on Marks Avenue, that was named in honor of Uncle Allen's brother-in-law, Mr. Marks, who was the first to settle in that particular section. One day news came to us that a terrible earthquake had occurred in Charleston.[7] Grandmother McFall wanted to leave at once to see what had happened and how her children fared. It was some time before we could get passage for the railroad tracks near Charleston had all been demolished and in addition, the earth tremors were continuing.

Finally, we got away and reached Charleston. Father met us at the station where we took the streetcar for home. When we reached the corner of King and Warren Streets I saw two or three buildings that had been gutted by fire during the earth- quake. People were still under the excitement from their expe- rience as the tremors had just about ceased. Many people were still living in tents of all types and descriptions rather than face the danger of being in a home that had suffered damage from the heavier shocks should another shock occur. I became infected with fear anticipating that an earthquake shock might come at any moment and so for the first two or three nights following my return I lived in dread.

Many tourists were visiting the city to view the effects of the earthquake and many of them bought souvenirs that con- sisted of "earthquake sand" which came from the Summerville area where the earth developed crevices out of which erupted varied colored sand. Practically all of the genuine sand was sold in shops but many small boys with whom I numbered pro- duced and bottled their own by powdering red brick, putting a strata of that in a bottle overlaying it with one of wood ashes and next with one of clean sand. My product though extremely

---

7   The earthquake occurred on August 31, 1886.

satisfactory to me proved a miserable failure as I could never persuade anyone to buy it.

I don't recall that our house suffered any serious damage from the earthquake. A few fallen chimneys and much broken plastering was the chief damage in our section but in the lower section of the city where brick buildings predominated the damage was great.

The following year I was sent to the Mary Street Public School where I was placed in one of the classes on the ground floor on the east side of the building. I have forgotten much of what my experiences there were. But I do remember that we would usually tease the old white policeman who was supposed to maintain order in the vicinity of the school. "Old Goat" we called him and made his life a miserable one, by running away from him and yelling "Old Goat can't catch me."

Perhaps the most impressive experience I encountered about this time was seeing and hearing Frederick Douglass, who came to Charleston to deliver a lecture at Mt. Zion Church. He arrived in the city a day or two before his lecture and stopped at the home of Dr. Crum, on Coming Street just around the corner from ours. One afternoon he was taken for a drive about the city. All along the line of drive the sidewalks were lined with Negroes who had assembled to do him honor. He had a splendid figure, a man of medium stature, dark brown skin, his head covered with grey hair worn somewhat long, so that it gave his face a leonine expression as he rose from his seat in the carriage at frequent intervals to bow to the crowds in acknowledgement of their plaudit.

Father took me to the lecture. Mr. Douglass held his audience spellbound and even I, though somewhat sleepy became wide awake when he told of his experiences while a slave, and how on one occasion when his master whipped him severely and remarked during the whipping "Give a Nigger an inch and he will take an ell," that he then and there determined that he would run away. Of those present at the lecture were many who had had their experiences as slaves and so could fully comprehend the sincerity of his talk. And as I write this, I wonder, how many of the present generation know how truly great is the life of Douglass and how far reaching were the results of his efforts to destroy slavery and to gain the rights of citizenship for the Negroes.

Of course I had my series of daily chores to do. One of which was going to the meat market to buy our daily supply of meat for we did not have refrigerators in those days in which to store food. Madodo was in charge of the kitchen and ordered the buying. She still retained some of the folkways from Upper South Carolina by clinging to the English monetary system and though we never used English money she would always direct me get "three pence or six pence" of this or that. It was highly confusing to me and yet I dared not ask her to clarify her meaning. She would then give me a clean piece of white cloth in which the meat was to be wrapped, since the paper then used was a very cheap type of brown paper and at times old newspapers. She always directed me to a particular butcher for her purchases but I soon substituted him for one who would give me a penny each time I bought from him. I never confessed this to Madodo though sometimes she would scold about the meat being underweight.

Mother kept cows when we lived on Calhoun St. They gave us an abundance of milk and clabber. When there was an accumulation of milk she would churn it for its butter and then we would have buttermilk. It was often my job to work the plunger up and down until the butter rose. Then she would gather it and salt it. We never colored it but enjoyed it much more than we did that bought from the store for often that would be rancid.

Mrs. Howard soon came to pay us another visit and this time she brought another sister. This one was named Thomasina but was called Tommie for short.

A short time after Tommie's arrival we moved from Calhoun Street to our new home on Palmetto Street. It was always the desire of Father and Mother to own their home and this was the first chance they had after selling the F Street place to do so. The section into which we were moving was in the extreme western portion of the city. Much of it had been reclaimed land which formerly was flooded whenever high tide was in. Palmetto Street was the entrance to a bridge that led to the causeway which connected the city with the old Savannah railroad wharves, and the old ferry docks that were used before the "new bridge" was constructed. In reclaiming the land the discarded chaff from the West Point Rice Mills was the principal filling used and so the section derived its name "chaff lot" from that source.

Our new home, No. 7, was formerly owned by a family by the name of Jackson. Of which three brothers owned separately No. 7, No. 9 and No. 11 Palmetto St. There were two houses on our lot, the front house contained four rooms, two up and two downstairs which the smaller one to the rear contained three rooms and a small kitchen, all on one floor. The front portion of the lot was fairly high and was seldom under water when the tide was high, though a portion of the rear lot and the rear portions of Nos. 9 and 11 which had not been fenced off were still overgrown with marsh grass in which the tide water sprang through the ground on very high tides.

The conveniences we found on Palmetto Street were far less than these we enjoyed on Calhoun Street. In truth the change was perhaps as great to us as were those encountered by settlers who left the east to the undeveloped areas of the far west. There was no water supply to the Palmetto Street home and so, for a while we begged water from the people who lived across the street at No. 6 as they had a well which gave plenty of potable water. Father's first effort towards getting a water supply was by constructing an ingenious arrangement of whiskey barrels, about six of them, on a platform. Each barrel at a lower level than the one before it and connecting all with overflow pipes from one to the other. A wooden gutter pipe leading to the roof of the house entered the first barrel and when it rained, the water collected in the barrels. But six barrels of water could only last a short while and since we brought two cows with us from Calhoun Street, it became my daily task to lug water from across the street every morning and afternoon to keep the cows supplied. Father's next attempt to solve the water supply problem was by constructing a huge wooden tank. He built it of planks, caulked it with oakum and coated it with pitch and tar both in and outside but despite that it leaked and so the problem remained unsolved. Then he had a well dug in the front yard, where the probability of finding fresh water was best, but when it was finished, we found much to our disappointment that the water it gave was salty. And so I was doomed to be both drawer and bearer of water for many years to come. In periods of drought when the well across the street went dry, then I had to go to the corner to Rutledge Avenue and Calhoun Street to get my supply.

As the milk business grew, I was automatically advanced to the positions of chief nurse and attendant upon three cows, cleaning their stalls, boiling cow peas, passing out cow pea vine when it was obtainable, and mixing their bran and about three times a week adding to it the spent hops that we bought from the brewery. Of course we did not know anything about vitamins then or that brewer's yeast held a content of it, but empirically we did know that it improved the cows' milk giving ability. Of course those duties were but a small part of my daily chores, for in addition to those I was the delivery boy for most of it, except for the short while when Willie, who was only known as "Willie, Willie rat tail" was employed.

The second year after we came to Palmetto Street, Father built a small shop, where we sold wood, some vegetables, horse cakes and "gungers." Since I was now growing, the added duties of clerking in the shop and delivering wood, not to mention storing it in the shop after the wood cutter had split into penny sticks, going to Knobelauch's at King Vanderhorst Street for the horse cakes, and my usual share of scrubbing were not deemed overtaxing on my strength.

But through it all there was room for enjoyment and play. In the wintertime, I would get some of the boys to help me and when we had finished, I would take them in the shop and build a fire in the stove and beneath its grate bars, roast sweet potatoes and eat them from the skins. My new companions brought a variety to these sessions as each took turn in telling a story. Most of them were the folk stories of the Uncle Remus type and thus Brer Rabbit, Brer Fox and the other inhabitants of the briar patch became the heroes of our evenings. Sometimes the program was varied to one of song in which "the buzzard that cross the river to see Sallie King" was voted too effeminate and was succeed by a weird rendition by one boy who had recently come from the Jacksonboro section, that had a refrain that went somewhat like this: "Gone to Green pond For watah; Meet a Bull frog da hollah..." but in which the [rhythm] and syllables were made [to] take on the slow beating of a drum.

Our elders and their children and the neighborhood were a far more lowly group than those I knew on Calhoun Street. But lowly only in so far as low wages, poor housing and meager education could contrive. For beyond these their friendships and neighborly qualities were sincere and free from the vices that so often infest the average poor neighborhood. In reality they comprised a democracy of the poor in which honesty and kindliness prevailed. I doubt if a single house in the entire "lot" had a lock and key to its doors. Certainly ours did not and it would frequently happen when we were out and a rainstorm occurred that one of our neighbors would enter and close the windows and on our return inform us that they "had shut up the house for us" and never once was anything molested. For the folks in "chaff lot" never stole. At time they would fight but usually only with their fists, sometimes rocks and bricks were used. But never did they seek to carve an enemy with razor or knife. I never saw a pistol fired there except on the celebration of Christmas at which time bullets flew fast and wide. Drinking was occasional—usually only on Saturday nights with Sundays to recuperate on and so be ready to answer the 7 o'clock whistle and mill bell call to work from Halsey's Mills.

A number of those whose intimacies and relationships were linked with those of the "lot" lived in the company's houses at the West Point Rice Mills about three blocks away, separated from the main group, by the newly constructed Roper Hospital.

Many changes have since come to "chaff lot." Passing events and the march of time have both succeeded in obliterating its name and changing its contour. The bridge that once connected Palmetto Street with Six Chimneys is gone and where it stood is now the site of a home, built there originally by Old Lady Holmes who lived in Simmons lot and sold vegetables. The pond that extended southward from Doughty Street, along Lucas to Meyers Wood Yard is now largely filled in, giving rise to lower President Street and that area on which a new addition to Roper Hospital has been erected. While the old plank road that once covered a part of Lucas Street has given place to modern asphalt.

Likewise have many of our neighbors of former years disappeared leaving behind them only memories. Some were unique and some can never be forgotten. One of them are the Grants. The husband was janitor at the downtown market. He was a little man who always wore a long brass keychain on which was suspended a varied assortment of keys and other trinkets. Mrs. Grant was Amazonian in size and build and on days when the street was flooded with tide water would meet him at the corner of Ashley Avenue, barefooted and with her skirt tied up above her knees, pick him up in her arms, as one would a baby and bravely wade through the water with him and land him safe at home. For she always said that "Francis is a weak man and he mustn't get sick." And next to her in Simmons lot lived Mrs. Holmes a very gentle and industrious lady who peddled vegetables. She weighed about 200 pounds, all solid muscle and woe befell any man who irked her. For she could and on many occasion did whale the daylights out of men who exceeded her in size.

On our side of the street lived the Middletons, the Morrisons, the Coaxums, the Simmons, the Johnsons and on the opposite side the Spearings and Johnsons, another family. One white family lived on the street—the Cravatts, a widowed mother and daughter.

Compared with its backyard neighbors in "chaff lot," Ashley Avenue at the head of Palmetto street was a different world in which resided Negroes and whites, some in pretentious homes and some that were not quite so fine but all seemingly with one accord imbued with the idea of avoiding the "lot" for few of them ever passed through it. This however did not bar our friendships—only restricted it for we occasionally visited them while they seldom visited us.

At the northwest corner of Ashley and Palmetto the Chaplins lived and at their rear in a little cottage dwelt a brother Aiken Crum. Mrs. Sarah Chaplin was a sister of Dr. Crum. Also living with them was a sister, Miss Florence Crum, who evidently was a very beautiful woman who unfortunately had developed a facial cancer compelling her to keep the greater portion of her faced bandaged from view. Mr. Chaplin was a "head waiter" who made semi-annual trips to summer and winter resorts, taking with him on each trip a full crew of waiters and bellhops. At No. 153 Ashley dwelt two families, the Taylors and the Johnsons. Each family had a boy, the Johnsons had Arthur and the Taylors one whose name I never knew but only knew him as "Bubber." On the opposite side lived the Parkers, the Fordhams and a white family, the Smiths.

As time from my many arduous duties permitted, I found opportunity to become acquainted with my neighbors and to make playmates among them. One of my earliest companions was "Raggy nine" one of the best scrappers I ever knew and across the street from our home, Johnny Spearing and Peter Richardson who lived with his mouth organ in his mouth and was always improvising musical ditties that were more annoying to me than beautiful to my ears. For he dedicated one to me— so we always fought whenever he would play and sing "Maussa McFall to pull your wagon." And also were the two Pinckney boys from Doughty Street, Mose and John, and from across the street in the arsenal, (The Porter Military Academy), "Tonkie" Robin- son whose father was the school's cook and dwelt there. Since "Tonkie" lived on the campus we automatically acquired a right to play there and so we had our baseball diamond there, away from the portion where the students played.

These boys taught me to swim, to row a boat, to fish, to knit nets, to rig fishing lines and also the mystical methods of avoid- ing cramps while swimming, by taking the [skins] from eel and tying it about the waist and around the wrists. One day while wearing my protective skins I happened to pass by Mother when she got a whiff of me and from then on I was divested of my cramp protecting odor. However I still know that when swim- ming should you smell watermelons that sharks are about and that you had better get out.

Together we would roam the neighborhood, going through the lumber and rice mills, watching the men while they worked and picking up whatever came handy. In this way I got my first job, to clean the *Anna Julia*, a fishing boat. Each day when the boats returned from their trips to the "black fish banks," the fisherman would leave small fish in the boat as a reward for the cleaner. I would first string my fish, rinse them off in the creek, then proceed to flush out the boat and dry everything. Perhaps I did a better scrubbing job for them than I ever did at home.

However my fish were always a welcomed addition to the family larder.

In the company with these boys, I would go to Halsey's Mill and gather waste lathes from the saws and drag them home. And which after several washings by rainfall would be rid of the salt that was in them and then became fit for firewood.

In the meanwhile I had acquired an immunity against taunts for being a cross-eyed boy. Not that I was no longer sensitive to the taunts but that through the tutelage of "Raggy nine" I could whip any boy my size or weight who dared to cross their fingers in my presence, or style me "Cross-eye Maussa McFall."

Our principal playground was the waterfront which included the pond that stretched from the Savannah wharf causeway on the south to Spring Street on the north and from Lucas Street out to a causeway that separated it from the Ashley River; the creek which flowed from the Ashley up to the rear of Roper Hospital then swinging to the left went under a small bridge at "Six Chimneys" and emptied into the pond, and last, the river itself. Where at the head of the causeway were the four Savannah wharves. Three of them were then in use by the Ashepoo (Bradley's) Fertilizer Companies as warehouses for phosphate rock. The causeway connected with the wharves over a small bridge under which the incoming tide would sweep at terrific speed until it reached the "horse hole" about two hundred feet away. Only the more experienced swimmers would swim there and so it became the aspiration of every boy to dive from the bridge, swim under it and either catch the brick siding of the bridge and pull out or continue to the "horse hold" and around in its eddy to the shore.

This was a favorite shrimping ground and at ebb tide we would gather to drop our nets when the incoming tide started to flow, for that was the best time to catch shrimps. From the head of the wharves we would fish. Sometimes our luck would be good and we would bring home crocus, whiting, sheep head and occasionally a small shark. At other times only toad fish would bite and then we would return empty, for the toads were inedible but nevertheless happy for then we could chant the luckless fisherman's tune, "a soaking wet ass and a hungry gut."

Opposite Six Chimneys, on the causeway lived "Uncle Judge" a man of mystery to everyone who lived alone in his "squatter's cabin" that he had built from raft ties and other salvaged odds and ends. Uncle Judge was an enigma who seldom spoke to anyone. In stature and appearance he was similar to the orthodox depictions of "Father Time" and to the people about him he was ageless for none knew when he first came to dwell there or who his relatives were. He had built a boat, as unique as was his cabin. It was about fourteen feet long by four feet at the beam. The stern held a small cabin in which he could crawl and sleep whenever and wherever he chose. Towards the bow he had a box of sand on which he made a fire for cooking. He propelled it by oars and made frequent trips up and down the river catching raft ties. Sometimes he would be gone for a week and on his return would be towing a raft of ties that he had caught. The river was his universe; it gave him food and the ties he got from it provided for his other needs. Sometimes Uncle Judge would catch a bateaux and these he would sell. I bought mine from him. It was a four-board bateaux to which I added a mast, built up [its] stern, and installed a crocus bag sail. I usually tied my bateaux at the corner of Doughty and Lucas Streets where Harry Pinckney, an older brother of Mose, kept his rowboat.

One day while sailing it in the pond, an ill wind caught me near the Spring Street side and tide began leaving me. I managed to get near to the channel that led to the "horse holes" and there anchored my craft by sticking the paddle in the mud and tying the boat to it. I took off my clothes, which were few, and made a bundle of them and fastened to the back of my neck and started to wade a shore. I never knew until then how deep one could sink into "pluff mud" for soon I was bogged to above the knees. After much effort I succeeded in reaching the channel where about fourteen inches of water lay. I decided to try swimming but only succeeded in having my belly badly scratched by oyster shells. Finally I reached the shore bathed my wounds put on my clothes and painfully took the way to home.

That summer Father was elected a delegate to the Odd Fellows Convention which met in Boston. It was Father's first trip to the far north. So Mother began to prepare him for the journey. Her first attention was to his overcoat, since Boston was in the far North where the weather was intensely cold or at least was supposed to be. So his overcoat, which was a pretty heavy affair and extremely warm for he would use it as a covering when weather was very cold, had a heavy flannel lining installed so that he could not take cold. He took it with him on the trip and I have often since wondered how he stood the sweating—for it was summertime in Boston.

While Father was gone, Mother's thrift and economy practices reached their highest level. Each morning I got up at 4 o'clock and took my net and caught the meat supply for the day. When Father returned I told him that Mother would not spend any money for our food that all we ate during his absence was shrimps, milk, and hominy, and at night "cold water tea" and bread. At which everybody laughed, especially Mother. But I later learned that every penny she saved went to the payment of the building loan mortgage on the home.

When we came to Palmetto Street, I was transferred to the Morris Street School while Laura, being a girl, was sent to Avery. I do not recall that I did any spectacular work at Morris Street School, for I only won the weekly award medal once. Beyond that I had had one or two conferences with Mr. Doty's cane and even though I had rubbed by hands well with rosin the memory of the contact lasted long. Mr. Doty, who was [the] principal, was an exacting disciplinarian. He exacted good behavior from his pupils at all times, both while in school and even on the streets after school if within his view. Mr. Doty lived on Mill Street near Lucas and so he came to know me well and I to know his usual routes. So I often sought to avoid him, for any misbehavior that he saw on the streets became a punishable offense, the same as if committed in the school. He was equally exacting of his teachers as he was with pupils. I recall that at one of his periodic examinations in spelling his ire rose when he called upon a pupil to spell the word "bacon." Now it must be understood that Charleston folks pronounce words differently from all others, especially Mr. Webster. So when the first child arose and spelt it "ba-ba-con" his ire new no bounds. He went through the entire class and then turned upon Miss Mustard, our teacher a sweet and mild-mannered lady, and bawled her out for teaching us in that manner. Miss Mustard immediately fainted, at which he made the class stand and turn its backs. And then from over our shoulders we saw him pick her up and take her to the office. It happened just after the morning recess and there we stood, forgotten by everybody until 2 o'clock when the assistant principal came through and asked what were we doing there. In the meantime the floor had become well-watered and not from tears.

The following year Mr. Doty died and was succeeded by Mr. Hill, who was formerly his assistant. Practically every child at school went to his home to view his body. Somehow the entire atmosphere of the school underwent a change with the passing of Mr. Doty. Maybe it was that a weaker personality had taken over who lacked the rigid requirements insisted upon but which always held full justice.

The next year I was in Miss Mackenzie's class. Miss Mackenzie was Scot, a rigid disciplinarian and an earnest capable teacher. One day a stampede occurred. A Christianized Fiji islander had come to the city and was lecturing on the customs of his people. Which as the children knew consisted mostly of cannibalism with special fondness for the feet of little girls.

That morning he came to the school and finding no one in the office walked into the girls' yard hoping to find someone who could present him. One of the small girls saw [him] approaching another child and immediately she raised an alarm that the cannibal was eating a child. In her fright she ran upstairs yelling her fear as she ran. In less time than it takes to tell it pandemonium ran riot and children were jumping from the lower windows and rushing down the stairs. The noise was like distant thunder. In our room which was on the fourth floor, the children started to run for the door but Miss Mackenzie placed herself there and with her pointer struck several of the foremost and compelled all to return to their seats. Two or three of the boys climbed to the windows and one named Freelain made as if to jump out. Perhaps the distance to the ground caused him to change his mind about jumping for he took second look and went back to his seat. In a few minutes quiet prevailed and it was all over so far as we in our class was concerned. But in the meanwhile the fire alarm had been sounded and firemen and policemen had arrived. A number of children were injured but fortunately none, seriously. Grandmother McFall who then lived downtown on Church street had learned of the happening quickly arrived uptown to learn if I was injured.

Morris Street School, then a grammar school, gave a very good course of study of which I regret to say much escaped me with the exception of what was [in] my Swinton's Sixth reader. For in that I took a keen delight and so its lessons which began with Milton's *Paradise Lost*, [*Il'Peneroso* ?], followed by Bacon, Shakespeare and on through the great works of English literature.

The attendance at Morris Street School came largely from the poorer families in the city. But despite that there was every effort made to simulate cleanliness even though its actual existence was absent. Practically every girl came to school dressed in a clean white apron with a bib attached. The boys however were often overlooked in these matters for sometimes one or two would show evidence that his face was unwashed and then the teacher would compel him to go to the yard and wash his face in the sponge bucket. Head lice were more or less a constant companion to all and found ample opportunity for widening their circle of contact through the "hat closets," where hats and caps after being collected by the "hat monitor," were piled one within the other and stored until closing time.

It was while I was at Morris Street School that I learned the social differences. Not that between races but the more inimical one within race groups. For it was not long before I became one of those who was supposed to molest and to beat, when it could be safely done, any male pupil from Avery Institute. For they were the supercilious ones, usually well dressed and always ready to sing, "Morris Street ravens, Mary Street rams, Can't associate with The Bull Street lambs" and equally capable of protecting themselves except when outnumbered or attacked with more rocks than they had.

The year following the cannibal's visit Mother decided to send me to Avery as my progress at Morris Street School was unsatisfactory to her. I took the entrance examinations and much to my disappointment could only make the seventh grade which was the one in which my sister Laura was. The humiliation from this soon wore off and gave place to pleasanter things. The novelty of having a Colored teacher after so many years under white ones, stimulated my methods. For my new teacher, Miss Mary L. Deas possessed so many ways of attracting her pupils to her that few could resist. So I did my best not only with the intent to please my teacher but also to keep Laura quiet.

The year before I entered Avery a very important happening occurred to me—it came about while I was reading a serial story that ran in the Sunday newspaper, "Nada the Lily" by Rider Haggard. It was about a Zulu princess and a most exciting story it was; even more so than "She" by the same author. One night while reading it, I unconsciously placed my hand over my right eye and found that I could not see the print. So I asked Mother if people only saw through one eye, the right eye only. At which she became alarmed. The next day she took me to Dr. Kollock, an eye specialist, who after examining my eyes pronounced that the optic nerve was in bad shape and that an operation to correct my cross eyes should be done as that would help the other eye. A couple of days later I underwent the operation at his office and then had glasses fitted. The results were highly satisfactory in so far as the operation was concerned though vision in the left eye is almost totally lost.

Having become a member of the "the Bull Street lambs" my contacts widened and though I found companionship, I also became aware that my clothes were of poorer quality than those worn by many of them. Neither did I have the spending money that some of them had. I noticed that the boys who worked in white barbershops were always better dressed and had more money than those who did not. I had the urge to be as they. So one day I saw Mr. Rufus Felder who operated the finest barber shop in the city and asked him for a job. He said that I could have the job if my father wanted me to work for him and that I must have my father speak with him about it. That night I told Father about it and asked if he would see Mr. Felder. He said that he would think about it and let me know his decision later. A few days later Father told me that he was glad to learn that I wanted to learn a trade but that he did not want me to be a barber and that he had talked with Mr. Sanders who promised to accept me as a tailor's apprentice and that when the summer vacation began that I would go there. And that was that.

Arthur Johnson, who lived on Ashley Avenue had already started his apprenticeship to a tailor. The Pinckney boys, whose father had recently died, were going to New York where their brother Harry and an aunt had gone. Several of the other boys who usually played with me had found jobs at Halsey's Mill.

Mother had disposed of her cows which gave me more leisure and more time for study. The prospects of a lonely summer vacation caused me to welcome the opportunity for becoming an apprentice. I was now in the eighth grade with Mr. Edward A. Lawrence my teacher. At the close of the year I was promoted to the normal department.

My duties at Mr. Sanders' were somewhat disappointing, but not quite so much as was that encountered when I received my first weeks wages, only one dime. Father told me not to worry about that for I was there to learn and that money could not be earned until the worker knew how to do the work. Mr. Sanders had three tailors in his shop. There was Lionel Holmes, who was a vest and pants maker; Heyward who made pants; and his brother-in-law, Mr. Attles who made coats and vests. Mr. Sanders only worked on coats. Most of his work came from Mensing's tailoring establishment on King Street near Queen. Mensing carried an extensive line of woolens and tweeds from which he would sell made to order suits. He did all of the cutting and trying on. But the actual making of the garments was done at Mr. Sanders. Heyward had a similar arrangement with Woolfe-Banov who conducted a men's furnishing shop at the corner of King and Calhoun Streets. But the work from there was of a cheaper quality and did not require the close attention to detail that Mensing's called for. Neither was the pay the same so Woolfe-Banov's work was always referred to as "buzz" and "buzz" it was for on Saturdays, Heyward could make three pairs of trousers at a dollar each—which was big money in those days.

My work consisted of keeping the shop clean, keeping the fire going in the irons, trips to and from to Mensing's with suits, and on occasions to the well at Wentworth and Meeting Street for a jug of "iron" water. My training required that I sit on board (table) with knees crossed and sew pieces of rags until I learned the various stitches. First was the "back stitch" which had to be learned until it was as neatly done as a sewing machine could do it. Next was "felling" by which linings were sewed to the fabric without the stitch showing. And this had to be done on the thinnest of rags. Then came the "herringbone" stitch and finally the making of buttonholes. Mr. Sanders would not allow his apprentice to use the sewing machine for he said, "you can't learn to sew on a machine." My first contribution to the making of a garment, was the sewing of sleeve linings by hand, and later the felling of coat linings. Heyward taught me to make pants' flies and do the buttonholes. Sometimes we had cleaning to do. And cleaning in the old days was done thoroughly—with a scrubbing brush and plenty of hot water. After which the garment was given a good rinsing and hung on a line to dry. Then it would be pressed and held until called for. In my second summer I did most of the scrubbing, some of the pressing and most of the felling of linings. In the meanwhile my weekly wage had been increased to 25¢ a week.

August 18, 1893 brought a hurricane. The most destructive I have ever seen. It was a Sunday. I had gone with Arthur Johnson to his home after Sunday school. The weather was cloudy a stiff wind was blowing and showers fell in between. I left his home about 5 o'clock in the afternoon and in between showers made it home without getting wet. When I reached Palmetto Street the incoming tide had reached our home and was rapidly rising. I managed to get in the house without wetting my feet and went upstairs and changed my clothes. By then the wind had increased to a gale and the rain was coming down in torrents and it could be seen that we were in for a storm. The water continued to rise. Mr. Jesse Martin and his family lived in the house in the rear. The water was going into their house and he brought Mrs. Martin, his daughter and his youngest son into ours. He asked me to go and help his son Walter pile their furniture so that the water could not reach them. The water in the yard was then above my waist so I waded through it and made their house and began piling furniture above the water. As hard as we tried to do this, the higher the water rose. So I decided to quit trying and get Walter to the front house. The water was then about my waist in the house and when we reached the yard, I found that it was deeper than my head. Walter could not swim. The yard was filled with floating debris for fences had fallen and the boards and everything else that could float was coming in with the wind and tide. Though the distance from the Martin's house to ours was not over twenty feet, it took me nearly half an hour to swim the distance with him. Fortunately he was cooperative and did not get frightened. When we reached our house we found that the water had reached the fourth step on the inside stairway. So everybody went to the second floor to wait out the storm I was so fatigued from my struggle with the storm, that I laid down on the "chest" and slept soundly until morning came. The storm had subsided but the wind and tide was still high. I went down to the head of the street, to the old bridge, and since several boys were swimming there, I peeled off and went in. Father had been watching me, and after me he came, with a piece of sash rope waving in his hand. He yelled for me and I came and got the last licking of my life. Father thought that I might have been drowned and though it was only a difference in opinions he won.

The following day was one of general house cleaning. Everything had to be scrubbed for slime and had covered everything on the lower floor. Our fences were down and all of our firewood had floated away with the outgoing tide. When I got a chance I went strolling to see what damage had been done. The new bridge was wrecked and piled upon it was an English tramp steamer. On Calhoun Street nearly opposite to Emanuel Church a three-masted schooner lay high and dry. The entire waterfront of the city was a mass of wreckage. At the old Southern wharf, where the Shriner's home now stands a three-masted schooner had broken itself in two over what remained of the wharf. It is this ship that is depicted in "Porgy and Bess." "The Battery" was a wreck if such can be said about a boulevard, the heavy flag paving stones of the high walkway, had been washed away and laid on the opposite side of the street. The iron railings along the walkway were bent and broken away by the force of water. While the paving in the center of the street had been broken and floated away. Only the heavy wall stones remained. Few buildings escaped damage. Fallen trees were everywhere and damage by rising water which flooded buildings and ruined their contents was enormous.

The following year, during the Easter holidays, Mr. Martin gave me a job, that of laborer at 50¢ a day, to carry bricks and mortar, on a bricklaying job he had on Rutledge Avenue. The two houses, the third and fourth, south from Doughty Street on the west side were under construction. Mr. Martin was building the chimneys. And my job was to carry the bricks and mortar he used to the scaffold where he worked and in between time straighten up the yard. It was hard work but I wanted the money. For some time I had been hankering for a pair of long pants, and had become somewhat self-conscious about my height and the thin tightfitting short pants I had. So that Saturday afternoon when I was paid off, I went shopping. I went to David's, he then conducted a small shop on King Street in a one-story building near Wentworth at the sign of the "big hat." I went in and asked for a pair of long pants. After searching his stock he brought out a pair of cream colored serge trousers and told me that it was the only pair he had at the price I wanted, that could fit me. I tried them on and found them to be too long. He told me that they could be shortened. I then mentioned that they were too large in the waist, but he called my attention to the draw straps at the back and told me that all that was necessary was to bring them in closer. So he took my $3, shortened the trousers and I went home rejoicing. I thought that mother would die when she saw my purchase but it was too late to do anything about them since they had been altered.

The next day, Sunday, I felt like a peacock when I went to church. Perhaps my appearance warranted comments, since my coat, a rather tightfitting hard worsted one of gray color tinged with pink strips, with sleeves that were two inches too short, and so tight it could not be buttoned, and the pink china silk tie that Jennie Grant made for me, were not quite in harmony with the trousers. But what care I for I was now in long pants and once there the die was cast.

Peoples' Pharmacy

INTRODUCTION TO A PHARMACY

In the spring of that year Father arranged with Dr. McClennan for my apprenticeship in his pharmacy. Father had been employed in the manufacturing department of Dr. Baer's wholesale and retail drugstore, for perhaps his entire married life. Certainly he was there during the time we lived on F Street and ever after. And so his ambition for me was to become a pharmacist. Dr. McClennan was not only our family physician but was also a friend of Father. For years it was my habit to go down to Dr. Baer's on Saturdays at noon to await the half-holiday closing hour and then walk back home with Father. On these visits while waiting for him I would roam about the plant and through the laboratory. Poking my nose into everything, until one day, seeing a large apparently empty carboy I removed the stopper and placed my nose to the opening the bottle to my surprise I received a knockout blow from the ammonia fumes that were in it. After that experience I restricted my curiosity to only seeing things. It was from these visits that I learned much about crude drugs and the original import packages in which they arrived. Father would tell me their names and where they came from. Dr. Arthur Speissegger was in charge of the manufacturing department. He was a kindly man and in after years proved his friendship to Father and to me. Three white women were employed upstairs—whose duties were to package and label medicines. Two Colored men, Mr. John Lawrence and Mr. Taylor were employed upstairs. Downstairs were the prescription and sundries departments. Dr. [Charles E.] Bullineau was in charge of the prescription department and Lawrence McBride, then a young man, was in the sundry department.

Dr. Baer was a German Jew. He had accepted Christianity and was a member of the Methodist Church. He was highly educated and was a linguist of no mean ability for he was a master of seven languages. He never participated in active politics though for many years he served as School Commissioner with supervision over the Morris Street School. Mr. Levin was bookkeeper. Dr. Baer was a friend in every sense of the word, as in later years he proved to be.

One of Father's duties was packaging crude drugs and labeling them. He had acquired a broad knowledge of their official names as well as their botanical names and families. He could instantly recognize any of them and could make them into tinctures and fluid extracts for such was his daily work.

These were the incentives that prompted him to seek for [me] the opportunity to learn pharmacy.

Dr. McClennan's drugstore was known as "The Peoples Pharmacy." It was located in the two-story building next to the one now occupied by O'Rourke's jewelry store on King Street near Warren. The building was about seventy-five feet in depth and twenty-five in width. The drugstore occupied the front portion and the doctor's office the rear. On the second-floor front was Dr. Robert J. Macbeth's dental office and to the rear of it, the editorial and composing rooms of the *Charleston Enquirer*, the second Negro paper to be published in Charleston. Rev. George C. Rowe and C.C. Jacobs were the editors and Robert Wainwright its printer.

The store was located in the midst of the uptown drug business section with Almar's Drugstore [409 King Street] at the corner below it and Dr. Schwacke's across the street [426 King Street] at the corner of John. Its patronage though general, came largely from the patients of Drs. McClennan, Thompson, Rankin and Robinson. Its stock and equipment were complete. Some of its fixtures, its prescription counter and iron stand show cases, had come from the Dingle Pharmacy, the first Negro-operated pharmacy in Charleston. When Dr. [Moses] Dingle closed out his business, Dr. McClennan bought most of his stock and fixtures and opened a prescription dispensary in the basement of his home at the corner of Woolfe and Meeting Streets, under the management of Dr. Edwin Elfe. Julius Mayer, the doctor's nephew, received training there and also at Howard University. After his graduation there he was brought back to Charleston and was placed in charge of the store, second however to Mr. Elfe. Dr. Ehren, who had also served under Dr. Dingle was employed at the dispensary and for a while longer at the Pharmacy. He left the year I started and went west, and across the [color] line.

When I entered, William (Billy) Birney was senior apprentice. He welcomed me to the store and gave me a mortar containing sulfur and chlorate of potash and told me to rub them together. He had placed a piece of cardboard over the mixture with a hole in its center through which the pestle went. My extreme care in not being rough with the mortar prevented the expected explosion and Bill after a moment of anxiety, repented of his act and took the mortar and dumped its contents into a pail of water. Such was the routine of initiation at that drugstore at that time.

My first duties were at the soda fountain. A new outfit had been installed that year and was complete with convenient tumbler washer, the ornate fountain type, a milkshake machine that operated with a hand crank, a hand ice shaver built on the order of a carpenter's plane but inverted and the necessary service supplies. Ice cream soda and soda straws were then unknown in Charleston. Cracked ice was used in all drinks, as neither the carbonated water nor the syrups were refrigerated. One afternoon just about dusk, one month after I started a boy entered the store and asked for the doctor. He was about the most bedraggled and filthy boy I had ever seen. I directed him to the office where the doctor was. About an hour later, he and the doctor went out and on their return brought several packages back with them. The doctor took him upstairs where he unearthed him and dressed him in the things he had bought. It developed that the boy was Alonzo Robinson, a nephew of the doctor. He had trampled all the way from Barnwell to Charleston walking most of the distance with hope that the doctor would take him in. He was not disappointed for Dr. McClennan was one of the most generous of men. Sometimes his magnanimity went to excess for at times he never paused to measure his [illegible] or extent of his [produce?], and so it would often happen that his generosity would be given at personal sacrifice. Dr. McClennan was one of the first appointments to Annapolis Naval Academy. But after a year spent there in which fighting and every other persecution was encountered, the Senator who appointed him suggested that he resign from the Academy and enter Howard University School of Medicine, which he did. Graduating from there with the degrees of doctor in medicine and doctor in pharmacy. He began practice in Charleston during the late 1880s and built up a splendid if not profitable practice, as Charleston with the rest of the country were then in the beginning throes of the Cleveland panic. In addition to his good qualities he was possessed with two faults, the first, a love from alcoholic stimulants, and the second an uncontrollable temper. And when the two were in simultaneous action trouble was on. He was highly respected in the community by both whites and Colored and it was hinted, even venerated by some whites for it seems that they saw in him a duplicate picture of their lamented Wade Hampton.

"Lonnie" [Alonzo] Robinson's coming promoted me to the drug department as he was given charge of the soda fountain. Mr. Elfe presented [me] with two implements as an induction into my course of study. The first was a cleaning rag with which I made weekly trips over the stock medicine bottles on the front. The second was a notebook in which I recorded the name from each bottle, its Latin name, its English name, its synonym, usage and if poisonous, its antidote. These I had to memorize and in addition note any particular character by which the preparation could be easily identified. The front shelves contained about three hundred such bottles. When these were memorized he quizzed me on them and next introduced me to the *Dispensatory*, a behemoth book containing about 2,800 pages of detailed information about all of the more important drugs and their preparations. All in alphabetical arrangement, beginning with "Absinthium and ending with Zingiberia." That was my course in theory. My practical training started with the making of seidlitz powders, waters, syrups and then tinctures. In those days the druggist manufactured most of what he used and under Mr. Elfe's tutelage I learned to make things that were not even taught at college. For we made our cologne water. And at Christmastime would package it in imitation cut glass bottles and seal the top with kid skin tied on with baby blue ribbon. We made most of the tooth powder that we sold. Which usually were in 5 or 10¢ packs. Face powder—the highly scented, high price variety was unknown. Since a nickel's worth of "[illegible] eyes" with a spraying of cologne water filled the need. Though coated pills had been in use for some time, many of our customers insisted on "handmade" compound cathartic pills and so it became my job to keep the week's supply an adequate one.

One Sunday night, while I was on with Julius Mayer, we had a prescription rush and Julius passed me a prescription and told me to fill it. It happened to be for magnesium carbonate to be made into twenty powders. It also happened that magnesium carbonate was one of the things I had not studied. The name had been abbreviated on the prescription to "MagCarb," which made it all the more confusing to me. I looked at it and with some degree of pomposity, I believe, asked Julius where the "mag carb" at which he laughed and said "quit bluffing" get that can from the top shelf. I humbly brought it down, weighed out the quantity, tritusated it, divided my powders, all the while wondering if my first prescription would be correct. For many of the frequent disorders, especially malaria, we usually kept Dr. McClennan's prescriptions readymade. The making of these was my particular duty. By the end of my first year I had acquired as much practical training as the average college student gets in four years of college work.

My work at the drugstore brought me in contact with all types of people and gave me opportunity to learn something about the life of which I was a part. It also brought to light difficulties of pioneering a profession and getting the confidence of people, many of whom had never before employed or even saw a Negro engaged in pharmacy. And so it required tact, perseverance and at times just plain bold effrontery to convince them that we were equally competent with the whites. I recall that once, a Negro from the rural section, asked if we filled doctors' prescriptions. I replied that we did. At which he expressed surprise and then asked "When unnah git you medicine—white folks wont gie you?" For a moment it stumped me, for a moment only for I quickly adopted a condescending attitude and asked, "You can read, can't you," knowing at the time that he could not, but he answered "yes." I reached [for] a bottle of a patent medicine that was made in New York and pointed to the label and said "See here" all of our medicines come from the North—from New York. Which both astounded and convinced him that we were competent.

And which was all the more effective, for the North was, to the simple Negro of the South, a place of mystery as well as wonder, as it had sent the Union armies throughout the South to give them freedom. And also the missionary barrels that contained clothing and shoes and was freely given to all who asked. Also were there other obstacles to overcome chief of which arose through petty jealousy from some of the doctor's colleagues who would not allow their prescriptions to come to us. Two of them sent all of their prescriptions to a white drugstore insisting that we could not fill them. Though their real reason for so doing was that they received a ten percent commission on all of their prescriptions. A practice which Dr. McClennan would not condone as he held that it was unethical.

The store was the usual gathering place for many of the doctor's friends. Several of them were men who held political positions or were otherwise men of prominence in the community. In this way I came to know many men who had shared in the making of history in South Carolina. Among them I may mention General Robert S. Smalls from Beaufort, who usually stopped with the doctor on his way to and from Columbia. General Smalls was a unique personality who at times would pause to tell me anecdotes of his life. There was General Sam Lee, the most outstanding Negro member of the South Carolina bar. Mr. Lee possessed one of the most remarkable memories of any man I knew, for with a single reading, he could memorize and repeat verbatim, pages of references without further reading. My first experience with dangerous illness was with him—on a Sunday he came to the store suffering from a heart attack, the doctor was out and I was alone. So it was up to me to do something for his relief. I gave him some digitalis and bromide and sent him home, with the understanding that I would have the doctor visit him at the earliest time. Mr. Lee's condition grew worse and he passed away a couple of days later. His law office was the training school for most of the Negro lawyers who have practiced in Charleston. His ability was far beyond the average and it was common knowledge that many white legal firms consulted with him about their cases. I recall that one that was told about—it was a famous murder trial in which Dr. McDow was the defendant. A Mr. Dawson, one of the editors of the *News and Courier* and Dr. McDow had an altercation in which McDow shot Dawson. Self-defense was claimed. And it is told that Gen. Lee advised McDow's attorneys to stress the fact that the bullet entered between the trouser waistband and the vest and that such could only have happened with the arm raised to strike a blow.

Another frequent visitor was Congressman Thomas E. Miller whose home was in Beaufort County. He would regale me with accounts of his political life, especially the part he and Rev. Bruce Williams played in preventing Tillman from closing the Citadel. During my last year [in Charleston] Mr. Miller sent his son Thomas Jr. to live with Dr. McClennan so that he could attend the city schools and also learn something of the drug business. But Tom's stay was short for he nearly wrecked the drugstore when he injected turpentine into our cat's rectum. Tom was merely uncivilized then as he said he "meant no harm."

Occasionally Mr. Whipper would call in but I never knew him closely. Dr. Lee, a white physician who with Dr. McClennan constituted the U.S. medical examiners for Civil War pensioners, was also a frequent visitor.

THE TILLMAN EFFECT ON NEGROES' RIGHTS

Another outstanding member of the legislature who would occasionally stop by with Gen. Smalls was Mr. Wigg from Beaufort. These were busy days for the Negro members of the legislature. Tillman had recently come into power by defeating Haskell for the governorship. Tillman had built up a powerful political machine with the avowed purpose of eliminating both the Negroes and the aristocratic whites of South Carolina from government. His organization consisted largely of the poor whites and were organized as "The Farmers Alliance" and functioned along lines that were similar to those followed in Mississippi. One of his campaigns boasted that "he would make grass grow in Charleston's streets" and there were indications that he could.

He succeeded in having a constitutional convention called at which the state's constitution would be changed so that the franchise rights of the Negroes would be cancelled or so restricted that but few could vote. Another measure which he had enacted and which was specifically aimed at Charleston, was the "Metropolitan Police Bill" which permitted the Governor to assume control of the city's police force whenever such was deemed expedient (to the governor).

The vicious purpose of his intent did not go unchallenged. The small group of Republican leaders then left in the legislature planned a campaign of protest as that was their only means of going on record against the vicious legislation Tillman proposed. Robert G. Small[s], James E. Wigg, Whipper, Thomas E. Miller and Rev. George C. Rowe who appeared as a representative of the people attended the convention. All of them with the exception of Rev. Rowe were duly elected delegates. It was apparent from the start that an almost unanimous vote would be given for whatever Tillman asked for. And that happened.

And so in the year 1895 the right of franchise was taken away from the Negroes of South Carolina by the adoption of the iniquitous "grandfather clause" and the insertion of a property and education qualification for Negroes, none of which affected the whites.

Early that year Tillman vented his spleen against Charleston by putting into effect the "Metropolitan Police Bills." It came overnight. The Central Police Station was but a block away from the drugstore and so we were among the first to learn that J. Elmore Martin had been to the city to take charge of the force with the rank of chief and that Chief Golden had been summarily deprived of office. The city was stunned but could do nothing about [it] as it was all under state law. Lieutenant Fordham's resignation was the first to be presented and quickly following was that from Sargent Brown. Within the next two months nearly half of the Negro patrolmen had been dismissed.

Needless to say, the entire city and especially its Negroes, became depressed as these happenings presaged what was to follow.

During that summer Timothy Patterson did observation work at the store. He was a student at Howard University, School of Pharmacy and was home for the vacation period. That fall he returned to college. But I never heard more of him as he also crossed over. Bill Birney having completed his apprenticeship went to Brooklyn and entered the Brooklyn College of Pharmacy and successfully [finished] its course. After which he like Patterson crossed over.

I was now the senior apprentice. Edgar Howard had been taken on as junior but Howard had other aspirations and soon left, going to Tuskegee Institute as a student. My duties had now assumed responsibilities as at times I would be left in sole charge. Mr. Elfe seldom stayed after 6 o'clock in the afternoon while Julius Mayer would usually have some social engagement or a poker game in view. Hence it fell to me to remain on duty until closing time. I did not mind the work but sometimes it brought me difficulties which were somewhat embarrassing. I remember one Sunday night when a customer handed me a prescription and said that he would wait for it. I took it to the rear and read it. It was for one-hundred pills and contained phosphorus. I knew that phosphorus was inflammable when exposed to air and that it could only be compounded in an atmosphere of chloroform vapor. Again I knew it to be extremely poisonous which gave me doubts as to my ability to accurately apportion the quantity in each pill. So I decided not to take the risk. But how to do it was the problem. For a moment I pondered the situation and then a brilliant thought came to me. I took the prescription out to the customer and told him that it was a very expensive medicine and that it would cost him two dollars and a half. He reached over and grabbed it from my hand and said, "Never mind" and out he went. I breathed a sigh of relief and immediately closed the store, though it was a half an hour before our usual closing time. The effect of my pricing the prescription at $2.50 can only be estimated by telling you that the current price then charged for such a prescription was only 85¢. His facial expression as he left convinced me that he thought that I was crazy, while I wondered if he would be crazy enough to let me fill his prescription.

Philadelphia College of Pharmacy

We were still suffering financial difficulties that followed in the wake of the Cleveland panic. Wages were low, the price of commodities the same but despite these conditions there was no actual suffering. My wages had reached the magnificent sum of $2.50 a week. I started planning for college. For nearly two years I had been a diligent reader of the *Druggist's Circular* and of *Merck's Index*. These magazines then devoted themselves chiefly to the scientific phases of pharmacy and chemistry and from time to time commented on the achievements of several schools of pharmacy. They also carried the advertisements of these schools. Gleaning what I could from these sources I had determined that I would endeavor to go to the Philadelphia College of Pharmacy. It was the oldest school of its kind in North America, its faculty was considered the best of all American schools and best of all its tuition charges were no higher than other schools. Its curriculum was so arranged that each pupil would have time to work and further that it was customary in Philadelphia for drugstores to employ two students who could alternate their hours of employment. So I decided that I would go to Philadelphia. I told the doctor about my plans and why I had chosen Philadelphia. He thought that it was practicable and in a burst of generosity told me to notify him when I got there, what book I needed and the cost and he would send me the money.

For several months I had been buying clothes. I had bought an overcoat; secondhand, for $10, dollar down and a dollar a week, and it was a beauty—dark navy blue beaver cloth, lined inside with wool, and a velvet collar. So good was it that it lasted me for the next ten years and was only discarded because I had outgrown it. My supply of woolen underwear was ample. I also had some woolen socks. These I felt would protect me against the extreme cold of the North. My other belongings I thought sufficient for my needs. I had saved up about $6 in cash.

So I spoke with Father and told him what I had planned and asked if he could help me. A look of sorrow came over his face, as he told me that he could not promise to give me aid. And then he told me of the meager wages he earned and how all of it was needed to support the home. I told him that I expected to work and knew that I could earn my support at least and perhaps some towards my tuition, at least what was needed after my first year. I also told him that I knew that I could get a job to work my way there on the Clyde steamship line and that I believed that Uncle [Allen] in Philadelphia would let me live with him until I got settled. My arguments won his consent and then he told me that he would see to borrow the money for my tuition and believed that he could get it.

I gave up my job at the drugstore on the last of July and then started to hound the Clyde Pier in hunt of an opportunity to work my way to New York. Very early one morning a few days later I met the *Seminole* (the old steamer, a new one by the same name has since taken her place) as she docked. I went aboard and found the steward and asked if he wanted a man to work his way to New York. He asked if I had ever worked on a boat, as he asked the question, I spied the *Wisteria* going out the harbor, so I replied that I had "waited" on the *Wisteria*, which in part was truth as on many occasions I had waited for the boat to dock so

I could go to the galley to see Mr. Porcher, the cook and enjoy whatever he had in the form of leftovers. He asked if I had a black jacket. I said yes. Then he told me to be at the dock before 10 a.m. and he would take me. He also directed me to have my trunk there early.

It was 4 a.m. when the boat docked that morning. My interview with the steward ended at 5:30 a.m. From then until 7 I pondered about "my trunk" for I had never owned one. Neither had I ever given thought as how my belongings would travel. So I decided to buy a trunk. I stopped in at Mays General Store on King Street near Calhoun just as it opened and asked to see a small trunk. After much bargaining, I found one that suited me. Its price was $2.50 and could be delivered immediately. It was a beautiful trunk, about forty inches long and twenty-four inches deep. It had a curved top, and black iron lock. It was covered iridescent metal in two tones of color, one beautiful blue, the other, a near tan. I rode on the wagon with the man who delivered it and immediately started my packing. Everybody joined in to help me. My overcoats went in first, the one I had bought on the dollar weekly plan, and a smaller older one that I had, my woolens, a copy of the *Dispensatory* that Dr. Harry Hancock, who worked at Dr. Baer's had given me, a bottle of Fellows Syrup of Hypophospites that Mother insisted I take along with me and use whenever I caught a cold, for if taken in time it could prevent tuberculosis, and all of my other clothing, save what I wore, and the black coat, which I had told the steward I had when he asked about "black jacket." Now this black jacket was the coat to a suit I had. It was of black diagonal cloth, made in the semi–cut away style, then in vogue, with black braiding sewed on its edges. I was totally ignorant of the style of black jackets waiters wore and honestly believed that anything black would answer. The coat and an extra shirt I wrapped in a newspaper that I could take with me. I went around the corner on Mill Street and arranged with Mr. Thomas to take me and the trunk to the dock in time for the *Seminole*'s sailing. After which we had breakfast and goodbyes.

On my way to the steamer, I felt some trepidation as I began to realize that the work I was to do was altogether new to me. I had never before been inside a public dining room and the nearest to that was only when I had passed the Charleston Hotel dining room and looked in from the outside. However the die was cast and the Rubicon of Atlantic water from Charleston to New York awaited. When I put the trunk aboard I neglected to have it checked. That did not worry me then but later it did. I shook hands with Mr. Thomas and bade him farewell and then went aboard the boat. There was none of the red tape about boarding a boat then as we now find, so I found it possible to get aboard without any questioning and then proceeded to the steerage, where I decided I would stay until the ship reached the ocean, as I knew they would not turn back merely to put me off.

As the ship was crossing the bar, the purser came in and asked for my ticket. I told him that I did not have one as I was working my way to New York. He asked to know who hired me and why I was not at work. I told him that the steward had hired me and that I was waiting for him to send for me. He said, "You come along with me." I did. He found the steward and asked if he had hired me. The steward said yes, but this is the first I have seen of him since he asked for the job. He asked where was my jacket. I told him that it was in the steerage. He told me to get it. When I brought it, he gave me a white apron and a towel and told me to put them on. When I put the jacket on he looked and asked, "Is that a black jacket?" I said yes, it is black. He merely said "Hell," then he told me to go to the dining room and set up a table. As I said, I had never before seen a dining room and so it was a new world into which I entered. A number of waiters were there and were busy setting up their tables.

So I approached one of them and asked if he would show me how to do it and explained that I was only working my way

North to go to school. Under his direction I got everything in good shape, the silver properly placed and the napkins in position. A few minutes later lunch was announced. The steward came in and took a station opposite me for as fate would have it, the number of passengers on that particular trip was large, while the number of waiters aboard were inadequate to meet the passenger demand, so the steward had to perform the duties of a waiter. I had six people to serve. Soup was first on the menu. Three ordered oxtail and three ordered consommé. I took my tray and followed a waiter to the pantry and called for the soup. I got my six plates but for the help of me I could not distinguish oxtail from consommé. But that did not phase me and even though I brought my tray in by holding it front of me instead of above my head it did not cause noticeable comment. I asked each passenger what was his soup and gave him the first that came to hand. I doubt if any of them knew the difference between the soups. If they did none showed it. Then all six ordered different things, of which I could remember but one, a glass of iced tea. One of the waiters showed me. I filled a glass with it and started off, when one of them yelled "put the glass of iced tea on a saucer," then another said put ice in it and lastly one told me to put lemon in it. I spied the plate of sliced lemons and put in about six pieces at which another waiter cried, don't take all the lemon, one piece is enough. By then I was giddy but despite that I started off for the dining room with that lone glass of iced tea in the center of my tray. When I reached my table each of my diners asked, "Where is my order?" to which I replied by asking, "Did you order the iced tea?" Eventually I found the person who had ordered the iced tea but she instead of being thankful at receiving it, was angry because the rest of her order was not there. During the while I was seeking to find the iced tea diner, the steward had gotten himself as red as a beet with beckoning me. So I went to him, he took [me] outside and asked in no unmeaning terms "How the hell you told me you could wait?" I answered, "I could." He said, "Wait hell," and immediately demoted me to dish wiping.

Now dish wiping in the days before dishwashing machines and hot-air dryers was neither an art nor a science, it was just a sweating job. So I peeled down to my undershirt and wiped until I had wetted two or three dozen towels and completed the drying of over a thousand dishes. The pantry asked if I had had dinner. I told him no so he fixed me a dinner and it was some dinner, none of the guests fared better. I asked where should I eat it, and he told me to go in the dining room. Which I did. No sooner had I gotten started than a waiter passed and asked, where was my jumper? I told him that I did not have one, he said "You had better get one for if the captain sees you eating in the dining room in your undershirt he will throw you overboard." So I donned my black jacket and finished my dinner.

Necessity compelled the steward to reappoint me to my former position. So the next morning I was ordered to set up the table for breakfast. As I have said before, life in the early 1890s did not embrace the niceties and refinements that it now has, for it was then a rather simple life and somewhat democratic. Table napkins when once issued were supposed to last a passenger for the trip. After each meal they were placed in tin napkin holders, each bearing a number which corresponded to the seat number of each passenger and reissued at subsequent meals. Few passengers received the same napkin twice in succession and yet none ever complained or turned noses up about it. The towel that was given me to wipe dishes with as they were placed on the table came in very handy to me as in the absence of a personal towel, I used one end of the dishtowel as a face towel and that end became too soiled for my face, switched ends, and no one ever complained.

That morning brought another problem, the differentiation between cold meats, when one of my passengers asked me to pass him the cold tongue, I reached him a plate and he said, "No, the tongue." I offered another and that didn't answer, then a third at which he got up and took the particular plate he wanted. And though he frowned, his neighbors merely smiled. That day the weather got rough and my "tongue" passenger could not come to dinner. I was called to his room and found him retching, I had a small bottle of paregoric in my pocket, so I gave him some. He gave me a quarter. He asked what I was doing on the boat. I told him I was working my way to school, that I intended being a druggist. He told me to keep on as from what he had seen of me that I would never become a waiter.

In between meals I had to wash the ceilings. And if one has never stood upon the top rung of a stepladder on a ship that is rocking in a rough sea and swabbed a ceiling with soap and water there can be no understanding of what that task means. But I did it and while there, Mrs. Joe Freeman, a second-class passenger passed and I didn't like the way she looked at me so I sloshed some water her way at which she went. But that was not as bad as lugging one end of the garbage tub over the engine room gratings and dumping it into the furnace for that was both hard work and hot work.

The next morning I was tired and fogged out. So I told the steward that the sea had made me sick. He looked at me and asked had I had breakfast, I said, "No!" He said "You are not sick, you are hungry, go get breakfast." After breakfast that day, I went back to steerage taking a couple of oranges with me for the "lamp man" who also had charge of the steerage for men passengers and who kept an eye on my clothes. I gave him the oranges and went to sleep. When I woke we were on the Jersey coast and rapidly nearing New York. After lunch was served, I returned to the steerage and got my things together. Then I sneaked forward to the "glory hole" where the waiters lived, borrowed someone's shoe brush, shined my shoes, used some one's comb and brush and by the time ship entered the narrows, was waiting and ready to debark. On the way in I had my first glimpse of the Statue of Liberty. As we approached the dock which was the near the Brooklyn Bridge, the view of the city with the gilded dome of the New York World Building, then the highest building in the world, and the plying traffic in the harbor astonished me. I had never before seen so much activity. It was a Sunday afternoon and the weather was intensely hot when compared to the delightful sea breezes we had left behind us. As the boat neared the dock, I edged up to the gangplank and was the first to leave the ship. In my haste to land, I had even forgotten to thank those who had aided me or even the steward who had allowed me to come.

As I reached the pier, with my newspaper bundle under my arm, a white man came up to me and asked, "Cab sir?" I had no idea of what he was talking about, so I replied "Nah," at which [he] paused and asked where was I going. I told him that I was going to Second Avenue near 42nd Street. He told me that I would need his cab to take me to the Second Avenue el and which would take me to my destination. I asked the cost and he told me it would be 75¢. Rapid mental calculation informed me that if I took his cab it would reduce the sum total of my cash to $2.00 even. So I told him that I would walk at which he turned and went away. His approach impressed me as it was the first time I had ever had a white man to address me as "Sir." But even that could not impress to the extent that I could pay 75¢ for it. I found a policeman and asked him to tell me what streetcar to take. He directed me to the Second Avenue surface line and told me to stay on it until it reached 42nd Street. Most of the surface cars in New York were then horse drawn. Some of the streets had "cable" cars. The trip uptown was a revelation. I had never before seen so many high houses, three, four and five stories high. All of brick and without front yards. As we passed through the "bow-ery", dead horses were seen all along the streets for New York was just emerging from one of its hottest hot spells and that Sunday afternoon was its first respite in several weeks. I was amazed that all the people I saw were white and that the signs on many business places were sometimes in foreign languages. On reaching 42nd Street. I left the car and found Uncle Paul's home. I rang the bell and "Aunty-ma" met me at the door. She was surprised to learn that I was able to find my way to her home unassisted and being fearful that I could not do so, had sent Tom Pinckney to meet me at the boat. About two hours later Tom came back and reported that he was at the wharf when the boat docked, and saw the passengers come off but did not see me and that he had inquired about me and was told that that boy got off the boat before the gangplank was down good. That night we had a small size family reunion as it was over eight years since I had seen either of them. And too, I had to meet my new cousin Raymond, then a baby and some of the neighbors, those living in the same house, the Steadmans and—I have forgotten the other. Then to bed but not to sleep, for the roar of the elevated road that passed our door kept me sleepless.

The following morning I told Aunty-ma that I was going down to get my trunk. She asked if I thought that I could find the way. I told her yes, that I was sure I could. When I reached the deck and found the baggage room, a small one-story shed, I was asked for my baggage check. I told the man that I did not get one when the trunk was placed aboard the ship and that I had worked my way up. That did not impress him for he insisted on getting a check. [Barney] the "lamp man" came in at the time and I asked him to identify me to the baggage man. I had spotted my trunk and pointed it out to the baggage man. He looked at it for a moment and then said, "If that is your trunk you can take it." I found an expressman outside the building and asked what would he charge to carry a trunk to Second Avenue. He said 75¢ which I paid. I gave him the number of the house and he promised delivery by 7 o'clock that evening.

When I got back home Aunt Lizzie (Aunty-ma) asked if I had succeeded. I told her yes and that the trunk would be up at 7 p.m. She asked for the check. I asked what check. I told her that I had none that I got an expressman to bring the trunk up. She was horrified at learning that I had given the trunk to the first wagon driver I found and that it was not coming through an "express company." She warned me that I could tell my trunk goodbye and that I would never see it again. To which I could only reply that the man looked to be honest and I was sure that he would bring it. And so the afternoon passed with neither of us saying much. About 7 o'clock the doorbell rang, and it was the man with my trunk. He brought it up and I thanked him for being prompt. Aunt Lizzie looked at the trunk and remarked, "He had to bring it. He couldn't do otherwise, even a thief wouldn't want it." I could not understand the real meaning of what she said for I had told her that the expressman impressed me as being honest, and I knew that the trunk was a beautiful one.

I spent nearly ten days in New York sightseeing and visiting. New York was not nearly so large then as it is now. Central Park was its uptown boundary at the center of the city and Grant's tomb, then undergoing construction, the westerly. Harlem was mostly fields with here and there a house. The Grand Central Station was a one-story structure while trains entering it ran on tracks on street levels. Walkway bridges crossed these tracks at every other street. One of the most unique of New York's character was that in which people of like races dwelt in settlements. For there was the Jewish section, the Irish section, the French and the Italian sections. Negroes were most thickly settled in three areas: the old Thompson Street section in downtown New York, "Hell's Kitchen" on 37th Street sandwiched in with Irish, and in an uptown area about 98th Street on the west side. A large number were elsewhere scattered in some instances occupying apartments in houses in which whites dwelt.

When I reached New York the McKinley-Hobart campaign for the presidency and vice–presidency of the United States was in full swing. Banners spanned the streets at many corners urging all to vote for them. In some of my walks, I would leave what money I had at home taking with me only a nickel or two. One day I took the streetcar down to the Exchange Place, near Wall Street to see the office where Uncle Paul worked. After leaving there I found that I did not have return car fare and so had to walk the distance back to 42nd Street. The farther I walked the hotter I got and the hotter I got the thirstier and hungrier I became. Despondency got me for I still had some miles to walk. I happened to pause near where a "hurdy gurdy" organ was playing. I was eight hundred miles from home tired and hungry and that "hurdy gurdy" had to peal forth,

> Just tell that you saw me,
> and they will know the rest.
> Tell Mother dear I am coming home some day
> etc.

I could bear no more and so the tears came flowing from my eyes. I finally made it home but never did I tell Aunt Lizzie or Uncle Paul about the incident.

Uncle Paul had a friend who was employed on the Pennsylvania railroad. He was kind enough to "dead head" me over to Philadelphia on the Pullman of which he was conductor–porter. It was my first experience in a Pullman coach. I took no chances by taking off my clothes or even trying to sleep. And so through the long night I laid awake listening to the click clack of the train as it rolled over the tracks. The following morning I reached Philadelphia where much to my surprise a brass band welcomed me and also the great Chinese statesman Li Hung Chang who happened to be on the same train. Li Hung Chang went his way while I took the trolley car for Darby. Uncle Allen welcomed me and once again I had the pleasure of meeting Aunt Elvira, Sadie and Oscar and the several other cousins who were born after I had returned to Charleston at the time of the earthquake.

I had placed my trunk check with an express company for its delivery to Darby before leaving the Pennsylvania station on my arrival. The following morning the trunk arrived. No longer did it show the beauty of its iridescent color nor was its shape intact. As it had been brutally treated. Its top had been smashed in and one of its sides broken. Someone had thoughtfully tied it together with heavy twine. For the first time in my life was I really mad. I told Uncle Allen of what had happened and that I would present a claim to the railroad company for its value. He went upstairs and looked at the trunk and turned to me and said, "I wouldn't bother to do that if I were you."

So ended my first trunk. But strange to say, despite the rough handling it had received, its contents were intact, even the bottle of Fellows Syrup remained unbroken.

I immediately got busy hunting a job. For though Uncle Allen was willing to have me stay with him, I could not rest until I found employment. I got a copy of the *Philadelphia Inquirer* and searched its want columns for prospects. I found two, one of which was from a drugstore in the Tioga section, some distance out in North Philadelphia. I decided to try that one first. I had with me two nicely typed letters of recommendation, one from Dr. McClennan attesting my diligence and ability as a drug clerk, the other was from Prof. Morrison Holmes, principal at Avery Institute, who testified for my scholastic standard and my personal character, and believed that they would insure me a reasonable hope for getting employment. When I reached the Tioga store the position had been filled or at least so I was told. At the other store I met with a similar answer and even though I showed my recommendations, they just didn't help.

The following morning I found one prospect, a small store on Woodland Avenue in West Philadelphia. I saw the owner who told me that the position had not been filled as yet but that he feared he could not give me the position for he had never heard of a Colored man being a druggist and in addition did not know what reaction his patronage would have to one. So that was that. And it caused me to wonder how a white cab driver could address me "sir" and offer to drive me for 75¢, and on the other hand why a white man would refuse me employment because I was a Negro. It was all new and strange to me, for in Charleston Negroes worked for whites and whites worked for Negroes. Many of the whites who lived near the Peoples Pharmacy when I worked there, patronized it and several of the white stores there employed Negro clerks, and so I wondered at the difference shown in Philadelphia from that which I had known in Charleston. I returned home somewhat sadly disappointed and went upstairs and had a good cry.

That afternoon while we were sitting on the front porch, Mrs. Marks, Aunt Elvira's sister called and told us about her visit that morning to the recently opened Douglass Hospital on Lombard Street and that it had a drug dispensary attached. I asked her for its exact location and said I would go there the following morning and seek a job.

Bright and early the next morning I was there. I introduced myself to Dr. Henry M. Minton who conducted the dispensary and showed him my recommendations and asked if he could give me work. I told him that I was in Philadelphia to attend college and that I would shortly matriculate at the Philadelphia College of Pharmacy and that I would need to work as I did not have the means to go through college without assistance. He was intensely sympathetic and after telling me that he was a graduate from the Philadelphia College and of the difficulties he encountered in getting practical training in pharmacy, he promised to do whatever he could to help me attain my aim. He said that he could not pay me much as business was small. But that he could offer me $2 a week. I jumped at the offer and immediately started to work for him. I doubt if I was ever so happy, either before or in after life, for somehow or other, his offer of help when compared with the repulse I had received the day before, restored my faith in mankind and stimulated me to greater effort.

The Douglass Hospital was the first community effort by the Negroes of Philadelphia to establish an institution where medical care would be available under the direction of Negro physicians. It was then housed in a modest three-story rented building on Lombard Street near 15th. The first floor provided space for a reception room-office, the drug dispensary and the kitchen-dining room. The second floor contained a male ward and an operating room, and the third floor, the female ward and the nurses' dormitory. The basement floor contained the heating plant, a small laundry and a corner in which stood a table with equipment for urine examinations.

Needless to say, the hospital was named in honor of Frederick Douglass. It is one of our oldest medical institutions and is only preceded by a nursing home that was founded, a number of years earlier in New Orleans, the Dixie Hospital at Hampton and the Provident Hospital at Chicago. I do not include the three teaching institutions, Howard University's Freedman's Hospital, Meharry Medical College Hospital nor Shaw University Hospital since they were not established solely for community usefulness and so I hold that the Douglass Hospital is the first community effort by Negroes to provide medical care under the direction of Negro physicians for its group.

The idea for its establishment arose in Dr. N.F. Mossell, who is rightly termed its founder. Dr. Mossell was chief of the staff of physicians and Medical Director of the hospital. I do not now recall the name of its President nor the full name of Mr. Lee, a member of an old Quaker family as well as a member of the old Quaker Society that sponsored the Laing School near Charleston, who served as Treasurer. Dr. Minton was secretary.

The consulting staff of the hospital included the most prominent physicians, surgeons and teachers at the several Philadelphia medical schools.

The services at the hospital included the usual in-patient department, a free outdoor clinic department and a drug dispensary.

My interests revolved chiefly about the dispensary, where prescriptions for in-patients, and those from the outdoor clinic were filled at special prices, and such prescriptions that came to us from outside patrons. Most of the physicians, whenever they could, would advise their patients to send their prescriptions to Dr. Minton and very often brought them in themselves and have them delivered. My duties therefore consisted not only in filling prescriptions, manufacturing preparations but also in delivering them to the homes of patrons.

A few days after I started at Dr. Minton's I received a letter from Father and in it was a check from Dr. Baer for my year's tuition. Dr. Baer had agreed to advance the full amount of my tuitions under an extremely elastic loan arrangement. Had it not been for Dr. Baer's generosity and helpfulness in doing so, it would have been impossible for me to even begin college. And so I immediately went to the college and matriculated and paid the tuition for the year. The apprenticeship system was still in vogue in Philadelphia and was one of the requirements of the Philadelphia College. Dr. McClennan's certification that I had served two years under him in Charleston was accepted and Dr. Minton's name entered on the records of the school as my "preceptor" for the ensuing years. For except [unless] a student had four full years of prescription training outside the college, he would not be eligible for graduation.

When the class first met one day in October in 1896, I found myself the only Negro among a group of more than two-hundred. A large number of nationalities were represented, Jews, Germans, English, Swedes and Russians. The majority however were American born, mostly from Pennsylvania but yet representing a majority of the states in the Union. Although no overt act was directed towards me, I could feel that my presence there was looked upon as an intrusion. This induced me to assume an air of unconcern towards my classmates. So I would never address one unless he first took the initiative in a conversation and even then would always strive to have it seen that the rest of the class was of but little importance to me. Because of the technical training I had received under Mr. Elfe, I was able to perform my laboratory work with ease and aptitude without ever once seeking the assistance of a fellow student.

One of the requirements for entrance was the completion of the high school course of study or the passing of a satisfactory entrance examination. It was the prerogative of the student to take the examination on entrance or with his first-year finals. I chose the latter, since I had had only one year of high school work and felt it necessary to do additional study if I expected to successfully pass the test. I secured a card to the Chestnut Street branch of the city free library and so gained access to the books I needed for my extra study. I had written Dr. McClennan sending him a list and the prices of the textbooks I had to get, and which he had promised me. After waiting two weeks without receiving a reply, I again wrote him but wishing that my letter would not appear to be an insistent request for money for my books, sent a glowing description about the Douglass Hospital and its aims and purposes. I also sent him one of its catalogues and hinted that he could do the same for Charleston by organizing a hospital there. But more about this again.

I never received the money for my books and was compelled to believe that once again, as I had witnessed many times before, the doctor's generosity had exceeded his assets. However Dr. Minton allowed me the use of his books and so I was able to carry on.

My greatest difficulty was in learning to study, for the work was heavy covering a daily average of from eighty to ninety pages of text each day. I soon learned that merely memorizing the text was almost worthless but that if I could visualize the subject and clearly see it, that I then would fully understand its meaning and could express it accurately in my own words. We seldom took notes as each professor was the author of his text and usually followed his book. So one little stenographer's note book sufficed for an entire year, since only what was newer than that in the textbook required taking down.

At the close of my freshman year, I succeeded in passing all of my examinations. I did not however do as well as I had hoped to do for I made two or three "satisfactory" and the others an even lower "sufficient." But I did not consider the achievement bad, for after all I had been giving time to study of my high school subjects that had been successfully done.

Time had flown rapidly by since I first arrived in Philadelphia. I had not acquired many friends for since I was always pinched for money, I feared that if I sought new friends that that might embarrass me. Perhaps the loneliness of my position prompted me to seek the associations of the doctors who frequented the hospital I found them all sympathetic and interested in my efforts. Most of them were men of elderly age. Dr. N.F. Mossell who was in charge of the Hospital was the first Negro to finish the course in medicine at the University of Pennsylvania. Associated with him in the active task of directing the work of the institution were Drs. Ogden, Howard and Hilton. Dr. Minton was a much younger man, and of course more companionable. Miss Minnie Clement, was the first graduate of the nursing school at the University of Pennsylvania. Of other Negro physicians who occasionally frequented the Hospital was Dr. Warrick from Germantown and Drs. Imes and Abel, the two latter ones were homeopathic practitioners. One or two medical students also frequented the hospital. One was Samuel P. Stafford a very earnest student, who after his graduation spent a year as the institution's first intern, and then McDougall, a graduate of Shaw University who had punched out before the State Board and was busy studying for the next examination and on whom

I pulled one or two tricks with the microscope but who on his next attempt successfully passed the Board and established himself in practice and later became one of Philadelphia's outstanding surgeons. Another was Dr. White an early graduate of the University of Pennsylvania who had gone to Arkansas and started practice but had neglected to take the Pennsylvania Board before going there. Unfortunately his Arkansas venture had been disappointed for after staying there through two bad crop years, and one river flood, he found himself penniless and [illegible] prospects for any betterment. So he returned to Philadelphia and spent the time while awaiting the meeting of the examining board in "brushing" up for the examination. He would tell us about his experiences as a country doctor and once how in response to a call that took him fourteen miles away from his office, through a rain and windstorm, he found his patient under a fallen tree, with a badly crushed leg. And how he directed the onlookers to dig a trench about the man that he could be removed more easily than if resort was had to cutting the tree away. That the man was bleeding and his only hope was in the immediate amputation of the limb. He did not have his surgical kit with him, only a knife but he found a "buck" saw and some needles and thread in the cabin where the man was taken. He operated and dress[ed] the stump [and] returned home. One of the fellows who was listening, laughed and said that that was "butchery" not surgery, at which White only remarked that the patient recovered. It was many years later before I realized that White was then a master surgeon, capable of meeting an emergency with only that which was at hand.

Among some of the other students in Philadelphia at the time was Wainwright Birnie from Charleston who was taking medicine at Penn. Also John Hall who later acquired prominence by making one of the first studies of infantile paralysis when the first outbreak occurred in the Boston area where he practiced.

And there was Tom Coates and Jonathan Philips at Medico Chi.8 Philips was from the West Indies and after his return home became prominent in politics and was elected to the legislature in Jamaica. Philips spent a year at the Douglass and while there tried to teach me to play tennis, in which he failed.

And then I must tell about Dr. Jackson, who unassisted constituted the "dental department" at Douglass. The doctor was the first Negro to practice dentistry in Philadelphia. His was a most unique career. He started it as janitor at the Philadelphia Dental College and by dint of perseverance rose to position of keeper of the dissecting room and in full charge of reception and final disposition of all cadavers. He would tell me of his experiences—one of which recited how on one occasion he had to transport a "lady" to the top floor. There were no elevators in the building and the "lady" being too heavy to take in his arms, he strapped her about his middle and started the upward climb and stumbled and that he and the lady rolled down three flights of steps together when he laid unconscious for a while until several of the students arrived and unloosened him and the "lady" away. As time passed he absorbed much dentistry and so impressed some of the faculty with his desire to learn, that they enrolled him as a student and allowed him to do part time work. In time he graduated and opened his office on Pine Street. I once went to him for a treatment. Asepsis was then a minor adjunct to dentistry so the doctor fastened a large cork to the back of his dental chair and while at work in the mouth, would often pause, and ask if the mouth was tired, if the answer was "yes" the cork would be immediately placed in your mouth, irrespective of who used it before and without washing. He was a good dentist but entirely devoid of humor for he could take a red hot "broach" stick it in your tooth and complacently ask "Do it hurt?" and so he became familiarly know[n] as "Do it hurt?".

---

8 Probably Medico-Chirurgical College of Philadelphia (1881–1916).

Of course Dr. Jackson was not the only Negro dentist then practicing in Philadelphia at the time I was there. For there was Dr. Cox who nearly put me out of business with cocaine one time while extracting one of my molars. Cox, though an able dentist was then fighting his way against race prejudice at Jefferson Medical College, where as the first known Negro to gain admission, he was beset with every obstacle that the student body and some members of the faculty could devise. Cox faced it courageously and eventually graduated there. Two of my newfound friends were students at the dental colleges—one was Royster, who came from North Carolina and the other was Warrick who after completing his course opened his office on South Sixteenth Street.

I was indeed fortunate in being a "penniless" being for thus I gained a host of friends, many of whom were much older than I whose counsel and guidance led me along lines that perhaps might have been different ones had I had opportunity to seek companionships elsewhere. Dr. Minton introduced me to the members at the Citizens Club and the Meteor Wheelmens and though not eligible for membership at either, I was given the privileges there and especially so when Dr. Hilton said "Let the kid" have it.

And so gradually I became part of the "who's who" of Negro Philadelphia. One or two of whom were old Charlestonians. For there was Mrs. Petty Piece, a sister of Mrs. Hurlong in Charleston, at whose home I held a standing invitation to eat "rice," the way it is cooked in Charleston and through her met the Williamsons from Greenville, South Carolina and the Ferrettes who had migrated from Charleston shortly after reconstruction, and some who had come from other southern points. For there was Mae Wilson, who came from New Orleans and later married Lem Cowdery. And so my circle of friends grew. By the end of my second year of residence I was in the "Entre Nous" of which Meta Vaux Warrick, then a student at the Academy of Fine Arts was the winsome miss. Of the older ladies I met, Miss Helen Stevens and Miss [illegible] Campton impressed me most. And another was Miss Fanny Jackson (Coppin) who conducted a private school in South Philadelphia. It was she who had taught Robert S. Smalls the rudiments of the three Rs. Neither can I forget that sweet old lady, who would often visit the hospital, Mrs. Harper, who was a poet of local reputation and who had recent[ly] published an anthology of poems.

One day I had occasion to make a delivery to Flora Batson, the great American Negro soprano of her day. I had heard her sing in concert recital at the Morris Street Baptist Church in Charleston and remembered her as a splendid vivacious person, dressed in satin and bedecked with diamonds. When I reached her residence, I found it to be a single room over a barbershop on Lombard Street near Fifth and in the center of one of Philadelphia's filthiest slums. There was no one to admit me for she was there alone and in bed, suffering from the last stages of tuberculosis. And there she laid amid dirty sheets struggling for breath while reaching under her pillow for a dirty handkerchief from which she took the money to pay me with. I left as quickly as I could but I could not forget the scene of abject poverty and filth that I had witnessed. I saw her physician a few days later and inquired why was she alone and learned that her husband, a white man, had abandoned her and had absconded with all of her jewels and money and that all of her former friends had forsaken her because of her marriage to a white man.

That summer Dr. Minton decided to close the dispensary at the hospital and open a drugstore at the corner of Sixteenth and Rodman Streets not far from the hospital. The location was an admirable one as it was in the center of Philadelphia's Negro population. The store was small and its appointments modest but it contained all of the necessary adjuncts for prescription work. Since it was the first drugstore to be opened in Philadelphia by a Negro, it received from the start a very satisfactory patronage from the physicians in the neighborhood. We had a small soda fountain, cigar stand and the usual line of sundries. And also a porter who did the cleaning and made deliveries. My salary had had several increases and things were now getting much better with me.

Most of the drugstores in Philadelphia had night bells and a clerk who slept on the premises, so that prescriptions could be filled at all hours of night. We discussed the feasibility of having such a service and decided to get a hammock in which I could sleep. Suspended behind the prescription counter and have the electric night bell near its head. I was in hearty accord with the plan, for in addition to allowing me to sleep a little longer each morning I would also save the daily car fare to and from Darby, where it was necessary for me to leave home at 7 o'clock each morning to reach the store by 8 o'clock. Under the new arrangement, I rose at 7:30, went to the "Old Virginia" restaurant around the corner. Ate a ten-cent breakfast and returned to the store by eight.

I stored my belongings in the basement. A woman who lived above the store did my laundry for 50¢ a week. Once a week I went to Green's Barbershop on 10th Street for a hot tub bath, at two bits a bath. Beyond that the drugstore sink met my needs. Not only was I able to meet my actual living needs but I could also save something each week. The night calls were infrequent and never seriously interfered with my sleep.

There was one incident however which did. And that happened one morning about four. When I heard a knocking on the rear door, just above my head, where I saw a piece of board being downward driven so that it could spring the lock on the door. At which I foolishly and still half a sleep arose and silently drew the bolts which held the door and stepping out into the hallway met a man and a woman. The man dropped the hammer he had and the woman ran upstairs. I assumed an air of bravado though I was shaking at the knees, and asked what was he trying to do, break into the store? He denied it and said that he was only going upstairs and with which he left me. I picked up the hammer and went back into the store and I locked the door behind me, thankful that my burglar was only an amateur for had it been a professional, he may have knocked me in the head and proceeded with his purpose without further fear of interruption.

The next morning I told Dr. Minton about the happening and asked if he could get me a pistol. He said he had one and that he would bring it with him that evening. The gun he brought me was a little rosewood handled, seven-shooter 22 caliber pistol. The kind that I played with in "chaff lot." I laughed when I saw it for the cartridges in it were green from corrosion and could not be extracted. So I knew that it was worthless. But never again did I open a door until I knew who was on the other side of it.

Until then our advertising had been done by notices in the Colored weekly paper and with circulars, which were distributed about the neighborhood. Dr. Minton decided to enlarge his advertising area and so it was decided that we would distribute advertising souvenirs made with sachet powder on the Sunday excursion train to Atlantic City. I was promised my railroad fare and an extra dollar if I would do the distribution. It took us a week to make up the packages. By Sunday all was in readiness. I took the Camden ferry and crossed over to the Jersey side where I bought a round-trip ticket for Atlantic City and back. The distribution of advertising matter on railroads was prohibited but despite that many did so. So I kept my bundle out of sight until the conductor had collected the tickets in my coach, which was the last, and giving him a start, commenced my distribution. And then the unexpected happened, for as fast as I could pass one out, it would be thrown back at me and some even cursed me and told me to take "this damn thing back." By the time I had reached the third coach ahead, I was exhausted and so gave up work for the morning. And then I learned why I was so treated, for it seems that it was the custom of train "butchers" to pass through each coach leaving their articles with passengers and if it was not returned immediately, to retrace their steps and demand payment for the item. And then it dawned on me that I had been mistaken for a "butcher."

I spent a lonely day in Atlantic City awaiting my return to Philadelphia. It was intensely hot so I spent most of the time beneath the boardwalk. That afternoon I got a 25¢ fish dinner. After which I went back to Mississippi Avenue where the excursion trains stopped. On my return trip I was careful to announce with each package I gave out, that it was free and then everybody wanted one.

College reopened in October and again Dr. Baer's check arrived in ample time. I was better prepared for study than I was during the first year. For during the summer I had taken a special course of study in chemistry under Professor Moerk who had accepted a class of ten students. The course consisted of ten lectures on inorganic chemical reactions. Prof. Moerk's method of teaching made it easy for me to understand chemistry and what it was about, and made my future work in analytical chemistry relatively easy.

That October I took the Pennsylvania State Board examination for a "registered qualified assistant pharmacist" and passed. But the funny thing about it was that my ability in passing the examination was not from what I had learned at college but almost entirely from what I had learned under Mr. Elfe and by roaming through Dr. Baer's laboratory. And some could be attributed to my year at Douglass Hospital for the ten questions asked by the examiners on urine analysis, which I answered correctly, were based upon actual work I did in that field at Douglass. It was a proud moment for me a couple of weeks later when I hung my license up in Minton's store.

Not long thereafter I had my first unpleasant happening at the college. I had rigidly adhered to my policy of refraining from showing a desire for companionship with my fellow students and so what contacts I did have remained those of mere mutual courtesy. But one day while I was seated in Professor Remington's lecture room, one of the students who sat on the row below and to the right of me and eating peanuts, began tossing the hulls in my lap. I was then engaged in conversing with two other students, and realized he was one with whom I had never before even spoken to. So I said nothing but merely picked up the hulls and dropped them on the floor, without stopping my conversation or deigning to look at him, at which one of the boys I was speaking with smiled. That smile provoked embarrassment and the peanut tosser became chagrined and turned his head away. At the beginning of the following lecture he did not take his usual seat but sat in one at the rear of the room. When the class assembled he stood up and yelled, "What's the matter with the coon?" A complete hush fell over the room. I sat still and so did the others, a few moments later Professor Sadler came in and began his lecture. My insulter was the first to leave the room. A couple of days later at one of Professor Remington's lectures, he returned to his usual seat. When the lecture was over and he had reached the aisle way, I stood in front of him and demanded that he apologize for the insulting remarks he had made. He answered by saying "Who is going to apologize to a damn nigger?" At which I landed a hook to his jaw which sent him reeling to the bottom of the room. Professor Remington who had witnessed the altercation called for immediate order. I went down and told him that I would like to speak with him in his office, which was to one side of his lecture room. When the professor came in, I told him that I wished to apologize for creating a disturbance in his lecture room but that I had no alternative in my action since it arose through an insulting remark which I could not brook. I told him of what had previously happened and that I was not hunting friendships from any student but only the opportunity to perform my studies without interference or insults. Professor Remington told me to sit down, that he wanted to tell me something. He then told me that a few years previously when the first Negro matriculated at the college that the entire student body presented a petition requesting that the student be refused admission and threatened to resign in a body if any Negro was granted entrance. He said that the faculty met and unanimously decided that Negroes were included as announced in the school's catalog "that all applicants, irrespective of race or creed who met the entrance requirements were eligible for enrollment" and that the faculty notified the student body to that effect and informed them that any who wished to resign could do so. Also that the faculty would not tolerate any interference or annoyance to Negroes because of racial identity. He told me that four Negroes had graduated from the school and in each instance had proven themselves to be worthy students. He told me go on and that he would assure me that I would have no further annoyances.

When Professor Remington told me that four Negroes had graduated, I wondered if the number might not have been more as I had recently found Frank Stokien from Charleston a member of the class ahead of mine—but Frank crossed the line.

After I left Professor Remington's office one of the students came to me and said, "McFall that fellow is waiting for you down in the locker room, you had better watch out." Also that some of his friends were with him. I told my informant that I was going there and that I believed that there were too many gentlemen in the class who would insist on fair play and would see to a fair fight if it happened. So I took off my glasses and buttoned my coat and cautiously made my way down to the locker room. As I neared the bottom landing I found my adversary waiting for me. I immediately took the offensive and in a few minutes had him well licked. And then John, the janitor came and parted us. I then returned to Professor Remington and told him what had again happened, that I was not seeking any actions from him, only to acquaint him with the happening for I did not believe that I would have any further trouble from that particular student. From then on I met with no further insults but instead found a closer friendship with many of the students. And again I must record that what I did there that day was not from anything that I had learned at college but was all due to the intensive training I had received at the hands of "Raggy nine" in the old "chaff lot" days.

My experience at the Philadelphia College of Pharmacy was not my only embarrassing one. For shortly after that one happened, I met with a somewhat similar one at the Jefferson Medical College. It was the custom during those days to permit the students of one professional school to attend lectures or clinics as visiting students. Usually I would go to the Medico Chi. But one night in company with another student we decided to attend an anatomy lecture at Jefferson Medical College. We entered the lecture room and took our seats and enjoyed the lecture but just at its end as we were leaving, a cry arose, "Let's lynch the nigger." Discretion being always the better part of valor, and since he who runs, may live to fight another day, we ran out of the room and down the hall. I tried the first door that came to hand and went in. It was dark in there, my companion had gone another way and so I was alone. I could hear the crowd passing by and since no one entered the room I was in felt somewhat safer and leaned upon a table that I could rest and get my wind back. After a few minutes had passed I struck a match to see where I was at and then I found that I was in the Anatomy professor's dissecting room leaning over a couple of half dissected stiffs. I question which were stiffer they or I. However, I quickly left the building and went my way homeward. Needless to say, that incident prompted me to avoid future excursions with any of my classmates.

Had I known how bitter the feeling against Negroes was at Jefferson I would have avoided the incident but it was not until Dr. Cox, the dentist, told me more about it and how he was then fighting to break it down, that I fully appreciated that my reception was much more than an empty threat.

In the meanwhile the business at the drugstore had increased nicely. We were filling a daily average of twenty-five prescriptions and had our share of the neighborhood's general business. We had secured the room above the drugstore and fitted it up as our living quarters. We had two single beds, a study table and two chifforobes. We built corner closets for our clothes. We alternated the night-service shift, Dr. Minton taking one night and I the next. To avoid any disturbance from the ringing of the night bell Dr. Minton arranged for me to sleep at his home on the nights when I was off night duty. He did the same on his off nights. And so I became a part of the Minton household which consisted of his father, Mr. Theophilus J. Minton, his cousin Miss Kim _____ and the housekeeper. Their home was on Tasker Street between 15th and 16th.

Mr. Theophilus Minton was a lawyer and had lived in South Carolina during the early Republican administrations. He held a position in the attorney's general office but had moved to Philadelphia when the "carpetbaggers'" administration ended. He was a gentleman of culture and integrity and was never too busy to lend a cheering word or give advice and guidance when he thought it necessary. Sometimes I would stop in at his office to chat with him and always found it a profitable visit. He was a man of high ideals whose friendship was most helpful to me in some measure he imbued with the ideals he maintained.

Though I did not connect myself with any church in Philadelphia I would sometimes go to services. Sometimes it would be to Shiloh Baptist Church and sometimes to the Catholic at 11th and Lombard but mostly it would be to St. Thomas Episcopal Church, whose membership was something similar to that of St. Marks in Charleston.

I attended the theater frequently—that is the Chestnut Street Theater, where one of my friends served as keeper of the fire-escape exit, through which I could sneak and see a show whenever I had the inclination. Elsewhere but seldom for I still found need for every penny I earned.

My circle of friends and acquaintances had widened considerably some were men and some were women. Some have been forgotten, both by me and by history. There was one I remember, Ernest Hogan was his name. He was one of the first Negro popular songwriters I knew and had written "All Coons Look Alike to Me" and thereby became famous. Unfortunately he sold his song outright for $25 while the publishers earned thousands from it. A most amusing and interesting conversationalist was he who never once expressed bitterness over the bad financial breaks that fate gave him.

And there was R. Henri Strange, a dramatist of no mean ability who had he lived in the age of Robeson or Harrison could easily have attained fame. But some of his habits and his love for liquor were handicaps that limited his efforts. The last time I saw him was one morning while on my way to work, I saw him draped about a lamppost.

Neither can I forget "Bun" Abel one of the most brilliant graduates from Hahnemann Homeopathic School of Medicine, who started a "brilliant" practice on the strength of a write up account of an accident that appeared in a Colored weekly paper and which described how the victim's leg had been severed from the body and how Dr. Abel sewed it on again and the patient recovered. Of course such did not happen as the victim, a child, was only badly [bruised?] and far from any danger of ill effects. However it made him the "miracle man" for the time being and also the butt for many jokes from his colleagues. Dr. Abel was the first Negro practitioner to be appointed to the staff of a white hospital in Philadelphia. For many years he was chief of the G.U. clinic at Hahnemann and was one of the first men in America to advocate the use of methylene blue in gonorrhea. Unfortunately he became a victim of cancer, and through the irony of fate, of the type of cancer which had been one of his special studies, in which he had had some good results by operative measures with patients. His condition became progressively worse. The pain became as it always does in such cases, almost unbearable. He refused to resort to morphine as he feared a possible addiction habit, preferring whiskey and its evil to that from morphine.

Which brings to mind a recollection of Lorine Palmer who was then attending the University of Pennsylvania's medical school. Palmer came from Atlanta, Georgia. His father was a white man, who was pharmacist at the Jacob's Pharmacy of that city, and who later developed "Palmer's Skin Whitener," but who never spared either time nor money to provide his son with the best medical education obtainable. After his graduation Dr. Lorine Palmer went to Chicago to intern at Provident Hospital. He wanted me to join him there but I did not since I had other plans for my future. Dr. Palmer returned to Atlanta after completing his internship and established a very lucrative practice there. It did not continue long, for he like Abel was fated for the untimely checking out from a brilliant future. Palmer developed paresis and amnesia and disappeared from Atlanta. A few years later he was found, while working as a steward on a transatlantic liner, and returned to Atlanta, where he died shortly after.

When the Spanish American War began I was in my senior year. The army and navy wanted pharmacists, the former designating them as "hospital stewards" and later as "pharmacist mates." Several of my classmates wanted to volunteer for the positions but members of the faculty advised them against doing so, as they believed that an adequate number could be found among present graduates. The war however was brief and but few of the volunteers except the "Rough Riders" and some of the "immunes" took active part in it.

Several of my old friends from Charleston had volunteered. They were Dr. J.A. Robinson and L.H. Lindau who with Dr. Stoney from Augusta, Georgia were attached to the "immunes" at Macon, Georgia. They held the non–commissioned status of "hospital stewards" and constituted the sole corps of assistants to the Surgeon, who they described as being of French extraction and more or less always drunk. A habit which I think was contagious, as from what I heard, the stewards were usually so. It seems that the principal medicines in their hospital tent was C.C. pills and whiskey, of which the patients received the former and the medical staff took the balance.

I happened to be passing the Union League Club on Broad Street one night, while the peace conclusions were being celebrated. It was raining but a small crowd had gathered about the building in which the leading military and naval officers had met to celebrate America's victory over Spain. The crowd began yelling for speakers and in response to their demand, the principal assembled guests came out to the porch to greet the crowd. It was truly an auspicious moment and one never to be forgotten. Among those present and who spoke were Admiral Dewey, Admiral Sampson, Admiral Schley and General Joe Wheeler.

A couple of days later, I witnessed the "peace parade." Broad Street had been profusely decorated and triumphal arches had been erected at several intersections. A very large representation from the army had been gathered together for the parade and included several regiments that had seen conspicuous action in the war. Among them were the 9th and 10th cavalry that had rescued Teddy Roosevelt and his "Rough Riders" at San Juan Hill and also the 24th and 25th infantry, somewhat depleted for their number had been seriously reduced by typhoid fever and many more were hospitalized at Montauk Point on the Jersey coast. Of course the cavalry, the 9th and 10th were the great heroes of the occasion and were loudly cheered and also stopped at frequent intervals along the line of march to partake of sandwiches and champagne and in such plenty that I wondered if they ever reached the end of the march. But of all the companies that took part in the parade, none was more conspicuous than the 9th

Ohio under the command of Major Charles B. Young (later Colonel) for theirs was the best drilled battalion and all wore while
gloves. I met a number of the men and officers and obtained a
souvenir, a Krag Jorgensen bullet from Sargent Bivans of the cavalry, who said it was one that he had with him when he went up
San Juan Hill.

I entered college the year that the curriculum was extended
from a two- to a three-year course leading to the degree of Doctor in Pharmacy. One of the requirements for the degree was the
presentation of an original thesis on some one of the subjects
taught. It was required that the thesis be presented by February
15th, so I started work on my research when the term began. I
had selected the yellow jasmine, gelsemium sempervirens, as a
suitable subject and planned to make an exhaustive study of the
plant, for though it had been used in medicine for many years I
could not find any evidence that a complete study of the plant
had been made. I planned to make, first, a microscopic study in
which its histology and other [characteristics] would be compared with those of two other related species I had heard about,
one of which grew in China and other in Louisiana and second
a chemical study of its active principles. I secured quantities of
the drug from the Smith, Kline company, and got some of one
of its related specie from Louisiana but could not get the sam-
ples I desired from China. When I got started on this extensive
research, I found to my amazement that laboratory fees would
perhaps reach $50 or more as the charge was 25¢ an hour. So,
though I had already invested several dollars on the project, I
was compelled to abandon it and seek a less expensive direction for my research. I chose "A method for the valuation of compound jalap powder" which I completed in ten days and with
an outlay of only $6.00. Before presenting it, I asked Professor
Moerk to criticize it. He did so and checked my computations,
he told me that he considered it a comprehensive outline and
that it was an excellent subject. He also told me to present it to

the committee without any change. With my thesis out of the way, I was able to concentrate on the current work and also to make a review of the entire course as I had to meet the "Committee" and their comprehensive examination.

The requirements for graduation at the Philadelphia College of Pharmacy were three in number, the first being a "meritorious" thesis, the second the satisfactory passing of an examination before the faculty and finally the third, a satisfactory examination before the "Committee." For it seems the membership of the College retained the right to determine not merely the proficiency of its students but also to inquire into the efficiency of its faculty and so they sent a "Committee" to give a comprehensive which covered the entire course of training and was all the more fearsome to the students because it sought to determine more about what had been taught and what had not been taught than it did to determine what we had learned.

As our finals approached I found that I was becoming somewhat popular with one of my classmates. He was from the coal-mining region of Pennsylvania. During our first year he was all right but the following year after being elected to the football team he became rather snobbish. So when he began making advances of friendship, I became suspicious about his intent. A few days before the finals began, he asked me to help him with his examinations and that he would pay me for doing so. I could not fully say to him what I thought about his offer, so told him that if I could aid him in any way that I would do so but that no compensation would be accepted. The more I thought about his request the more it troubled me. Certainly I could not think of jeopardizing my career by aiding him for if I was caught assisting him in any way it may have meant my disqualification and I could not afford that. After thinking the matter over I decided to talk to John, the janitor and asked him to change my seat as it was his duty to arrange the members of the class according to their registration numbers. He asked what was my number. I told him number 97, and then what was the number of the man who wanted my help. I told him that I only wanted to be moved to some other place. He said all right that he would fix it. And John did for doing [sic] during all of the written finals, my aid seeking classmate sat at a small desk all by himself and directly in front of one of the instructors.

And then the period of waiting for it would be at least ten days before the results would be given. About a week later I received a letter telling me that I was eligible to compete for the Maisch Prize and that if I wished to do so to report at the microscopical laboratory on a given date and time. It was this particular subject that I had feared most and so when I was notified of my eligibility to compete for the Maisch Prize, I became satisfied that I had passed in all subjects. So I bought my few invitations, addressed and stamped them but withheld mailing them until I received official notice that I would graduate.

Notice came three days before commencement. I did not attend the baccalaureate sermon for somehow or other I could not bring myself to feel that there was that oneness between me and the other members of the class that could make it an event that I would really enjoy. I did attend the faculty dinner beyond only those affairs which were mandatory.

Neither Uncle Allen nor Aunt Elvira cared to attend, but Oscar my cousin did. Other than he, I cannot recall if any of the few I invited did. The commencement exercises were held at the Academy of Music on Broad Street. Quite a gathering of people were present. I was agreeably surprised when I read a program to find that I had attained the grade of "meritorious" an honor in which only eight members of the class shared and also that I had been given an honorable mention for my participation in the Maisch Award contest. I recall but little of the commencement address as my attention kept straying away from the speaker and centered itself upon what might otherwise have been my attainment had I had my full high school training and had not been compelled to divert so much time from my studies during my first year to make up that deficiency.

However I quickly recovered from that for as the names of the graduates were announced, I realized that ninety four of the number who had started with the class had fallen by the way-side, which made me realize that I was indeed a most fortunate person. I wished that Mother and Father could have been there and also Dr. Baer whose help had made my success a possibil-ity. These thoughts were interrupted by the call to proceed to the rostrum to receive our degrees—as we went up in groups of twenties each—President Bullock of the college conferred the degrees, mine was Doctor in Pharmacy (P.D.).

Diplomas were not issued at the time the degrees were con-ferred since each graduate had to receipt for his at the office of the registrar. I delayed several days before going for mine as I was somewhat fearful if it would be delivered until I reached my twenty-first birthday and which was several months off. When I reached the office I met Miss Taylor, the assistant reg-istrar, in a rather weak voice, I started to explain to her that it was necessary for me to leave Philadelphia and that my twenty-first birthday would not arrive for a few months. I doubt if what I said made sense or if it was intelligible to Miss Taylor but she knew what was troubling me and was sympathetic for I could see it as she turned and said Mr. McFall, I am too busy to hunt up the records of your age, here is your diploma, please sign for it. Which I immediately did. Then we shook hands and said goodbyes.

I remained with Dr. Minton a month longer. But home was calling and yet I did not care to leave Philadelphia as I wanted more than anything else to study medicine. I had made several inquiries and found that I would be given one-year partial credit against the first year studies at any of the Philadelphia medical schools, with the [proviso] that I double up anatomy and physi-ology, which could easily be arranged for I would be exempted from certain second year courses, and so could spend a full year at both subjects. However I did not have the money to do it with and part time work was out of the question for there would not be time in which to do it. I could not ask father to seek further funds for me, as he had already done enough. And moreover I had received a letter from him in which he told me that he had been speaking with some friends and thought that it would be possible for me to establish myself in business in Charleston.

Life as a Druggist

RETURN TO CHARLESTON AFTER GRADUATION

And so I decided to return to Charleston. After bidding farewell to all my friends and relatives in Philadelphia I left, going to New York where I spent a few days with Uncle Paul. I took passage by boat for Charleston a few days later. When I reached the boat, I found that the passenger who shared my cabin was a white man. We introduced ourselves and I learned that he was going to Charleston to supervise the removal of electrically controlled mines that had been laid in Charleston harbor during the Spanish American War. While we were talking the purser came in and said that some mistake had been made in the assignment of our cabins. I showed him my ticket and told him that there was no mistake with mine. The white man did likewise. The purser spluttered and said well we can't let white and Colored sleep together and that a change would have to be made. It was my first experience with "Jim Crow" on common carriers and it made me hot. So I told the steward that I had paid for the accommodations and intended to use them and if I was deprived from using the space my ticket called for that I would immediately institute a damage suit on my return to New York. He then turned to the white man, who without waiting for a question, told him bluntly, that he would not leave the cabin for he was satisfied with it. The cabin we had was on the upper deck and adjoined those occupied by the Captain and by the First Mate. They were nice and cool and had sitting chairs on the top deck. I am convinced that these comforts induced the white man to cling to his space and not a wish to insist on equal treatment for me.

The trip down was pleasant. We arrived in Charleston about 11 o'clock at night. I started to leave the boat but when I looked out the stillness and darkness that enveloped the city deterred me on the boat and taking my suitcase proceeded to the trolley line to East Bay, took a car and proceeded home.

Mother greeted me, Father had gone to work, but my numerous sisters, including one I had never before seen and my brother Paul were on hand to make me welcome. Perhaps I astounded them for my dress was the latest in Northern fashions. In contrast with New York and Philadelphia, Charleston appeared to be the smallest, crudest dump I had ever seen. The stillness jarred me, while the slow staring glances my former friends and neighbors bestowed upon me made me restless. At that moment I wanted only to leave Charleston and beat it back North. When my trunk arrived and I unpacked it and showed my diploma everybody gaped. Father came home and after our greetings, things became as they formerly were, just one family with "bubber," back home.

Father told me to have a talk with Dr. Crum who had assured him that he would advance the money that would be required opening a drugstore. So I went around and spoke with him about it. I found the doctor to be no philanthropist but only willing to put up some money, maintain full control over it, allow me to do the work and he to take the profits. He wanted to have the store at the corner of Coming and Calhoun Streets, a few doors from his office, where he said all of his prescriptions would go. He wanted me to agree to receive a very moderate salary until the amount he had advanced was repaid, after that to continue on the same salary and divide the profits equally between us.

Since the amount the doctor would advance could be returned to him within one year, the proposition simmered down to one in which my efforts were to be used for the sole purpose of enrichening the good doctor. When I explained it to Father he told me to wait that he would try to think up something else.

A few days later he told me to look for a location, that he and Mother had agreed to mortgage the home for a loan of $500.00. and that amount should enable me to get started. After a short search, I found that the corner of Smith and Morris Streets could be rented at the very low rental of $8 a month and in addition to that stood at a very strategic location, as it was in the direct line of traffic that led to several drug stores, for there was one at the corner of Smith and Cannon, one at Cannon and Rutledge, one on Rutledge several doors north of Morris, one on Rutledge at the corner of Doughty and no intervening stores between them and King Street. And so I believed that should I open at the corner of Smith and Morris that I could benefit from the drug traffic which passed that corner daily. At first father thought I should seek a neighborhood in which there were no drugstores in preference to what I thought best, as he believed that the absence of competition there would be a help. At last I succeeded in convincing him that the prospect of doing business was always best in the areas where most was done and that it was competition that made one's business thrive best. So I took a lease on the first floor of the building and proceeded to arrange for fixtures and stock. On one of the walks about town, I had seen two counters at an auction house at the corner of Wentworth and Meeting Streets which were held for sale at $9.00. I bought them and had the auctioneer agree to hold them in storage until I wanted them delivered. I spoke with several contracting carpenters and arranged with one, Mr. Lawrence Hollings to build the fixtures I needed. He agreed to build me what I wanted and to alter one of the counters into a prescription counter for the sum of $120.00 I asked would he start the following morning. He said "No" he would not start for its [sic] was Friday the 13th and that he had never started a job on Friday that it was bad luck and perhaps would be worse [?] when Friday fell on the 13th. So I had to accept the delay, though I always believed that 13 was my good luck number.

I had a paper hanger by the name of Green put in a ceiling for me which cost me $12.00. Grandfather McFall supervised the painting. He hired a painter and I joined in and so we got the inside painted at a very nominal figure for it was under $20.00. I went to Powers and Holtz, a newly established furniture store and bought a linoleum floor covering, one small table and three chairs for the front. Had a pair of hanging signs made for $9 and also a few other incidentals that included Welsbach gas lamps at a further expenditure of about $15.00.

In the meantime I had spoken to Dr. Arthur Speissegger, who was then Secretary of the State Pharmaceutical Examining Board about taking the examinations. He told me not to go to Columbia for the examinations but to give him $8 and he would have me registered on my diploma from the Philadelphia College of Pharmacy and that I could save the difference between that sum and $25 it would cost me to go to Columbia and take the examinations. I jumped at that as I needed every penny I had. And so I was duly licensed but instead of being licensed under the provisions of a current act I was licensed under a repealed sections of an older act which made my license a perpetual one, and today it stands the oldest and the only perpetual pharmaceutical license in South Carolina.

The net amount father received from the loan, after deducting attorney's fees was $475.00. I had used nearly $200 of it for fixtures and conditioning the building. I had placed an order through Dr. Baer with the Whitall Tatum Co. of Philadelphia for a set of stock bottles, The old-style glass labeled bottles in which drug stores of the 1890s kept their tinctures and chemicals, and for a few graduates, mortars, pestles, pill tiles etc. That order amounted to about $80.00. I had less than $200 left with which to buy my stock of merchandise, patent medicines and drugs. I had placed a listed [?] order with Dr. Baer's for only what I thought would be absolutely necessary. And that order exceeded the amount of money I had left. So I went down and told him that I would be compelled to delete some items from the order I had placed. He told me, "Don't do that for you may need some of those things." And further, that he would extend me a monthly account, payable one month after I opened. That helped me out immensely for I had overlooked the necessity of ordering labels and prescription blanks. I got Robert Wainwright, who then conducted a small printing shop to print my labels and some prescription blanks and at his suggestion and offer of credit, some advertising circulars for distribution on my opening day. My luck continued to hold for Dr. Speissegger had the men in the sundry department make up some "bargain assortments" for my special benefit. I had planned to have everything in readiness for my opening on September the first but met with a delay in the shipment of my stock bottles and did not receive them until the fifteenth which was a Friday. I immediately got busy transferring my stock to the bottles and arranging them on the shelves. All of the other stock had been placed in the cases and my front windows dressed. I worked until late that night and was on the bright and early the following morning so that I could get everything in readiness for opening at 6 o'clock Saturday afternoon. I had hired a boy, Moses Smalls, a brother of Edmund Smalls of Paradise fame in New York City, to distribute circulars through the area from Rutledge Avenue to St. Philip Street and from Cannon to Vanderhorst Street. A few days before I opened I filled my first prescription in my own store and though it did not offer opportunity to exhibit my technical skill it did bring me encouragement. It was for Mrs. Kate Weston and was written by Dr. A.B. Baker, and though the good doctor has long since passed away his patient still lives and now resides in Rock Hill. The prescription called for an eight-ounce bottle of Wampole's' Homogen, a rather popular proprietary remedy at the time. In setting 6 p.m. Saturday for my opening I had hoped to catch a crowd who would be through with their days work and also on the day [they] received their weekly pay. During the time I was arranging the store I visited many of my future neighbors especially those with nice looking daughters hoping that I could gain customers in that [manner?]. I managed to catch a few but before I knew it, one had caught me. However that is [beside] the point, the main thing is that my opening was a complete success and while many of those who came did so merely to wish me luck in my venture and to assure me that I would have their patronage, that many came and bought. When I closed that night my evening receipts totaled $9.54. As I have stated before money was scarce in those days and a little bit went a long ways. My afternoon work excepting the prescriptions compared very favorably with the business we did at Dr. McClennan's.

Among those who came in on my opening night was Dr. Crum, who brought a patient, Mr. C.M. English and had me fill a prescription for him. I had had some blanks printed for Dr. Crum and had been given his promise that he would use them. I had made no effort to persuade all of the Colored doctors to use my blanks because several of them were under obligations that compelled them to send their prescriptions elsewhere and instead had determined upon a policy of making my appeal for that type of business directly to the homes.

I had teamed up with Dr. L.H. Lindau who had recently started practice in Charleston and in return for his prescription sent him every prospective patient that I could. This arrangement and my direct advertising appeals soon created a daily average of fifteen prescriptions coming to me. I was disappointed at the small number I filled from Dr. Crum and soon learned that neither sympathy nor good will could be expected from him. For as a matter of fact he was under an agreement with the Hummell Pharmacy, a white drug store, where he received a ten percent commission on all of his prescriptions. The business prospered from the start and though I was not able to pay my drug bill in full at the end of the first month, I did succeed in paying the greater part of. It did not take me very long to get out of the red and also to anticipate some of the payments coming due on Father's mortgage. By the end of 1901, I had paid off the mortgage, paid Dr. Baer the amounts of the tuitions he had advanced and had installed a small Lippincott soda fountain.

I had two clerks in my employ, one was Robbie Brown and the other Eddie Plowden who had had some experience at Dr. McClennan's and was a very dependable prescription clerk. I also had one boy who did the general portering work.

CHARLESTON EXPOSITION

In the meanwhile Charleston had been seeking a way to get out of the financial doldrums which had followed the Cleveland land panic. While I was at college the city had constructed a municipal auditorium on part of the old Halsey Lumber Company's tract on Rutledge Avenue and in 1898 had entertained the United Confederate Veterans Convention there. It then sought to become a "convention" city and succeeded in getting the National Educational Association to hold its 1901 convention there.

I was appointed a member of one of the entertaining committees having to do with the reception and housing of Colored delegates. There was absolutely none of [sic] segregation in the convention. And there was one delegation which came from a central western state that brought a Negro, I think, a Dr. Scarborough, an eminent Greek scholar, which had reserved rooms at the Charleston Hotel in which they and Dr. Scarborough stayed during the convention. Everyone who came had a nice time and no one called the other "nigger" as such wasn't done in Charleston then.

The success of the N.E.A. convention prompted the community to aspire to greater achievements by seeking to obtain nationwide attention whereby its port facilities could be expanded. Under the leadership of Capt. F.W. Wagner, one of the leading wholesale grocers of the city, the Carolina-West Indian Exposition was planned. One may well wonder why a small community of 50,000 people would essay such a prodigious effort. The city was by no means a wealthy community but despite that fact it went ahead with the project. Everyone was enthusiastic over it. Whites and Negroes subscribed generously to the capital stock of $250,000.00. I had bought $100.00 of it. Negro fraternal organizations subscribed and so great was the initial impetus that within six months from the inception of the idea, the site was obtained and the plans for the buildings completed.

It may be well to say here that faith in the probable success of the exposition arose largely from the fact that the Paris Exposition which had closed the year before had seen many of its exhibits and concessions transplanted to the Buffalo Exposition that was then in progress, and though the Buffalo Exposition had been the scene of a memorable tragedy, the assassination of President McKinley, it yet offered a source from which exhibits and concessions could be easily obtained for the Charleston exposition. That possibility gave added stimulus to the project.

Following the pattern established at the Atlanta Exposition, a "Negro building" was included in the general set up, under the direct control of a committee composed entirely of Negroes. Dr. Crum was the Chairman of that committee and I was one of its members. We had an office on Calhoun Street in a small frame building that stood where the service entrance to the Francis Marion Hotel now is. The committee secured the services of Mr. Jackson, who was then in charge of the Hampton Institute exhibit at Buffalo, to secure and to classify the exhibits to be placed in the Negro building. All of the plans for that building as well as its decorative additions had to be acceptable to the Negro committee, and there we had our first rub, for several of the plaster statues that the architect had designed for the Negro building, were deemed by the committee, to be more symbolic of the Negro of slavery days, than it did of the Negro of the day and time of the exposition. The objections were so solidly voiced that the offending objects were removed and other pieces of statuary substituted in their places.

While this discussion was under way, a far more insidious plan was discovered, for we found that the architect's plans and the intents of the Directors of the exposition, was to have separate rest rooms and eating places for Negroes and for whites. It was the first time that an openly planned system for racial segregation had been made in Charleston since emancipation and it created a wave of protest from the Negroes. The Negro committee bitterly opposed all proposals and methods for segregation and announced that if such was persisted in, that the Negroes would have nothing further to do with the exposition and in addition would use their every effort to prevent Negroes from attending it.

The committee was unanimous in its action, as it fully knew what import, the plan to segregate held. They knew that the Tillman regime had already succeeded in establishing segregation on common carriers operating within the state, the "Jim Crow" coaches. And if this further separation of the races was permitted, that it would be only a matter of time before it would involve every avenue of life.

Moreover, we had already suffered the loss of unrestricted right to the use of the ballot, and a few years later, the right to bear arms, as a part of the state militia. For the two Charleston regiments had been disbanded by order of Tillman. All of which had come about through the political control of the state that Tillman and the "Farmers Alliance" had achieved. It had been voiced around that the proposals to separate the races had come from prospective visitors from the upper section of the state who would takes offense if Negroes were permitted to use all facilities in common with whites. And that this attendance was necessary for the success of the exposition.

The Negro committee continued adamant in their attitude as they realized that if further segregation was permitted to take place in Charleston that it would become an entering wedge that would ultimately extend itself into every avenue of life.

It must be remembered that at that particular time that there was no segregation in the city beyond that which held sway at the beginning of the 1890s and also that the pattern of racial relationship in Charleston was far different from that which pertained in other parts of the state, and especially so in most Southern cities. As in Charleston its Negroes enjoyed the full use of the parks in common with all others and the same freedom in the use of seats on street cars. At the Academy of Music, the city's only theater Negroes and whites sat together. The only definite act towards segregation by local groups, was that at the Isle of Palms, a beach resort that had been opened by a company headed by Dr. Lawrence, a Northerner who was President [of] the Consolidated Electric Company which established the electric trolley car system to Charleston about 1897 and extended its lines to the Isle of Palms where the resort was established. During its first year of operation Negroes bathed there but that privilege was prevented after then.

These were reasons that compelled the Negro committee to maintain their position and so persistent were they in maintaining it, that the Directors abandoned their plans for segregation. And so when the exposition was opened, it was free from any restrictions because of color.

[Its] opening day was a huge success. Senator Chauncey Depew, one of the nation's famous orators made the opening address. I was present on that occasion and after the dedication ceremony was over, went through several of the buildings and through the carnival, "the Streets of Cairo" where I found several Negroes as concessionaires, there was "Jim Key" the educated horse and his owner, a Negro from Alabama, I believe, at "Fair Japan" was a Negro magician. His name was Sneed, he was originally from Charleston and was a boyhood playmate of Elias Robinson. Miss Maggie Claggett from Summerville who later became Mrs. Dumas of Washington, was a receptionist at U.S. Fisheries exhibit. At the Negro building, I found everything in splendid shape, the exhibits were all well arranged, and of varied types. Mr. Jackson had his Hampton Institute display arranged in the same manner that it was when at Buffalo. Mr. Jack Wheeler, who many years later married Mrs. Elise Forrest Harleston, was in charge of the Tuskegee Institute exhibit and his was a very complete one. There was also one that was rather unique, it was presented by a young Negro, and consisted of a model of breech loading, disappearing cannon. He claimed that he had invented the gun and had had it patented and that he was then negotiating for its sale to some of the countries, either to the United States or to a foreign one. I never knew whether his exhibit was a "catch penny" exhibit or not, but as he charged a dime admission fee to those who wanted to see it, I wondered if the model possessed worthwhile qualities or if it was only a gadget.

The coming of the exposition brought an immediate improvement to local business. During the period of construction, a large number of white mechanics were brought in as the local supply, mostly Negro, was entirely too few for a job of that magnitude. The street railway company extended its line from Spring and Rutledge Avenue, out Rutledge to Cleveland where the main entrance to the exposition was located. It also created a local real estate boom by which much of the farmland near the exposition grounds were sold for residential purposes. Many Negroes took advantage of the sale and bought a number of lots. Sythe Thorne bought three at the corner of Cleveland and

Rutledge, Rev. J.L. Dart bought a number on Maverick Street. Martin Middleton, Philip Bennet and Jessie Martin bought on Cleveland street. Almost it seemed that by overnight the city had extended its area from Sheppard street to beyond Cleveland.

Business was booming at my drugstore and I was making money. I found it necessary to employ another clerk thus bringing the number of clerks up to three. Thaddeus Hume was the newly employed one and proved himself to be splendidly fitted for his duties. He remained with me for the next two years and left to enter the New York College of Pharmacy.

Since I was making money, I no longer held on to hopes of studying medicine but instead began to make other plans, the first of which was the purchase of a home, and so on November 7, 1901, I made a contract to purchase No. 70 Bogard Street for the sum of $1,700.00, $50 down and the balance in monthly installments of $20.22 for the next 100 months. This change of mind came about through my efforts to catch customers among the mothers of the little girls who dwelt in the neighborhood of the drugstore, as one of them had caught me and we were thinking of marrying.

Having secured the future home, my next step was the accumulation of the wherewithal to furnish it and to assume the obligation of marriage and so I proceeded to save every cent I could, so that when the time arrived, I would be prepared to meet it.

In the meanwhile my circle of business associates had increased. P. Sheridan Ball from Jersey had come down and had established the "Metropolitan Life Insurance Company" with offices on King Street near John. And though his venture was not a new one to Charleston, for Rev. S.S. Youngblood's company had then been operating for seven or eight years, his proved an immediate success. Ball's company had no connection with the New York company with the same name nor had that company domesticated its charter in South Carolina at the time Ball started. Ball's company continued to operate for several years, until the North Carolina Mutual came into the field when it transferred it membership over to them.

J. Perry Seabrook, a Charleston boy had attended Atlanta University and had returned home after his graduation there, brought with him his friend and schoolmate, Joe Porter. Together they organized a co-partnership under the firm name of Seabrook and Porter and opened a retail shoe store, on King Street in a building, where a portion of Condon's Department Store now stands. They built up a splendid business and though they were not the first Negroes to engage in the shoe business in Charleston, for C.M. English had preceded him, theirs gave promise of becoming a more permanent one.

Like most good things, the Charleston boom did not last. Most of what we had made, had largely come for the expenditures that were made in constructing the exposition buildings and from the money that the concessionaires spent. That year the cotton crop was a financial failure, and in addition to that, we had an exceedingly cold winter. That combination of bad luck affected the attendance to such an extent, that several of the concessionaires closed down their shows and moved away. The exposition was rapidly becoming a flop for its receipts were far under the costs of operating. And had it not been for the personal sacrifices of Capt. F.W. Wagner would have closed its gates before the appointed time. How much of his personal funds Capt. Wagner spent for the exposition is not definitely known, but it was stated as being nearly $250,000.00. However the United States Congress subsequently appropriated $160,000.00 to reimburse those who had suffered the loss.

The spring of 1902 brought financial improvement to the exposition. Its racetrack attracted many out-of-town visitors and things began to look as they did when the show first opened, and though there was talk about extending its time, nothing came out of it. A special day had been set aside as Negro day and a very elaborate program had been arranged. It began with a parade by the Masonic lodges of the city in which they were joined by other fraternal organizations. The line of march started at Meeting and Market Streets from the Masonic Hall, which then occupied the third floor of the building that was subsequently used by the Louis Cohen company as an annex to their King Street store. I participated in the parade and being the Junior Steward of Prince Hall Lodge had the pleasure of carrying the staff of my office during the time it took to traverse the two-and-one-half mile distance we had to walk. It was a hot day and when we reached the grounds, most of us were too exhausted to participate in the ceremonies. So several of us strayed over to the race track where it was cool and exciting and when the afternoon was spent I returned home, happy and a few dollars richer for the horses had run in my favor that day.

Many interesting people spent that winter and spring in Charleston and their presence added much to our cultural life. Paul Laurence Dunbar was one. And it was my good fortune to become personally well acquainted with him. He stopped at the home of Mrs. Pauline Seba which was not far from the store and usually would drop in at night to spend the evening, sometimes playing cards but mostly just in conversation. His physical condition was far from being good as he evidenced the early stages of tuberculosis. He was under medical care and was then taking full daily doses of creosote carbonate under the direction of Dr. Crum. But despite his infirmity he was always affable, happy and a most interesting talker. At times he would show signs of despondency, and especially so whenever he consulted his watch in which he carried a picture of Alice, his wife, from whom it was rumored, he was estranged. On one such occasion he confided to me of his love for her. Beyond that his inner life was a closed book. He had one friend in Charleston to whom he had met elsewhere. She was Miss Jeannette English but their intimacy never passed beyond the bounds of friendship. Sometimes he would tell me about the local settings of some of his dialect poems and explained why the dialect differed in many of them, "because," said he, "I have found about twenty different Negro dialects in my travels and so I have used the dialect that is peculiar to a section, when composing a poem in which the scene is laid down there."

It is unfortunate that so little is known about his novels, for it was in that field he wished to gain fame. He finished two, *The Sport of the Gods* and *The Uncalled*. It is from his poems that his fame came, as in them may be found not only the descriptive but also the more sublime, and which, is the contemplative.

While in Charleston he gave several readings of his poems, [and] it was on one of these occasions that I learned why he so often indulged in alcoholic stimulants. On that occasion I accompanied him to Emanuel Church where the reading was given. That afternoon he suffered severely from his malady and should have cancelled the engagement. But he refused to do so and with the help of an ample supply of stimulant gave a very enjoyable presentation. I doubt if I shall ever forget that evening because of the embarrassment, I met with nor was it caused by Mr. Dunbar, but came about from a box of friction matches I had in my side coat pocket, which as I sat down, ignited and caused me to hastily beat it downstairs to the pastor's study where I could extinguish it without the audience knowing about it.

As usually follows, those who seek stimulus from alcohol often become addicts to the habit. And so it was with Dunbar. But even so, I cannot think of him as being merely a drunkard, but always, as a poor unfortunate who was possessed with an incurable malady and a firm determination to carry on, even when his physical body was incapable of creating the energy that his efforts required.

Shortly thereafter he left Charleston, going to Baltimore and later to his mother in Dayton, Ohio.

Another who came to Charleston about that time was Sidney Woodward, the great American tenor of his day. Woodward had studied music in Germany and had rendered parts of several of the popular operas while there. He was reputed as having made a concert tour of the musical centers in Europe but because of certain personal peculiarities became disliked and was subsequently forced to abandon his European musical career. Before coming to Charleston he lived in Jacksonville, Florida where he had achieved considerable popularity as a concert soloist. Woodward's coming to Charleston was ushered by a recital at the Morris Street Baptist Church where he demonstrated the fine quality of his voice and the splendid [technique] of a highly trained singer. He was in great demand among the whites and on frequent occasions gave recitals at the Charleston Hotel.

Shortly after his arrival in Charleston he was joined by Samuels Belboder, a native of the British West Indies. Mr. Belboder was an experienced musician and composer of promise. Within a short while they associated themselves with others in the community who were musically inclined and had embarked upon a program which brought to Charleston the best in classical music. They brought Madam Azalea Hackley, the then outstanding Negro soprano to Charleston and presented her with Mr. Woodward in a joint recital at the City Auditorium. It was a brilliant affair and was attended by a mixed audience of nearly twenty-five-hundred people. Madam Hackley remained in Charleston for [a] while and gave several other recitals at one which she interspersed her singing numbers with lecture talks that explained both the mechanical and musical requirements for voice culture.

It would be an omission should I neglect to include Mr. John D. Moore, a native Charlestonian and the immense part he played in assisting Woodward and his associates in bringing to Charleston the very best that could be had in music at that time. Mr. Moore was a teacher of piano and organ music who had studied under several of Charleston's teachers, especially

Mrs. Lee, who was a graduate of Oberlin. Mr. Moore provided the instrumental accompaniment for these recitals and later when the Woodward aggregation presented the biblical cantata "Belshazzar" at the Academy of Music to a crowded house, directed its string orchestra accompaniment.

But by far the most far reaching in its subsequent effects upon the political future of the Negro was the visit by President Theodore Roosevelt to the exposition. Ostensibly and from the proceedings set forth in the day's program, there was absolutely nothing that foreshadowed that that particular visit would at a later date partake of political significance. But such it did and in such measure did it exercise its force that it provoked a reaction within the ranks of the Republican party that reached such proportions that it came near to eliminating the Negro from any future position of rank in it. But about this and about the particular incident that happened that day I shall tell later on.

I did not attend the exposition the day the President visited it, as I had allowed all of my clerks the day off. I saw the parade as it passed the corner of Morris and Rutledge Avenue and had a glimpse of the President as he passed.

When the exposition closed Jack Wheeler who had charge of the Tuskegee exhibit confided to me that he had been instructed to dispose of the Tuskegee exhibit, as the school had no further use for it and that he would sell what he could and abandon the balance. Since I was planning to marry in June, you may imagine with what delight I received his message, and so I immediately arranged to purchase the entire kitchen exhibit, which contained a "safe" (the kitchen cabinet of the gay nineties) a table, a stove that had never had a fire built in it, and two chairs, all for the huge sum of $5.00. A little later when I was arranging the kitchen, Father got his first view of the stove and remarked "That girl is going to break her back trying to cook in its oven," so he built a box and elevated the stove to a level at which back-breaking toil would be averted.

One of my clerks had notified me that he would shortly leave my employ and go West which necessitated me getting another clerk and so Clarence Brown became my next. Clarence was a bright diligent worker but only remained with me for about eighteen months when he brought me his brother Charles and offered him to me in his place as my friend Perry Seabrook had offered him a more lucrative position in his shoe [store].

MARRIAGE

June the 18th, 1902 was rapidly approaching and with it the end of my days of single bliss. The young lady was arranging all of it told me to get a "groomsman," three "best men" and four ushers. So I asked Dr. Louie Lindau to serve as "groomsman," Elias Robinson, Perry Seabrook and Frank Baxter to act as "best men," and Joe Hare and three of my clerks, Robbie Brown, Thaddeus Hume and Eddie Plowden to serve as ushers, and so that Wednesday evening, we marched into Centenary Church with my sister Laura, as maid of honor, Janie English, Alice Robinson and Mary Brawley as maids, and I think it was Uncle Tom, who willingly gladly and quickly gave me my bride.

"Johnnie" Moore presided at the organ and played the old familiar march. Reverend Palmer performed the rites and my best man, I hope, gave him the five-dollar gold piece, I had entrusted to him for that purpose.

Our reception was held just after the wedding at the bride's residence, 199 Smith Street where only wine was served. I had closed the drugstore for the occasion, but had there an assortment of more potent beverages for those who disliked wine and had entrusted my keyring on which was the key to the rear door for the store to Dr. Lindau and requested him to preside at the end of the affair. I made one brief visit to the store and found that everything was progressing according to plan, and again later that evening when I wanted my keys for among them was the key to my trunk and it was also necessary that I find my "best man" so that he could escort the maid of honor to her home, when to my consternation, I found that the "best man" had vanished, taking with him what was left of the liquor and one of the carriages. All of this was most embarrassing to me as it was time for everyone to leave, especially the bride and the groom, for it was then the custom for the newly made couple to leave the house first.

Our new home was on Ashley Avenue at the corner of Condon's Court, just across from Palmetto Street. I was unable to get possession of the Bogard Street place as the right of tenancy did not permit me to oust the tenants before the first of the coming January and so I rented my first home at a monthly rental of $10.00 and had nicely furnished it. It contained six small rooms. Our floors had been covered with matting, window shades installed and the furniture placed in position. Sam Carr, Phenie's[9] brother gave her the living room suite as a wedding present. All the rest of the furniture, consisting of the bedroom set, the dining room set and a few other odds and ends I had bought from the Phoenix Furniture Company for $250.00 cash and so it was with pride and satisfaction that I looked forward to entering there with my bride, for we were beginning life free from any debt.

My embarrassment at learning that Lindau had disappeared increased when I realized that the key to my trunk in which my pajamas were, was on the keyring he had with him, and so I became somewhat perturbed over that but still held to the hope that Lindau would appear shortly. When we reached our home he was not there. The friends who had stayed there to guard it and to welcome us, congratulated us and then went their ways. And so I had to confess my dilemma to my bride. I found her to be extremely resourceful for she replied without a moment's hesitation, if you can't go to bed without pajamas, take that axe and break the trunk open and come to bed.

---

9   The bride was Josephine (Phenie) Carr.

Lindau returned my keys the next morning and life proceeded on its way. The customary formality of "making an appearance" was complied with on the following Sunday, when we attended Centenary all bedecked in our finest.

At the time we began housekeeping, it was a custom in Charleston to run accounts—and so the grocer, the baker, the butcher and vegetable lady, all extended us the privilege of monthly accounts. When the first of the month arrived, I found to my dismay that I had an enormous amount to pay. I paid the bills and after much pondering asked my wife how much would it cost to run the home for a week. After a little discussion we arrived at a sum, which I gave her. Five days later she asked for a loan against the following week's allowance and explained that she had run out of money and needed more. I couldn't understand why it had happened so as we had included in our "budget" everything we needed. It was a bit mystifying to me why a planned method of living could not be adhered to. Perhaps my attitude in that direction had developed through the necessities I had found essential in arranging my living affairs while I was at college and perhaps also because from the time I had bought my first pair of "long pants" at David's that I had almost entirely supported myself. I knew from the brief experience I had had, that if thrift and saving was not made a part of life that there would be no protection against adversity. I could not bring myself to the point of saying these things—so only asked how much is required to run the house for one day—and we reached an amount, and from that day onward I would leave whatever the amount was the day's expense, and the understanding that no more bills must be incurred and so we lived.

Shortly after my wedding both Robbie Brown and Eddie Plowden left my employment. The former going to New York to study pharmacy but instead embarked upon a somewhat hectic career which shortly resulted in his death. Plowden went to St.

Louis, but I never heard from him, only that he had reached and had "crossed the line."

FRIENDS AND ASSOCIATES

The mutual acquaintanceship I had made with Dr. Schroder, a white physician whose home and office was on Cannon Street, just opposite Smith Street had now extended itself into one of actual friendship. Dr. Schroder was an exceptionally skilled physician and perhaps had his wife been more cooperative by giving the proper care to his office and to his home, would have taken his place as one of Charleston's most outstanding practitioners. He was one of the best diagnosticians I have ever known whose ability as such contributed much to the success of Dr. R. Barnwell Rhett, the surgeon and to that of Dr. Hunter.

But despite these qualifications the doctor never made a financial success of his practice as the ill-kept condition of his office and the paucity of its equipment did not attract many patients and of those who came the majority were Negroes, and of these, the greater number were from the rural areas. It was thus that I came to know Dan Nesbit from the seven-mile bottom well. When I was at McClennan's pharmacy, I would occasionally meet him there, for he was the President of the Angel March Society for which Dr. McClennan was the physician. The Angel March Society was a cooperative membership of Negroes living in the area seven miles north of the city. Each member paid a monthly due of 50¢ and in return received the attention of a physician, all medicines, and the personal services, both nursing and housekeeping, by a fellow member in lieu of any cash benefit, when a member became sick, and in the event of death a suitable burial by the society. It was a somewhat communistic system of cooperative living and while it continued. It was a splendid arrangement while it lasted but unfortunately for them, when the sick benefit insurances started and offered a cash weekly benefit instead of the forenamed services the Angel

March Society quickly dwindled in membership and finally disbanded.

Among my many friends, I rank Dan Nesbit among the first. For his was a friendship that never sought or accepted anything in return for what he did for me. And he did aplenty, for it was through his influence that I obtained the patronage from so many people in his area, and even more so than the financial value that came with it was the constantly increasing number of friends it brought to me. I have known many men but none I knew possessed in higher degree the qualities he did. And they embraced all of the essentials—character, honesty, integrity and faithfulness.

I attended his funeral, only one of the older members of the family remained alive, his wife and all of the others had preceded him, and this remaining one, a sister took me aside, we were then in the cemetery, the body had been lowered into the grave and the grave diggers were filling it over, and said to me "Doctor you and Dan been close friends all these years and that the last except me. All of us are buried here," and then she added "and we all take your medicine." And I knew that though the latter expression may have been under any other circumstances something to laugh at, I also knew that it was meant as an expression of confidence that only many years of true friendship could express.

And as I think of Dan, my thoughts again return to Dr. Schroder and his diagnostic ability which he so capably demonstrated when he diagnosed an epidemic outbreak at the prison farm in St. Andrew's Parish as epidemic beri beri. When he announced his diagnosis many of his colleagues looked askance at it and the Health Office telegraphed to Washington for an expert from the U.S. Marine Health Service to come to Charleston to investigate the epidemic. By the time that expert arrived, Dr. Schroder had the epidemic under control, and though two patients had died he quickly succeeded in restoring twenty others to health.

Of course all of this took place years before vitamins and vitamin deficiencies were known about or when the functions of a Board of Health extended much beyond vaccination and the control of smallpox and the elimination of noxious odors that came from overflowing privy vaults by liberally dousing the puddles of filth that arose there from with a solution of copperas. Dr. Green, the Health Officer who appeared to have had a hereditary political right to the position, was in the minds of the community, largely a figure head, who relied upon old man Nipson to do whatever was necessary and the old man could be depended to do whatever was necessary for once he donned his black raincoat and mounted his old gray horse he would tackle anything from a living victim of smallpox and take him to the pest house, and as was known on one occasion to crawl under a house and drag the dead body of a smallpox victim and inter it.

I got possession of 70 Bogard Street early in 1903 and hastened to move there as we were expecting the arrival of our first born and wished to have ourselves settled there before the event occurred.

On the morning of April 7th, 1903 she came to light. It was a rather strenuous occasion, for Lindau had to use forceps and I had to act as anesthetist. We secured the services of Mrs. Anna D. Banks, who was then the Superintendent of Nurses at the hospital. Mother was also present and gave personal supervision to all that took place, as she was still skilled in obstetrics and had demonstrated her ability in that direction about eighteen previously by presenting me with my youngest sister, Charlotte—better known as Lottie.

That year I became a member of the faculty of the Hospital and Training School for [Nurses] and taught chemistry. I had been invited to join the faculty when I first returned to Charleston but had to decline at that time as I could not spare the time from my business that the position demanded.

About the same time, I became a member of the Sumner Literary Society, with the added honor of being its youngest member. The Sumners were an old Society and was named in honor of Charles Sumner, the great abolitionist. It met monthly at the homes of its members in alphabetical rotation. Its programs were restricted to discussions and to debates on timely topics. Mr. James Spencer was its President and from among its members I can now only recall the names of Mr. John Gregg, whose frequent letters to the *News and Courier* in protest or in correction of the tenor of many of its editorials, made him an outstanding critic of that paper, as well one whose letters were eagerly read when they appeared in that paper under his nom de plume "Nestor," Mr. Philip Lindau, the father of Dr. Lindau, Dr. Crum, Mr. Charles Craft and Mr. Swinton Bennett who conducted a real estate and loan business on Calhoun Street. Once a year the society held its annual [illegible] and on those occasions would usually invite one or two prominent white men to the function. At its annual celebration that year Col. James J. Kaufman, one of the old wealthy aristocrats of Charleston and Father Kraft, a Catholic priest who a few years later served at St. Mary's Church were the guests of the Society. The affair was strictly formal and its menu a splendid one. It started with crème de menthe served from frosted glasses and went through a dinner course and ended with black coffee. Dr. Crum acted as toast master and in fitting terms presented our guests of the evening and extended to them the welcome from the society, after which a series of toasts were responded to and then came adjournment—with "Auld Lang Syne."

At one of its earlier meetings, I made my "maiden effort" as speaker and gave a talk on "Haiti, its background and the probable effects that Dominican intervention by the United States would produce." (At that time President Theodore Roosevelt was seeking to prevent European interference in that Island.)

Economic and Political Decline

CHARLESTON LABOR CONFLICT

We were now beginning to feel the ill effects from the Charleston exposition upon the Negro mechanics of the city. It had been necessary to import many white skilled tradesmen into the city when the exposition buildings were under construction as the local supply of workmen was totally inadequate for the amount of work to be done. When the exposition closed a large number of these whites remained in the city and continued to work at their trades, and since the then available amount of employment, was somewhat less than that of the pre-exposition period it resulted in bringing about a type of competition between workers in which each would seek to underbid the other for work. Prior to the exposition the only union affiliations were those of the Carpenters and Joiners union and the Bricklayers and Plasterers unions. White union members who came to the city during the exposition period to work affiliated themselves with these two unions but as their number increased they established themselves into separate unions with the same national affiliation. The wage scale then in force averaged a $2.50 daily scale for ten hours work. At the close of 1903, the Charleston unions had become fully separated racial groups.

And in addition had established trade unions among workers in other crafts and also among the unskilled workers. An executive group known as the "labor council" was created and consisted of thirteen members, seven of them being whites and six being Negroes, and from their number chose a white man by the name of Cole for its Executive Secretary. The council next proposed that a citywide strike be called if a general wage increase with fewer hours to the work day which they proposed was refused. These demands were presented to the contractors of the city and were refused as the contracts then under construction were all based upon the previous wage and time scale. At which the unions declared a strike and every worker both white and Negro responded.

Application was made to the National offices of the unions for strike stipends on the receipt of which the National offices replied that the National office did not recognize that strike as it had not given it their authorization. On receipt of this announcement the white workers immediately resumed their jobs, but the Negroes persisted in remaining out and declared themselves in favor of a "walkout," which they proceeded to do. Somehow or other the Negro worker had acquired the belief that his labor and his efficiency was so far superior to that of the white worker that that alone would suffice in bringing about a compliance with their demands. They repeated their demands to the National office for their strike stipends and after considerable delay received for each member the sum of $3.00 and for two of its officers the sum of $6.00 each and notification that no further remittances would be made. In the meanwhile the white contractors were bringing in other white workers.

Realizing that unless something was done to reinstate the Negro worker in his job it would merely be a matter of time before white workers would be in such numbers in Charleston that they would be able to perform all of the work that the whites wanted done. I also realized that if the situation continued as it then was that a very large number of my patrons would be unable to meet their ordinary living expenses and that it would react disastrously against all Negro businesses. I could not afford to sit idly by and allow the condition to become worse as that would affect my personal welfare as well as that of many others in the community.

I had a conference with Cassie Smalls and Dan Whilden. They were the principal officers of the unions and held more influence over the membership than anyone else in the city. I called their attention to the gravity of the situation and warned them that if they elevated the scale of wages to the point where the white worker would find it profitable to live and work in Charleston that it would be but a short time before every Negro would be replaced by a white man. I also advised them against harboring the belief that the Negro was the only efficient and capable worker as that was only a delusion and was not supported by facts. I told them that I realized that there was need for betterment and suggested that the old wage scale be adhered to and only a reduction in hours of work demanded. My proposals were bluntly ignored and I was told that the unions would fight it out. Which they continued to do, as the "walk out" remained in effect during the following six months, at the end of which period the greater number of its members, most of whom had fallen in arrears with their union dues, became "scab" workers and took employment at whatever wage was offered them.

So began the economic decline of Negro Charleston. Less than five years had sufficed in which to destroy the majority control of the skilled trades that the Negroes formerly enjoyed and in addition to that there was no longer seen, the use of Negro foremen on white jobs.

And added to this was the subsequent tie up between the white labor unions and the newly organized political group headed by J. Elmore Martin, Tillman's chief of police for Charleston whereby the newly created office of "building inspector" was filled by the former Secretary Cole of the "Trades Council." But this was not all that came out of it, for more shall be told later.

In due time we began to feel the effects from the non–employment of Negro mechanics as our several businesses shrunk in volume. I was only using two clerks now, Charles Brown and Robert F. Morrison who had recently been taken on. Morrison did not remain with me long for the following as the following year [sic] he went to Fisk University. The desire for apprenticeship training was still a keen desire in the community, both with parents as well as with potential young pharmacists. One day, a young man by the name of Williamson, called to see me and told me that his guardian, Dr. Crum, had directed him to see me and request that I take him on as an apprentice. Though I could not say much to the boy, the request made me hot, for Dr. Crum had been giving my store some rather hard knocks recently. Sometimes it would be merely an insistent order that his prescription be taken to Hummell's Pharmacy and some-times it was by faint praise which was even more damnable—as when he would leave two prescriptions at the home of one of my customers and would tell, "You can have this one filled at John's but this one you must take to Hummell's as it is very impor-tant"—so you may imagine just how hot I was, I told the boy to go back to Dr. Crum and ask him to try and get Dr. Hummell to take him on as an apprentice, and should Dr. Hummell refuse to do so or if Dr. Crum would not ask Hummell the favor, to come back and let me know. Needless to say Dr. Crum would not seek that favor from a white man. When Williamson told me that Dr. Crum said that he could not do that, I told him to be ready to start on the following Monday morning. Williamson though a promising youngster developed tuberculosis within six months and later died.

A few weeks later I had another example of Dr. Crum's meth-ods, when Robbie Wainwright brought in a prescription for 2 ounces of Elixir of Iron, Quinine and Strychnine and asked if I had it. I said yes, then he wanted to know how long would it take to dispense it. I told him only a few minutes. So he said that he would wait on it. He continued to chat with me while I filled the prescription and when I handed it to him, he said, "I just wanted to see if you could, for Dr. Crum told me that you did not have this medicine and that only Hummell could fill it." I replied that I would speak to Dr. Crum and warn him not to continue his misrepresentations about my business. At which Wainwright replied "Yes and also tell him that I told you so." The next evening I called on Dr. Crum at his office and told him what had brought me, that I only wanted to advise him that he could not make any further statements about me, my business or what my stock included, and that I was not seeking any favors from him but only putting him on notice that should I ever again hear any statement from him concerning my business which I felt to be in disparagement, that I would proceed to settle it with him in my own way. With which I left him. Perhaps my manner startled him, but nevertheless, it was effective for I never again had need to complain about any of his actions and as time passed his attitude towards me changed and even became a friendly one.

FINANCIAL STRAIN

Had it not been that the lean years had then fallen upon me I would not have resented Dr. Crum's methods in the way I did, as I had usually attributed much of what he did to a silent resentment against my refusal to have him as my silent partner when I started business. And also that he may have been influenced in that direction by Dr. Hummell, whose prescription business, largely among Negroes had been seriously reduced when Dr. Wm. H. Johnson withdrew his support as well as from the inroads I had made upon it.

The business at the drugstore had dwindled to such an extent that I found it necessary to dispense with all of my clerks except Charlie Brown. I was on duty there from 7 a.m. until

11 p.m. each weekday. I could not take time away to eat my dinners at home and so they were sent to me. I had closed my banking account at the Dime bank as there was too little money coming in to allow me to maintain a satisfactory balance. I thought of selling out and moving North, and perhaps find opportunity to study medicine for I still had a desire to do so but could not find a buyer as no one in Charleston wanted to buy it. And so there was nothing else to do but to sit still and hope.

And then the twins came—Estelle and Allen, and once again I had to assist in giving the anesthetic while Lindau applied his forceps. Immediately after Estelle arrived, I hurried downstairs to get my breakfast so that I could get to the drugstore without further delay for it was then about 8 a.m. and I was then an hour late in getting there. Just as I started to eat, Lindau called from upstairs and said, "Come on back, you have got another chance for a boy." So startled was I by his call, that I could only mumble a reply and return again take up my duty with the chloroform mask. I was afterwards told that I had cursed Lindau, but if I did, I think that it was due to the financial stress under which I was.

The second was a boy. We named him John Allen, Jr.

By the time I finished paying the nurse, the maid we employed and for a twin baby carriage, I was pretty broke. I had been able to keep up the payments on the house and with my drugstore bills but after doing so never had more than a few dollars left. Shortly after the birth Estelle developed a pneumonic attack which left her a weakling. She never improved and died a few weeks later and I was broke. I borrowed some money from father to pay for her grave and got Elias Robinson to furnish her funeral on credit. But my hard luck did not stop there, as Allen then took sick. I secured the services of Dr. Cornell, the first baby specialist to practice in Charleston and under his care and through dint of hard work and special feedings he succeeded in bringing him back to health.

Lindau's practice was rapidly falling off. For some time he had been imbibing too steadily and had now reached the habit state where he was more or less always drunk. For years we had been very close friends and though I had used every possible method to restrain him from drinking there was nothing that I could do that would stop him. He was an exceptionally able physician and could easily have become Charleston's most capable doctor but fate determined otherwise. I could tell much about him and about the disappointment he brought to his parents and to his wife but from these I shall refrain.

And so I started "counter dispensing." I detested doing so for it was not in keeping with my ideals of ethical correctness but necessity compelled me to it and I had to live and feed my family. It was not long before my daily "clinic" averaged ten to twelve sick persons. The majority of them came from the rural areas and as each benefited by my administrations, would in turn send me other patients. And so the drugstore over which I had hung my sing, "apothecary" became in fact and in accord with the old Charleston jingle,

Oh dear mother what a pain I got
Take me down to the doctor shop
Get me something but I don't care what
To cure this awful pain I got.

I unhung my sign and threw them in the backyard and proceeded to make money. For I needed it badly. It was before the day of "sick blanks" and vital statistic blanks in the rural area, and since my patients never died I had no need to worry about death certificates. When a smallpox epidemic struck the city, the health department furnished me with free vaccines and on one single day, I vaccinated more than forty people free. During intensely hot weather when the cesspools overflowed and babies died in numbers from enteritis without receiving any medical attention, the coroner would phone me and ask me to investigate infant's deaths occurring in the neighborhood, and if death was from natural causes to certify it for him, that he could issue a burial permit without the necessity of coming up and viewing the body. I had bought several textbooks on medicine—a Tigerstedt Physiology, a Williams obstetrics, a Whites, on syphilis and an Osler's practice and from these and from my knowledge of therapeutics was able to carry on.

POLITICS AND DR. CRUM

Just before the twins were born A.J. Clement joined our community. He was fresh from College and came to our city to establish a branch office of the North Carolina Mutual Life Insurance Company. He opened an office on King Street near Morris and soon became one of our group, and shortly thereafter took over the business of the Metropolitan (Ball's) Insurance Co. and that of another insurance venture that had recently been started by Rev. Beckett (Bishop, later,) and a man by the name of Bryant from Savannah. His business flourished from the start and it was not long before it acquired a sustaining debit.

None of us were satisfied with the volume of business which came to each of us, Perry Seabrook was crying for more, so was I and our newcomer, Clement, though doing well wanted more. We had used Jenkins paper and other methods of advertising but yet was unable to reach any new business, when Perry Seabrook got the idea that if we could reorganize the Republican party in Charleston county and make it a young man's party, that we would be able to accomplish something in that direction and also get county-wide advertising that would help our several businesses.

And this we did and with so much vim that when the precinct meetings were held we secured a majority of the delegates for the city convention. But it was there that we met our Waterloo for we had reckoned our course without giving heed to what a corrupted "credential committee" could do, for when he got to the convention we found that the credential committee had unseated so many of our delegates that we only had left a minority control of the convention we immediately organized a "rump convention" and elected our delegates to the state convention with instructions to contest the legality of those who had been elected under the roll created by the "credential committee." It was then that I learned what a shrewd old politician Gibbs Mitchell was. For he was the Chairman of the old group and had directed the unseating of our delegates but in addition to that had retained Seabrook and Clement on his roll and had Seabrook, Clement and several others from our group elected as delegates to the Columbia convention but with instructions, attested copies of which had been sent to Joe Tolbert the State Chairman, that required the casting of their votes for only those whom Gibbs Mitchell wanted selected. All of which ended my brief political efforts. But I did get some notoriety if not advertising from it.

I was somewhat hesitant, a short while later when Dr. Crum called on me and asked what had become of the Board of Trade, a proposed organization that we were trying to organize but which had never gone beyond the "talking about stage." He said that he wanted me to perfect its organization and have it address a letter to President Theodore Roosevelt endorsing him, Dr. Crum, for the position of Collector of Port at Charleston.

The doctor's request astounded me and caused me to wonder if Tolbert was giving him the "run around," as I could not figure out how the doctor could secure the necessary backing in Washington to bring him the Collectorship. Which as I said caused me to wonder if it was only a "run around," for I had seen one such given a few years earlier when Tommie Grant had been promised the Postmastership at Charleston, supposedly with everything so well prearranged that all he had to do was to go to Washington meet Edmund Deas, the "Duke" of Darlington, who would present him to the Postmaster General, and there he would receive the appointment.

Deas however had no intentions of permitting Grant to get the position and as a matter of fact had been directed to block the appointments. So he met Grant at the station, and took him to his room and filled him on liquor and when Grant could but barely navigate, put him in a hack and took him down to the Post Office Department and had him ushered into the presence of the Postmaster General.

Needless to say, Grant was immediately ushered out, at which Deas cussed him out roundly for entering the Postmaster General's office "drunk as a fool," expecting to get an appointment.

However I talked with Seabrook and Joe Porter about it and we decided to organize the Board of Trade, temporarily at least, for that purpose. So we met and organized and drafted the letter the doctor desired us to write. We had it typed on a letterhead the doctor provided us with and I signed it as Secretary and delivered it over to the doctor for mailing. Through this manner the doctor was able to present some evidence that the business interest of Charleston, in some measure at least, wanted him appointed. After which the "Board of Trade" dissolved.

When the announcement came from Washington telling that the President had made an interim appointment of Dr. Crum to the position of Collector at the Charleston Custom House it aroused a wave of protest from the whites. Who then proceeded to make plans to defeat the appointment when it came before the senate.

At the time of Dr. Crum's appointment the compensation allowed the Collector was on a fee basis and not a fixed salary. The position required only part time service and was more one of honor than one of compensation. A number of the clerks in the office were Negro. Mr. Charles Purvis was a clerk. Practically all of the boatmen and janitors were Negroes. When Dr. Crum assumed his office he made no changes in its personnel. Miss

Washington, a very estimable white lady, who was stenographer to his predecessor continued in her position and served the doctor throughout his entire tenure of office.

During the first year of his administration, Clarence Brown, who had once worked for me, and who had since passed the civil service examination, received an appointment to the Custom House as Assistant Customs Inspector thereby adding another Negro to its clerical force. At the time of the doctor's appointment the gross business income of the office was extremely low. But during the second year a tremendous increase occurred. It came about largely through the increase importation of kainite from Germany and returning export shipments to foreign countries in ships which had brought in kainite.

This huge increase in kainite importation had come about through announcement from the "Kali syndicate" that the price of kainite would increase from the then $6.00–$7.00 a ton to $30.00 a ton and that the new price would become effective within six months. The local fertilizer companies sought to anticipate their needs by purchasing as much as they could at the old price, and so the volume of imports increased enormously.

It may be of passing interest to know that the formation of the "Kali Syndicate" was a German state affair and that the huge profits received from the increase charge for kainite did not all go to the individual owners of the potash mines but that the major portion went to the government and was one of the beginning preparations by the Kaiser for World War One.

However that is only a passing comment, the main thing is that after his second year, the doctor's salary became a fixed annual sum instead of a fee allowance. Dr. Crum told me that during his first year, that his fees were under $500.00. But I also learned that his fees during his second year amounted to nearly $40,000.00 [sic] and that this was the reason for the change.

During his last year several other changes took place in the custom house—the position of cashier was eliminated and Mr.

Smith's services were dispensed with. Mr. Purvis had resigned because of ill health. An altercation between one of the janitors, William Johnson and one of the white inspectors precipitated a disturbance in which the police shared by injuring Johnson, and resulted in much local criticism for Dr. Crum from many Negroes who held that Dr. Crum could have prevented it by declaring the custom house, a government reservation, beyond the reach of police law.

But these were all of minor importance when compared with the doctor's chances for reappointment under the newly elected Taft. Three days before Taft's inauguration, Dr. Crum sent for me and told me that he had received a telegram to come to Washington at once. He said that President Roosevelt had exacted a promise from Mr. Taft to reappoint him to the collectorship and that it then seemed that some difficulties were brewing over his appointment. The doctor went to Washington and held a conference with President Roosevelt and Mr. Taft but on his return to Charleston refrained from discussing anything that occurred.

Current rumors and local comment gave rise to several interpretations of what had taken place there but all of them agreed in that President Roosevelt's promise received from Mr. Taft was beyond recall and if Dr. Crum insisted on being reappointed to the position that Mr. Taft had been pledged to do so, and further that Mr. Roosevelt had demanded that the promise be fulfilled.

Mr. Taft's attitude on the appointment of Negroes to federal office was then well known, and is most clearly enunciated in the speeches he made at Augusta, Georgia and at Birmingham, Alabama, in both of which he announced that he would appoint no Negroes to office in any Southern section except when they were recommended for those positions by local whites.

It is only from the events that immediately followed Crum's Washington conference that conjecture gives some explanation for what took place there. To those of us who were then on the sidelines and had previously witnessed Mr. Roosevelt's attitudes along racial lines, not only the instance when he had Booker T. Washington to dine with him at the White House, but also by his appointments of Negroes to federal office in several Southern cities and to consular positions in foreign countries, other than the usual Haitian, Dominican and Liberian appointments. And also the full exercise of membership in the National Committee of the Republican Party.

The preinaugural break that occurred between Mr. Roosevelt and Mr. Taft was seen as one which predicted the elimination of the Southern Negro from political affairs and the transference of his prior privileges and exercise of power over to the newly created "Lily-white" Republican group. In favor of which Mr. Taft was one of the foremost.

The intensity of the clash between these two political leaders is best realized, when it is recalled that on that inaugural morning, and for the first time in the history of the United States, a retiring President chosen from the same party which elected the incoming president, left the White House without welcoming or witnessing the inauguration of his successor. For President Roosevelt left Washington at 8 a.m. that morning for Oyster Bay and as far as any reports show has never welcomed Mr. Taft to the nation's mansion.

Subsequent events showed that Dr. Crum had agreed to resign his position as Collector at Charleston and accept the post of Minister to Liberia. And though it brought a higher financial compensation to the doctor than the Collectorship did it also served as the entering wedge in eliminating the Negro from Republican political affairs. The consensus of local opinion was that Dr. Crum would have insisted on receiving the local appointment as by doing so it may have focused national attention to Taft's movement at the time when its defeat was a greater possibility than it subsequently became. To our local Negro group, his resignation brought a keen sense of disappointment and to some extent even embarrassment for when one read the newspaper comments on his removal from office it could not be helped.

At the time when these events took place I only gave them passing notice as I like many others too busily engaged in seeking to improve my own personal fortune and so could only give passing attention to them.

Our mode of life at that time was almost altogether the individualistic one, in which each one strived to attain the goal he desired. Much of the earlier methods in which group co-operation was foremost had disappeared, and of what remained, was largely that which took place within the confines of fraternal organizations and almost altogether for the furtherance of their particular activities. The keen sense of racial solidarity so conspicuously present during the 1880s had largely disappeared and in its place was spirit of indifference towards anything that was alien to the individual aspirations.

Many of our former leaders had disappeared from public life or had accepted positions which automatically retired them from the role of leadership. Mr. Thomas E. Miller had been given the position of President at the State A & M College by Governor Ben Tillman with the distinct understanding, that he was to keep out of politics; Rev. George C. Rowe had left the city, Congressman George Murray was seeking to evade trial on a felony charge, Robert Smalls had been retired to the postmastership at Beaufort, Colonel Robinson who had commanded the militia at the time Tillman ordered it disbanded, had migrated to New York, and so on down the line it went and in the wake of it followed disintegration of the solidarity that previously prevailed. My former adventure into the realm of politics had not altogether been one in in which I had hoped to improve its mores or to increase its activities. For I knew that that was beyond my power, as the majority of those who then directed the local affairs of the Republican party, consisting mostly of the "old war horses" who enjoyed a monopoly of the janitorships and other minor positions in the federal offices were all feudally bound to Joe Tolbert, the Republican National Committeeman from South Carolina, who ruled them with an iron hand and dictated every move they made.

Tolbert's power and leadership will always remain a conundrum. It was devoid of constructive initiative. Relatively speaking, he was a man of wealth and was one of the largest landowners in upper South Carolina and whatever incomes he derived from his political activities were but a small part of his total income. He was noted for his peculiarities, the chief of which was his disdain for wearing a necktie and his familiar boast that he "never wore a tie for no man could put a rope around his neck." In place of tie he always wore a two carat diamond stud button, a fashion that very few could emulate.

I knew Tolbert as well, perhaps as anyone else in Charleston did, except those who were his henchmen, and never once did I ever find him in anyway concerned with formulating a constructive policy for his party. His sole aim was the continuation of Republican party rule and his personal retention as a member of the Republican National Committee. To him the Republican party "was the ship and all else the sea."

So far as my knowledge is he never once has made a single proposal to any of the party's platforms during his entire career. His chief aim was always to maintain a complete control over the South Carolina delegates at a National Convention and to use that power to further his future aims. He wanted neither the intelligent Negro nor any new white adherents to join his ranks and so forceful was his power in that direction, that few of them ever could. And of those who did succeed in doing so, there was none whose voice was ever heard beyond the walls of a precinct meeting.

His methods only succeeded in bringing criticism and ridicule upon the Republicans in South Carolina. The intelligent and politically minded Negroes in the State wanted him ousted from office and from his position as National Committeeman. And that that position be made an actual elective one, instead of as it then was, the personal prerogative of a dictator. The Negroes were not seeking to create a solidly Negro political unit of the Republican party. For they were neither inimical to nor did they seek to bar fellow white Republicans from its ranks but only sought to insure to themselves the preservation and continuation of their political right as members of the party.

In the meanwhile a few of the white Republican leaders had rebelled against Tolbert's exercise of power and the method by which he had maintained it, and had deserted over to the newly organized "Lily-white" Republican contingent with whom they became actively engaged in the effort to build up an all-white following of such number that a two-party system, for the state, would result. And from which all Negroes would be barred, and that all rights and privileges to the holding of state and federal offices would thereafter be solely at the dictates of the whites.

Such was the political atmosphere in Charleston when Taft was nominated for the presidency and it was no mere local cloud that hovered only above South Carolina for it overshadowed Negroes throughout the length and breadth of America. And so it came about that we in Charleston felt its pressure and being without strength to resist it, became apathetic and fearful that future edicts would come from the National Executive Committee of the Republican party authorizing the extension of "lily whitism" throughout the entire South, and so could, as effectively as did Tillman's constitution of 1895, deprive us of exercising any of the rights of representative government. This condition of apathy was further increased by the economic decline which had set in with the mass unemployment of Negro mechanics who had participated in the 1903 "walk out." And which had taken place at a time when a large number of transient white workers were in the city and who had largely supplanted them in their employment. These transients had in the meanwhile taken permanent residency in the city and through their unions exercised a coordinated power in the Democratic primary that could not be overlooked. Neither could their demands for employment be ignored.

About two years after the beginning of the "walk out" the Negro unions, with the idea of conserving what work was available to them, enacted a union law, which restricted the employment of apprentices by any one contractor to a ratio of one apprentice to each six master workmen employed. So once again I went to Dan Whilden and to Cassie Smalls and this time urged that they have the unions rescind the apprenticeship ruling. For if it was adhered to that it would rapidly deplete the future number of skilled Negro mechanics, and would also lessen the efficiency of the union's older men by removing from their midst, the younger and stronger workers, whose physical strength could supplement the greater technical knowledge possessed by the older workmen and so could insure longer employment to the older ones.

I was most keenly interested in having the apprenticeship system of training continued for I knew its worth. But nothing I could say influenced them for they wanted none of it and said that if contractors were allowed to employ apprentices in the number they wished to, that there would be no work for the men. I asked, "how was it when you went to trade" and the reply came forth—"that was different then." And so far as they were concerned the apprenticeship system of training went into the discard.

A ray of hope brightened the situation, when a little later, a number of the younger carpenters who had left the union when the "walk out" collapsed, organized themselves into the "Carpenters Benevolent Association" under the leadership of Basie St. Marks. I assisted them in drafting their constitution and bylaws. They functioned as an independent union and since their membership included a majority of the really capable Negro workmen, they were able to offset to some extent the effects of the inroads which the whites had made upon the trades. The new association was far more liberal in its attitude towards apprentices and in known instances overlooked it entirely. The old union took offense at this and threatened to call a strike against the employment of any member of the association by general contractors. But the threatened strike never materialized as the association countered by threatening to bar all members of the union from working on any job with them.

I assisted in effecting a compromise between the two groups, and at the request of the association, drafted a "working agreement" in which the full autonomy of the association was recognized by the union, and a uniform scale of wage agreed upon. Both organizations signed the agreement and so brought an end to a struggle that had lasted nearly five years and had netted them nothing. But the most amazing thing about that struggle was that the Negroes, like robins, fought about the worm they had and in the bitterness of the strife, lost sight of the sparrow, who grabbed their worm and made off with it.

And so the monopoly which Negroes enjoyed in the building trades at the time the exposition was conceived passed from under their control and was never regained. Perhaps it may have continued longer had the exposition not attracted white workmen or had the Negroes [not] manifested a determination to starve out any and all competition for their jobs by refusing to join in the strike.

When the announcement was first made that President Roosevelt had appointed Dr. Crum to the position of Collector at the custom house, it leaked out that while the President was in Charleston attending the exposition that he had made several inquiries among prominent local white citizens about Dr. Crum's character and about his status in the community and had received very commendable replies [illegible]. And that it was largely on the strength of those replies that he had appointed the doctor and not through any political pressure that the doctor exercised. For the doctor's political strength was very little and his influence negligible. Which makes it evident that President Roosevelt then had the intent of giving Negroes, who possessed ability and integrity a larger place in national affairs and in public life.

The political significance of Mr. Roosevelt's questionings while at the Charleston exposition, and the incidents that surrounded Mr. Taft's inauguration, when coupled together brings to light the forces which were then working for or against the extension of political rights to Negroes. To say that the criticism which had been directed against the Tolbert party was solely responsible for the advent of the Lily-whites is erroneous. For the plan to eliminate the Negro from the Republican party had already been determined upon by the Taft machine and had only been held in abeyance until such time when it could be put into full force and effect. So long as Mr. Roosevelt exercised a power of direction within the party, the status quo of the Negro was not a pertinent issue. But as soon as he had accomplished the election of Taft to the presidency and announced his temporary withdrawal from public life and from active participation in the directing of the policies of the party. The anti Negro contingent within the membership of the National Committee manifested its intent by unseating several of its Negro members. To all of which Mr. Taft gave acquiescence.

PHOTOGRAPHS

John A. McFall, age twenty, Philadelphia (1899). He earned the Doctor of Pharmacy degree (P.D.) from the Philadelphia College of Pharmacy in 1899.

John A. McFall (middle row, third from left), with his graduating class at the Philadelphia College of Pharmacy. Courtesy of Philadelphia College of Pharmacy, University of the Sciences in Philadelphia

John A. McFall, age twenty, Philadelphia, Pennsylvania (1899). Courtesy of the Philadelphia College of Pharmacy, University of the Sciences in Philadelphia

Henrietta Alston McFall (1820?–1901), the paternal grandmother of John A. McFall.

Photograph of a drawing of Dr. John McFall's father, Thomas Alston McFall (1854–1927). The drawing bore the signature "Harleston." Charlestonian artist Edwin Harleston and Dr. McFall were friends. Dr. McFall purchased some of Harleston's paintings.

Dr. John McFall's mother, Mary Ann Hargrove McFall (1860–1942) was born at the King's Mountain Military School in Yorkville, South Carolina. John Allen was the first of their eleven children.

*Josephine Carr McFall (1881–1962) with the couple's
children, Edith (1903–1995) and John Jr. (1906–1995)*

Dr. John McFall (right) and his son Dr. Thomas Carr McFall (1909–1969). Courtesy of the Dr. John W. Work IV estate

Dr. John McFall's sister, Thomasina "Tommie" Alston McFall (1887–1964), helped manage the drugstore. Courtesy of the Dr. John W. Work IV estate

150 Ashley Avenue, the home of the Dr. John McFall family in 1930. Courtesy of the Dr. John W. Work IV estate

150 Ashley Avenue side view with garden. Courtesy of the Dr. John W. Work IV estate

This undated photograph shows the storefront of McFall's Drugs, located at the corner of Morris and Smith streets in Charleston. Courtesy of the Avery Research Center for African American History and Culture, College of Charleston, Charleston

Encroachments by Tillman and Taft

Within the short period of fifteen years, (from 1893) the Negroes had suffered two encroachments upon their rights to participate in government through the exercise of the ballot. The first was by Tillman, through the provisions of the Constitution of 1895. And the second that by the Taft machine which sought to create an all-white electorate.

Efforts were made to overcome the obstacles coming from the first encroachment by encouraging Negroes who could qualify through either the property requirement or through the "reading test" to register. But the number who did, never exceeded five hundred, and by 1905, through deaths and removals from the city had fallen to under three hundred. At which time Rev. John L. Dart called a small group of us together for the purpose of devising means whereby a larger enrollment could be obtained.

About seventy-five of us formed an organization, and each contributed the sum of $5 to an expense fund for defraying the costs of the proposed program. Rev. Dart was elected Chairman and Mr. Morris Richardson, Secretary-Treasurer of the Committee. We engaged the services of Mr. Robert C. Brown, an attorney for the purpose of being present at all openings of the county registration office, where he would assist all applicants for registration. We had ministers of the city urge their members to apply for registration and membership of the committee to do likewise.

Prospective applicants for registration were carefully instructed as to the procedure they should follow. Those who owned taxable property to the extent of $300.00 were directed to present their county tax receipts for the preceding year and demand that they be registered on that qualification alone. Those who presented themselves on the educational qualification provision, were instructed, that after having read the portion of the state constitution presented to them, if asked to interpret its meaning, that they should read it a second time, and reply, that that was its meaning. Mr. Brown's services were altogether satisfactory but the number who applied was not. For we only succeeded in getting about nine hundred to register during the twelve months through which the campaign continued. Which brought the total registration within the city to approximately 1,300 and that of the adjacent rural areas to about 150 more.

The total white vote in the city and county was then over 4,800 and rigidly being bound into a solidarity in action, could not be defeated.

While these political and economic encroachments were taking place, other restrictions had come about, the theater where we previously had bought seats freely, now refused to sell seats to Negroes, except those in its two upper galleries, claiming that it was forced to do so because of complaints, that Negro women who had bought seats on the lower floors were soliciting white men there and that that was the only way by which they could stop it. Of course there was no truth in that as we all well know that the chief purpose behind it, was the wish to comply with the insistent demands, from whites who had recently moved into the city, that Negroes be barred from using seats beside them. When this was done I swore that I would never again enter a white showhouse where segregation obtained. For [a]while it was bad enough to endure segregation where it could not be avoided, to pay a white man to do it to me, was something not to be thought of.

That summer a similar effort was made at the baseball park. Where the Negroes who usually occupied the middle portion of the open stand, were sandwiched in and among whites on all sides. One afternoon the management, without giving prior notice, erected a barrier near the lower part of the stand and designated the portion beyond it as "seats for Negroes." When the gates opened about three hundred Negroes bought tickets and entered but when they saw the sign, they stopped and stared, and with one accord immediately returned to the box office and demanded a refund of their admission and all the while vociferating at the top of their voices that they would never again enter the park.

Of course they got their money back and quickly too as the management had no mind to further enrage a mob of several hundred mad Negroes. And be it said to their credit, that the rank and file of the Negro "fans" never returned to the park. The management sought to induce Negroes to return, by giving complimentary tickets to a number of Negro ministers, and each afternoon about ten of them could be seen there, basking in the shadow of the "Jim Crow" sign. I won't give the names of these divines, as they should sink into oblivion.

The management soon found out that the admissions formerly paid by Negroes represented not only their net profits but also a portion of the expense they paid and that they were approaching bankruptcy. So they endeavored to lure their Negro patrons back. Matthews who was President of the club called on me and asked, if the signs were removed, would we not return. I replied that the erection of the signs was an uncalled for insult to us, and that in view of that insult, we saw no reason why we should forget that it was our patronage that made his venture a successful one. He tried to explain that it was not the local club's wish to segregate the attendance but that the other teams in the South Atlantic league had demanded that it be done and that they had to comply. Since none of us returned to the park, the season became a financial flop. The following year the park was closed and the Charleston franchise in the South Atlantic League passed to another city.

Thus did we feel the noose of segregation tightening around our necks, and little could we do about it. Either we could accept it as it was or as an alternative, withdraw ourselves into a more contracted mode of life. We had no power with which to resist it. Our political power had well nigh been extinguished. Our economic opportunities had been seriously diminished by the coming of white worker, who had brought with them, a new pattern for workers, a "white man's job" that was backed up by the power of the "labor vote."

During the fifteen years in which this had taken place many of our leading Negro citizens had moved away from the city. Most of them going North. Death had also taken its toll from the ranks of the worthwhile. Of ten who had served apprenticeships at Dr. McClennan or with me, only two, of which I am one, returned to Charleston, the others remained in the North. The personnel of the police department which previously included over thirty percent of its number, Negroes had been reduced to three, Policemen Carroll, Hazel and Bob Hutchinson. Lawrence Hollings, the last Negro to serve on the Public Lands commission went out of office that year. Only the Truck company No. 2 of the Fire Department remained intact. At the post office several of the Negro indoor clerks had been ousted, Robbie Gordon and Walter Mischeaux were out and Dannie Hines, only allowed to remain with the understanding that he would only work at night when the windows were closed, so that white patrons would not see him. The anti-Negro attitude of many white patrons at the post office, became somewhat amusing when one or two of its patrons, mentioned to Mr. Mushington, who was very fair complected, that they were glad to have him serve them, since the other man, "the nigger" who was also there, was insolent. The "nigger" happened to have been Chief money order clerk Blank, who though white was much darker than Mr. Mushington was.

Mr. C.C. Leslie had died. And his business, the largest wholesale fish business in the city, [illegible] sold to Tom Carroll. Thad Marshall had sold his business and had gone to New York. The Stokiens closed out their meat markets and had moved away. Thorne the printer had closed his shop and moved to Brooklyn. Barks, the merchant tailor had died and his business was closed. The once goodly number of stall keepers in the downtown market had dwindled to the point that they could be numbered with the fingers of one hand. And there were others too numerous to mention whose going left a void that has never since been filled.

The halcyon days of the 1890 period had vanished and perhaps may never again return to make life in Charleston as harmonious and pleasant as it once was.

Much Good Could Be Accomplished

COMMUNITY WELFARE SERVICES

As we passed into the more restricted life the need for Negro community welfare service received attention. Some of it was patterned after what had been done elsewhere and some there was that was altogether original. The Hospital and Training School for Nurses was organized in 1897 under the leadership of Dr. A.C. McClennan and founded along lines similar to those followed in Philadelphia when the Douglass Hospital there was established.

Dr. Robert J. Macbeth, the dentist, organized an independent Y.M.C.A. But it never attained the full scope which the national Y.M.C.A. held to and for years remained what its limited scope designed it to be, a Bible-study school until several years later when a large organization was created and national affiliation with the Y.M.C.A. was obtained.

Under the leadership of Mrs. Phyllis Goodwin, a group of ladies organized and incorporated the first Y.W.C.A. in South Carolina. The Committee bought the building on Coming Street and equipped it for the purposes of a Y.W.C.A. program. For a while I was a member of its Executive but when the ladies became sex conscious, I was legislated out of office. The entire conception of the Y.W.C.A. was to an extent somewhat original in Charleston, as the white organization was then unknown. A number of years later when the white Y.W.C.A. was established, the Colored Y.W.C.A. voluntarily surrendered its charters so that functioning under the new group. The title to the property on Coming Street is under that name, and became a branch organization.

OVER [Penned notation is in original manuscript, but it is unclear what it refers to.]

Altogether unique in its conception is the Jenkins Orphanage that was founded by Rev. J.D. Jenkins about 1893, as it is the first institution of its kind. Many orphanages have been in existence for a longer period of time but none were ever started in the manner which he did his nor combined with it both technical and mental training for children to the extent he did.

Beyond these our social life showed but a few changes. Our churches and the number of our ministers had increased. As also had the number of sinners, for somehow though the number of churches had increased, yet their attendances had all diminished. Our education facilities had remained the same as it was before, no better, no worse.

The color complex had abated somewhat, as most of the near whites had left the city for parts unknown to begin life anew, on the other side of the line, as free, white and twenty-one.

During the spring of 1907 our community entertained a group of visitors from Washington, at a banquet tendered in their honor, at the old Odd Fellows hall on Society Street. The party consisted of two Reverends Grimke [penned], Whitfield McKinlay, Mr. Kelly Miller and Mr. Richard T. Greener. These gentlemen were all former South Carolinians and were well known to most of us by the outstanding reputations they bore. Rev. Archibald Grimke and his brother, the Rev. Mr. Grimke had pastored leading churches in Washington for many years. Mr. Kelly

Miller was a member of the faculty at Howard University, Mr. McKinlay conducted a very large real estate business in Washington and at the time maintained two offices for the transaction of his business, one on U Street and the other in the business area on F Street. Mr. Greener was a member of the United States Consular service and had only recently returned from Vladivostok Russia where he held the post of United States Consul. Mr. Greener formerly resided in Columbia, South Carolina where he held a position on the faculty of the University of South Carolina during the 1870s when Negroes and whites attended the University. Mr. Greener had also had the privilege of serving in other quasi-public fields, as he had served as a member of the commission that had charge of the erection of the Grant memorial that stands on Riverside Drive in New York City; a memorial that was built by public subscription in memory of President U.S. Grant. The other member of the party, Mr. Miller who removed from the state at an early age, was devoting his entire time to education work, and several years later was destined to become one of the foremost critics and writers against the rising tide of Negro repression.

Approximately one–hundred-and-twenty-five of our group attended the banquet. After we had partaken of a very splendid repast, the toast master introduced and welcomed our guests of honor and then proceeded with the presentation of the evening's speakers.

The speaking proceeded smoothly until Mr. Seymour Smith attempted to make his speech, when it appeared that something out of the ordinary was happening. Mr. Smith was a graduate of the University of South Carolina, who subsequently studied law and had been admitted to the South Carolina bar. At all previous times he had amply demonstrated his ability as a very logical speaker who possessed a splendid flow of words and with no mean oratorical power. However when Mr. Smith began his remarks that evening, everyone could note a drastic change in his demeanor and in his speech, as he was then mumbling his words and they did not make sense. He was supposed to be presenting—"The position of the Negro in the then changing political situation in South Carolina." We had anticipated that he would bring us words of wisdom and perhaps some panacea that would alleviate the ills we suffered. Ordinarily Mr. Smith was fully capable of doing so but instead only disappointed us. That however was soon forgiven, as when a few days later, we learned that he was ill and suffering with a nervous breakdown, which had had its initial beginning during the banquet. Mr. Smith never recovered from the attack and died several months later.

Mr. Greener who had given close attention to Mr. Smith while he was speaking, was the next speaker to be presented, and in his introductory remarks looked towards Mr. Smith, with a glance, and without words, and on that instant it seemed as if I heard him say, "Now Seymour when I taught you at University, you could have presented that subject better, this is what you should have told."

For two and a half hours Mr. Greener held us spellbound. He gave us an analysis of what was taking place in our lives and of the forces that were then planning to concentrate our existence into that of a colonial status. He told us how propaganda had been used and was still being used for that purpose. First in Southern areas by coordinating Southern newspapers to the task of exaggerating the deficiencies of Negroes and of minimizing or withholding from publication any of our achievements.

He said that segregation was not devised solely as a means to separate the races but rather was with the intent to legislate a sense of racial superiority into the poor whites and cause them to become inimical towards Negroes and thus to be more potent tools in the hands of those who wished to further depress the Negroes.

Also how the ideal of "white superiority" was given added stimulus by white Southern papers whenever news items were published about Negroes, by emphasizing their racial identification and never using the title Mr. or Mrs. While the lowliest white when mentioned would always be designated Mr. or Mrs., for the sole purpose of having them feel a sense of superiority over their darker neighbors. And that from it would ultimately arise the full power of "white supremacy."

He also told how the "Southern Historical Society," an organization about which I was ignorant, had been created for the particular purpose of spreading vicious propaganda against the Negro, throughout Northern areas. And that it was largely due to that Society that anti-Negro attitudes were beginning to appear in the North.

Mr. Greener then described the conditions in South Africa and told us about the South African reconstruction measures whereunder the natives in the Dutch and English settlements there were being virtually enslaved and that a similar system was *being planned by the white South for all Negroes within its Domain*. And that that plan had been presented to one of the New York daily papers in 1898 with the request that it would open its columns for a forum discussion of methods by which the American Negro should be controlled but preferably a discussion about applying the South African reconstruction measures in the South.

In his summation, Mr. Greener expressed the belief that if these methods were permitted to take hold in the United States that it would be but a very short while before the Negroes would be re–enslaved, not as a chattel however, but as a restricted group bereft of all of the rights of freemen and of citizenship.

To prevent this from taking place, he said, it will be necessary to acquaint the entire country with the falsity of the propaganda that is being spread and in addition to that to make an appeal to those in the North and in the South for an unbiased attitude. That efforts should be made to check the spread of further segregation, especially in northern areas for if it should reach there that its extension would soon become nationwide. He advocated that we foster education and the learning of the skilled trades and seek to be industrious and thrifty. And lastly he said that every Negro should register and should use the ballot, for in that more than in anything else lies his hope for salvation.

There was little conversation between us as we wended our way homeward that night as I was busily engage, mentally, with thoughts from Mr. Greener's message. It was my first experience in thinking beyond my own personal existence and it provoked a new chain of thoughts, both for my future and for the futures of my children. I did not sleep much that night for it seemed that the noose of racial repression was even more tightly drawn about me than I had previously suspected.

His message had brought to me an awakening to the realization that the individualistic mode of life had many defects and invited danger and that a fuller life had to be lived if safety was desired, and so I began to ponder how I could extend my life into that of the community whereby I could most efficiently render the community a worthwhile service. I had no desire to become a "leader" since most of those I had met were either panhandlers or were like Don Quixote chasing windmills and, who after having made their spiels and gathered up the collections quickly made it off to newer fields. So naturally I centered my activities within the sphere of community health service, and later after some years had passed, towards improving our educational facilities. For I was convinced that through these two channels much good could be accomplished. For I believed that these two requirements, health and education were the basic essentials for further racial progress, as without health, the Negro could not survive, and without intelligence and culture could never become a worthwhile part of American life.

N.A.A.C.P.

Two young men had recently come to Charleston. They were Max Barber and Hamilton. Both of them were recent graduates of Atlanta University and while there [they] edited and published the first monthly magazine entirely devoted to the task of expressing the hopes of American Negroes. I suspected that Professor Dubois was their mentor and guided them in many of the things they did. The journal was named *The Voice of the Negro* and was a very commendable publication. Unfortunately its existence came to an untimely end for it seems that white Atlanta wanted none of it and so quickly found methods by which its short existence was terminated.

When Barber reached Charleston he got employment as editor of the *Charleston Messenger*, the Jenkins Orphanage weekly paper and Hamilton took charge of the printing department. During the time that Barber edited the *Messenger*, he published a number of articles that stimulated our community towards racial solidarity and towards aspirations for a freer life.

A few years later when the N.A.A.C.P. was organized and its journal *The Crisis* appeared, I could not refrain from feeling that it was but the old *Voice of the Negro* in reincarnation form, as its form and style were largely those of the *Voice*.

Max Barber only remained with us one year, leaving Charleston to Philadelphia where he studied dentistry and after completing his course practiced there. Aside from his professional work, he found time to participate in an active way with N.A.A.C.P. activities there, as well as time to devote to its national activities.

HOSPITAL AND TRAINING SCHOOL FOR NURSES

In the meantime, my services at the hospital had been increased by the addition of two teaching subjects, Materia Medica and Therapeutics, and in addition to those, that of financial Secretary-Treasurer, which included all of the duties of a superintendent. The hospital had been in a somewhat precarious financial position for several years and so had become somewhat annoying to Mr. Swinton Bennett, the former Treasurer, who had on several occasions been compelled to use his personal funds, temporarily, for its maintenance. For which reason Mr. Bennett resigned. With full knowledge of the responsibilities I would assume, as well as the difficulties to be incurred in striving to keep a community charity going, I accepted the position, and though at time it required me to use my private funds to an even greater extent than Mr. Bennett had, I managed to carry on. And so the work continued, despite its periods of financial stringency, until years later when assistance from the Duke Endowment and from Charleston county made its existence easier. Our medical staff, excluding Dr. McClennan, had been seriously reduced in number from what it was at the time it was organized. Dr. Brown was an invalid, Dr. Lindau was out, Dr. Crum had gone abroad, Rankin had died, and Johnson had become antagonistic, which left only Thompson and McClennan to carry on with. Of course, we had ample opportunity to supplement our needs whenever professional assistance was necessary by calling upon our white colleagues for help and especially on those who were members of our consulting staff. But we never cared to do that except when we needed the services of a specialist, as we had always been able to get along without doing so and had maintained a highly satisfactory record in our professional care of patients. One day Dr. McClennan came to me and said, "John, I want you to give the anesthetics for me after this." I laughed and told him that I had never given an anesthetic, and in fact had never even paid attention when one was given, except on the two occasions when my children were born. He said that I could do [it] and that he would bring me some books to study. And so I became the hospital's anesthetist and continued as such for the next two years. A few days after our conversation, he brought me a text on anesthesia, vintage of 1878, and told me to study it. So I proceeded to digest it, and with what I gleaned from it and from my other later text books, learned about as much about the theory of anesthesia as anyone else knew. But mark me, I said "theory." I constructed a couple of masks and then awaited a call from the doctor. About two days later, the call came and I responded. My first patient was a man who weighed about 200 pounds. He was a husky bird and apparently had the strength of an ox. He was in for a minor, a circumcision, so we used the emergency room with its wooden table. As I said, I had never before witnessed the giving of an anesthetic. In all of my visits to the surgical clinics at Medico Chirurgical College of Philadelphia while at college, the patients had all been anesthetized before they were rolled into the amphitheater. And even at the hospital, of many operations I witnessed there, I had only watched what the surgeon was doing and never paid attention to anything the anesthetist did. And so it was with only some knowledge of the theory of anesthesia and absolutely no knowledge about its technic [technique] that I approached the patient.

I told him to lay down and he did so. I grasped the cone and started to drop chloroform, when the head nurse asked, "Doctor, shall I grease his face and apply a towel?" to which I replied, "Certainly" and so got my first lesson in technic. I started him under, but when his breathing became the stertorous type of the first stage, I became hesitant. Dr. McClennan had disappeared from sight, and there I was with a great big bird who could easily have thrown me out of the room and who now was struggling to get away. He started cussing everybody out, at which the head nurse whispered to me "Push it to him," and I did and with such vigor that I soon had him sleeping as gently as a baby. I had spent nearly twenty minutes putting him under. We called the doctor and he proceeded to operate. I had never before seen him consume so much time with a simple operation as he was then doing. But he continued to do so, and after an hour and twenty minutes had passed told me to hold up, that he was finishing and that the patient had had enough. It was with a sigh of relief that I moved away from the table, for not only had I been anxious, but I had also swallowed a good bit of the anesthetic. And then I found out the doctor had deliberately used that particular patient and had consumed the time he did with the sole purpose of teaching me some of the technic of anesthesia. Mostly I used chloroform, as it is safe if freshly opened and not used from a quantity that has been exposed to air for some time. For it is from the oxidation products that may arise through exposure to air that most of its dangerous actions come. And again, it had added safety over the inflammable ether vapor when we had to use open flame heating stoves in winter as we often did. For long operations, I started with chloroform and after the patient was under would switch to ether. Many of the preanesthetic aids now used were then [un]known and so we had to rely upon morphine. Neither did we have the restoratives then that the present-day supplies, for then it was chiefly upon a hypodermic syringe of aromatic spirt of ammonia that we depended and H.T. of atropine. I shall never forget one patient, an old lady of 72 years, who was undergoing a major [procedure], and who, when I told her to "breathe it out if it chokes you," answered, "No, I want to see your face before I do." I told her that I was a pretty doctor, even more so than was Dr. McClennan, and just to take my word for it and go ahead and do as I asked. But still she refused, and since time was passing I told the nurse to remove the towel from over her eyes and let her see me. When this was done, the dear old lady took a good look at me and said, "I just wanted to see you so if I should not wake up again, I will know you when I see you." And so the thought of her standing by the River Styx, waiting for me to arrive, went with me throughout the operation. She pulled through all right, and I got a lot of fun by teasing her during her convalescence.

My teaching work was pleasant. Our student nurses were all diligent and evidenced a desire to learn. As a rule, none were accepted for training until they had reached 21 years of age. Most of them were in the thirties and some even older than me. Our greatest difficulty was found in the paucity of their elementary education, and so we had to present our subjects in such a manner that its intent, purpose of whatfore [sic] would easily be understood. The majority of those who came to us were poor, and one or two whom I recall brought all that they possessed in a pillowcase. But despite this, they were made excellent pupils and in due time became skilled in nursing. There was one young woman who came to us whose subsequent career I have watched with pride. She was Jane Hunter, one of our most diligent students, who in after life proved the ability of her character through the wonderful work she has done for young Negro women. In 1908 the stork paid us another visit and this time it was Carr. Dr. Thompson delivered him and once again I assisted with chloroform. We were quite a family now. Our neighbors were kind and congenial, and that made life extremely pleasant. Opposite our home, the Montgomery's lived, and with them was Mrs. Carter, Mrs. Montgomery's mother. Two daughters were with them, May and Virginia. They had several sons but these had gone North and over the line. Reverend Bruce Williams, who was in the legislature during Reconstruction days, and his wife lived a few doors away. Mrs. Gaillard, one of the early graduates from the hospital, was also a neighbor. We were sandwiched in between two white families on our side of the street. To the west, by the Vietts, a French family whose neighborliness will always remain a pleasant memory. They were very fond of our children and always expressed an interest in my welfare. The O'Neills and the Kanapaux lived to the east of us. These [were] Irish, but despite that were good neighbors.

UNITY AND FRIENDSHIP SOCIETY

Shortly after Estelle's death, and soon thereafter as I was able to, I joined the Unity and Friendship Society, one of the few active ones remaining of the old burial societies of pre-Civil War days. My main reason for joining was to secure a burial plot and not so much for the sick or death benefits the Society paid to its members. At the time when I joined, its membership had fallen to a very low ebb, and though its finances were in good shape, it was felt that unless a number of young men could be induced to join its ranks, that the Society could not long survive. A number of the younger men in the community, of whom I was one, were invited to join, and as an added inducement were accorded a reduced membership fee. About fifteen men accepted the invitation to membership and were duly elected. Shortly after joining the Society, I was appointed Chairman of the cemetery committee and in such capacity had charge of the records of the cemetery. I found that these records had not been properly kept, as neither its ledger accounts for lot assessment payments nor its burial register for internments were accurately entered. I opened a new ledger in which every lot carried a page and succeeded in getting it in balance. The internment register, however, was a far more difficult undertaking, as several years earlier, a portion from the easterly boundary of the cemetery had been reclaimed by the state as a part of the highway, and the bodies that had been interred thereon had been removed and reinterred on other lots within the cemetery. That procedure created much confusion in the register—both in the numbering arrangement of lots as well as in the internments thereon. I made a new plat for the grounds and renumbered all lots. With the assistance of Mr. Lindau, who was the clerk of the cemetery, and of Tinny, the gravedigger, I succeeded in designating the place where all burials had been made and verified these from the minute books of the Society. The task was not as burdensome as it first appeared, for after getting access to the older minute books, I found a mass of information about the customs and mode of life of the Charleston Negro that was not to be found elsewhere. The Society had been organized in 1844 along lines much similar to those of the other pre-Civil War Negro burial societies. A few years after emancipation, it applied for and received a charter from the state giving it the right to function as a mutual, cooperative body. Its minute books and its membership roster provided me with the names of many of the city's older Negro families and also much about their vocations, religious affiliations, and general status in the community. As I went through its rosters, I could perceive why its membership had dwindled, for it was not so much from death that it had occurred but more largely by the migration of many of its former members to the North. A few of those who had migrated maintained their membership with the Society for many years after their removal from the city, but the majority of them allowed their memberships to lapse. A number of those who had gone had severed their racial connections by crossing the line and thereby established a precedent that was later followed by a number who joined the Society when I did. The next few years passed rapidly by. Edith had been sent to a private school for her elementary instruction and, after a few years there, was enrolled at the Morris Street School. Her mother did not take kindly to the idea of having her sent to a public school, but I did so because I felt that there, she would have opportunity to contact people from all walks of life and through that contact acquire the wherewithal that could make her a human being free from conceit and selfishness. I allowed the religious training of the children to be under the full direction of their mother. And I know that she has done an excellent job, as their lives prove it so.

Conversations and Colleagues

TALK WITH A FORMERLY ENSLAVED CIVIL WAR VETERAN

During these years. I had little opportunity to leave the drugstore except during the quiet afternoon hours. It would have been extremely lonesome for me had it not been that I had one or two friends whose companionship helped to kill the monotony of being alone. Business was still slow, and the volume I did did not allow me to hire an experienced pharmacist. I had lost two of my close friends—Perry Seabrook, who while on a "drumming trip" on the sea islands contracted hemorrhagic malaria and died from it within a week, and Dr. Louie Lindau, who had developed paresis and then passed away. All of the once popular intellectuals who had come to the city at the time of the exposition had long since departed for greener fields. Not the kind that prevailed in Charleston, where Tillman's threat "to make grass grow in Charleston's streets" had come true, but to more fertile fields where financial reward could be found. One of my new friends was a Mr. Williams, who lived on Smith Street opposite Warren. He had married one of the Merchant girls, who died shortly after their marriage. Mr. Williams was well advanced in years and had retired from active work. His early experiences were well worth listening to. Evidently he had been a slave and had been apprenticed to Tony Weston, Negro contractor and millwright of pre-Civil-War days, whose business was the largest of its kind in the city. On one occasion he described to me the fall of Fort Sumter, where the Civil War began. He told me that he had been sent over to Fort Moultrie on Sullivan's Island, shortly before the action took place, to do some repair work there but that shortly after he reached the fort, Major Anderson, who was in command, removed all of his troops and the Negro workers, himself included, over to Fort Sumter in the center of the harbor. The transfer, he said, took place at night and during the early morning hours, and he believed was occasioned by a demand from the Confederates that Major Anderson surrender the fort, which the major refused to do. The Confederates opened fire on the fort and they, the Negroes, were sent to bomb-proof shelters. A return fire was directed against the battery on Morris Island, where the Confederates had erected a battery, but none was directed against the city. During the intensity of the firing, the Union flagstaff upon the fort was hit and [the] flag fell, but it was quickly recovered and nailed back to the remaining portion of the staff. He emphasized that the report that Major Anderson had lowered his colors at that time was false, but perhaps was thought to be true when the flag could no longer be seen from the city. He said that under the truce, Major Anderson was permitted to move the entire garrison, with side arms and with colors flying, from the fort and to take passage for the North on ships of the Union navy. He said that Major Anderson offered to take all of the Negroes with him, but that he "like a fool" wanted to get back to Charleston to see what his folks were doing. And that while the firemen from the city were endeavoring to quench the flames within the fort and he was doing what he could to help them, a policeman took him in charge and brought him to the city and placed him in jail. At the time it happened, he could not understand why he had been arrested, but later he learned that it was to prevent him from spreading any information among the Negroes of what had taken place on the fort. He remained in jail for nearly three weeks and then got word to Colonel Rawlin Lowndes (perhaps he was his owner), who secured his release and put him to work with the Confederate forces building earth-work fortifications. After spending two years with the Confederate army doing service work, he was transferred to a shoe factory in the old United States arsenal on Ashley Avenue, where he made shoes with wooden soles and canvas tops for the army. The old gentleman had a keen sense of humour and never hesitated to tell a joke at his own expense, but of all of his jokes the one he claimed to be his best was on him—when he passed up his opportunity to leave Charleston with Major Anderson—"because he wanted to see the girls" and instead of seeing them, found himself in jail. And then there was old man Hicks, a shoemaker, who lived and worked in a little shop in the rear of the drug store. He was all alone in the world, without kith or kin. His friendships were limited to a few lodge brothers and church members. On winter evenings, I would call him into the shop and when business had quieted would engage him a game of checkers, the Spanish pool variety. He was a marvel at the game but occasionally I would win, at which he would then concentrate all of his attention to "lynching me" by winning five consecutive games.

EMPLOYEES, A COLLEAGUE AND VACATION

Charles Brown was still with me. He was giving satisfactory service but could not see his way clear to enter college. His father was an invalid, more mentally so than physically, and so would not work. This necessitated Charlie, Clarence, and an aunt to assume that he would take the civil service examinations for the railway mail service, and if he received an appointment would resign his position with me. I was sorry to have Charlie leave, as he was diligent, honest, and faithful in all that was entrusted to him.

For some time I had had Oscar Smith in my employ as a delivery boy. He was about thirteen years of age when I got him. His people had come to the city from Mt. Pleasant. One of his sister[s] was in training at the hospital where she was doing nicely in her studies. Seldom has it been my privilege to see a family so eager to advance themselves in all directions as did his family. They were all very industrious and thrifty. But it is about Oscar that I must tell. Of the many boys I have had under me none have excelled him in any way. When he first came to me I took him to be just another one of the usual run of delivery boys who only wanted a job for a month or two and then would quit. But with him it was different for I soon found that what he wanted was a chance to learn. I made him enter Avery and allowed him to work in the afternoons and early evenings. After his graduation from Avery he was ready for college and by then had become an experienced prescription clerk. He entered Howard University and completed its course in pharmacy. He was to return to my employ after his graduation but was caught in the draft of the First World War and sent overseas. I did not have an opening for him when he mustered out of the service and so could not give him employment. Oscar went to Wilmington, Delaware and secured a clerking position in one of the stores there. A few years later he bought the store and has done nicely ever since. He has made a big success in life and I am glad of it. For of all the boys I have had, none started with less than he or in the years to follow acquired more than he did. Not only from the financial viewpoint but also from the measure of respect his community accorded him with for the splendid quality of his leadership.

When Oscar entered Howard, I secured the services of a Meharry[10] graduate named Freeman. He was industrious, capable and for a while made an excellent assistant. My sister, Thomasina was also with me and had charge of the books, which duty

---

10 Meharry Medical College, a Historically Black College in Nashville, Tennessee.

she subsequently extended by taking charge of everything else including me. Knowing that everything was now in such shape that I could take a short vacation. I planned one. It was my first opportunity in more than ten years to get away from the drugstore. So I decided to make it profitable as well as enjoyable by joining with Harry Boston and Thompson who were going to the N.M.A.[11] meeting in Nashville where Thompson would leave us and we to proceed to Chicago and return by way of New York. I joined the N.M.A. at Nashville and enjoyed and benefited by the sessions. When we arrived in Chicago Harry received a telegram telling him that Mamie (his wife) was ill and that he should return home at once. Which he did. I changed my itinerary and went to Detroit and from there to Niagara then down to New York and home.

For some time I had been seeking to find a young physician with whom I could tie up with at I was tired of "counter prescribing" and wanted to be rid of it. One physician from Columbia, South Carolina wanted the opportunity but I was compelled to pass him up as he had recently been involved in a scandal and was also addicted to too much alcohol.

In 1911 Bill Thorne came. He was a graduate of Michigan and had just completed an internship at Freedman Hospital in Washington. He was just the man I had been looking for. He had been well trained in his profession and was not merely a "prescription writer" as so many are but was always insistent that his diagnosis was correct before giving treatment. We found an office site on Coming Street near Morris and had it equipped and opened by October. Our friendship which started then remained unbroken until his death. His progress was rapid as I was able to turn all of my "patients" over to him. Some of them [squawked] but calm[ed] down when I told them that I was too busy to look

---

11 National Medical Association, which promotes the interests of physicians and students of African descent.

after them and had secured someone who could do all that was necessary for them and that they must go to him.

Two other young physicians came to town that year and settled there. One was M.M. Edwards and the other was W.H. Miller. Gus Purvis also came through but went to Anderson in the upper part [of] the state to take over, in the place of Dr. Earle, who had recently died. Purvis quickly tired of Anderson and after a year there returned to Charleston and opened an office on Anson Street.

The tie in between Thorne and me created some little jealousies among the other physicians as his success was dwarfing theirs. So I became the persecuted and as a result got but few of their prescriptions. But that did not bother me since they only wrote a few. And again, I was not the one who was responsible for their lack of patients but only a case where the best man won.

Thorne was added to the faculty and to the medical staff at the Hospital. Dr. McClennan gave him surgery. About two weeks after he started Dr. McClennan phoned him and told him to be at the hospital that afternoon at 4 p.m. to do an appendectomy and that I would give the anesthetic. Thorne came by on time but was as nervous as a chicken. He wanted to back out of it. I told him, that if a trolley car could knock a man down and mess him up and not necessarily kill him, then he could do no worse. That quieted him down. When we reached the hospital we found the patient to be one, who had been sent in from Georgetown had been suffering for nearly a week. He was toxic and not in any too good a shape. I put him under and Thorne started. McClennan was assisting. The appendix had ruptured and had been walled around by the momentum, and so it was necessary to install drainage and close up. The patient made an uneventful recovery for nature had done most of it. After that Thorne was all right.

Challenges and Opportunities

PROBLEMS AT THE HOSPITAL AND TRAINING SCHOOL

That year I was elected dean of the faculty. I continued to teach the three subjects I formerly taught I also changed the curriculum and included a course in dietetics which was given at Avery under its domestic science teacher. That year our school was accredited by the National Association of Nurse-Training Schools.

Some years previously the hospital had incurred a mortgage debt of $2,000.00 to avoid a suit being brought by Tommie Grant the butcher for supplies that he had furnished and which had not been paid for. The debt distressed me as nothing had been paid on the principal but only the interest. I wanted the debt liquidated. So I put on a three-night "bazaar" and got the ladies of the Lucy Brown Auxiliary to serve at the tables. The project was a success as I was able to pay from its proceeds $800.00 on the principal, the current and semi-annual interest, and to place on deposit with the Charleston Savings Institution the sum of $60.00 as a reserve for future interest.

Ridley McClennan, the son of Dr. McClennan, was the next young physician to join our group. He had recently graduated from Shaw University. A year later he was followed by Dr. H.U. Seabrook who was a third-year student at Shaw when the insurrection which led to its closing occurred. He took his final year [of] medicine at the University of Western Tennessee and after an internship in New York settled in Charleston. Which made us have ten practicing physicians in the city, eight of whom were associated on the hospital's staff.

Dr. McClennan, the elder, had been in failing health for some time. He was suffering from diabetes and was more or less indifferent to his condition. One day when I returned to the store one of the clerks told me that the doctor had sent for five glasses of lemon soda and wanted them made "very sweet." A few minutes later Ridley came in and I told him about it and suggested that he return home at once and send me a specimen of his father's urine that I could examine it, I had been doing such for some time, as I suspected that ill effects would follow the drinking of that much sweet. Ridley went home at once, only to find his father in [a] coma and to see him pass away within thirty minutes. Dr. Thompson had been called in and had given soda bicarbonate subcutaneously but without results. Of course this happened before the day of insulin, when soda bicarbonate was the only thing we could rely upon to combat diabetic coma with.

Dr. McClennan's passing was a definite loss to the community and to the Negro medical group. As no other man had ever done as much as he had to elevate the standards of practice. And though he had his faults, his good qualities and his unselfishness so far outweighed them, that they were lost sight of. To me he was more than an associate for he had been my tutor and much that I have learned has come from him. His untiring efforts and the great personal sacrifice he made that the hospital could prosper is largely responsible for the success it derived. When it was suggested that the institution be named "McClennan's Hospital" in his honor he refused to allow it to be done and insisted that its corporate name be retained.

The doctor's death brought about a reorganization of the staff and of the faculty. The very early breach that had occurred between Dr. Johnson and Dr. McClennan when the institution was first opened had never been healed. And now that Dr. McClennan was no longer in the picture and a majority of the staff were friends to Dr. Johnson, the inevitable happened, Dr. Johnson was elected to the position of surgeon in chief. The Corporation was likewise organized and Mr. Thomas E. Miller elected to the Presidency. The office of Secretary-Treasurer which I had held for years was abolished and separate offices created —the Secretary—to which Dr. M.M. Edwards was elected and the Treasurer in which I was retained.

The change was most unfortunate for it heralded the beginning of an era of decline. Much of which originated with the policies that Dr. Johnson and Mr. Miller inaugurated. Dr. Johnson's ideas involved an altogether Negro-manned institution with the elimination of the white consulting staff and the white Advisory Board. Which only resulted in the alienation of much of the goodwill that was expressed for the institution by the whites in the community. The Hospital had then but recently received two bequests of $1,000.00 each. One from the Estate of Mr. A.T. Smythe, a former mayor of the city and the other from Mr. A. Markley Lee, a law partner of Mr. Smythe, who also had recently died. Mr. Miller urged that the amount be expended for the erection of an annex to the brick building, the upper floor of which would house the surgical section and lower floor, a kitchen, dining room and laundry.

Mr. Miller voluntarily offered to defray the cost of installing the plumbing equipment for the laundry and directed that a contract be given for that work. When the $2,000.00, (the bequests) had spent, the work had not been finished and the contractor refused to complete the work, except the amount that was required to complete it, was paid to him in advance or guaranteed to him. Mr. Miller never did pay for the plumbing work.

Moreover a paving abutment levy tax for a balance of $100.00 was allowed to lapse. All of which only served to create a deplorable financial state for the institution. In addition to that current income was not being sent to the Treasurer as it should be which only added to the muddle. When the city became insistent that payment of the abutting tax be paid and threatened to sell the property for unpaid taxes, I and nine others from the staff contributed $10.00 each and paid the tax. Current operating bills were piling up without funds to pay them. Some of the more urgent bills I paid by using my personal funds to do so. I decided to bring matters to ahead by asking for a special meeting of the Corporation to which I would make a report of the transactions of my office and tender my resignation. When the meeting was held I presented my report, and the cash balance in the treasury and a bill for the expenses which I had paid for the hospital's account and requested that those be verified and the amounts reimbursed me. I also questioned Dr. Johnson's reports of income from patients. The doctor reported that some of the money he had retained and kept in his safe at his office but had refrained from sending it to the Treasurer, because he wanted to pay the mortgage debt with it. I asked, how much did he have? He said about $1,200.00. I asked what would happen to that money should he die, and his estate be ignorant of its ownership. And further that he had never been empowered to act as custodian of any of the hospital's funds and that there was no legality for him doing so. I moved and it was adopted, that the doctor make immediate payment of the mortgage and have the same satisfied and the satisfaction recorded. During the discussion it was revealed that the doctor was having supplies bought in the name of the hospital delivered at his office and from time to time would dole them out to the hospital. I questioned the propriety of such action. He said that he did so because they were not economically used within a quantity was left at the hospital.

I was so disgusted with the financial condition that I insisted that my resignation be accepted.

I continued as dean of the faculty for two years longer. One night Dr. Johnson asked me to call at his office that a matter of grave importance had to be discussed. I did so and learned that the matter involved a question of immorality at the hospital. He told me that I as dean was the authoritative head to which such was to be reported and that he was making a report about it to me so that I could call a faculty meeting at which proper action could be taken. I agreed with him but insisted that he put his charges in writing and sign it and when I received I would act. The following morning I received it from him and then called a special meeting of the faculty. I had the head nurse notify three of the nurses not to leave the building. I also arranged a questionnaire which covered the charges—leaving on it spaces where the answers could be inserted. The investigation took place that afternoon. There was no question that the doctor was correct in his charges, the evidence which the nurses gave confirmed that but when the doctor's turn came to testify he wavered and gave evasive answers to my questions. At which I turned to the Secretary and directed him to read the charges contained in Dr. Johnson's letter. When he had finished the reading, I addressed the faculty and told them that it was at Dr. Johnson's demand that the meeting had been called, and that the charges which he had made, had all been verified—not so much by the doctor's oral testimony but by contents of his letter and by the evidence given by the nurses. I reminded the faculty that my duties at the hearing were altogether investigative and reporting ones and that I had performed them. That the matter was now before them awaiting their action. And that I would entertain a motion for its disposal. After several minutes had passed with no action taken, I arose and tendered my resignation as a member of the faculty for the reason that I did not deem it fitting for me to continue as the presiding office and chief executive of a body, which through its silence had "whitewashed" the matter. With which I left the room.

Freeman, my pharmacist, resigned his position with me after two years of service. He said that he had an opportunity to purchase a drugstore in the town in Kentucky where his wife formerly lived. James Miller, whose mother lived in Charleston succeeded him. Miller was a graduate of the Connecticut School of Pharmacy. He had but little practical experience and so had to be taught. One of the delivery boys, Rudy Deas, took a keen delight in showing up Miller's deficiencies and by teasing him about it. I put a stop to it by threatening to kill him if he did it again. He left off from Miller but shortly after met his death by teasing a pervert who stabbed him in the heart one night while he was returning home from work.

Tommie was then capable of supervising the operation of the store. She understood the buying, could keep the books and best of all could manage the employees. Which made it fortunate for me, since it assured me, that whether I was present or not, that everything went on properly.

BUYING THE STORE PROPERTY

One day, Mr. Renken, my grocer neighbor from across the street came over and told me that his sister-in-law who owned the drugstore building had offered it for sale to his wife. But that he told his wife, that he thought that I should have had the first offer of the property since I was the tenant. And also that he told his wife not to buy it, if I wanted it. He suggested that I immediately see the owner and see if she would not sell to me. He told me that the place had been offered to his wife for $3,300.00 and that I should try to get it at that price. I expressed my gratitude to him for telling me about it and for his willingness to allow me the opportunity to acquire it.

I immediately went over to see Mrs. Renken, the owner and asked if she would sell the place to me. I told her that Mr. Renken had said that I would like to have the first offer. She replied that she would sell to me, if the other Mrs. Renken did not want it. But that the price would be $3,500.00 and not the $3,300.00 she had offered it at to her sister-in-law. I did not haggle about the price but told her that I would take it and have my lawyer arrange the details. I did not have the cash money for buying the place at the time. So I went to the South Carolina Loan and Trust Co. Bank where I carried my account and asked if I could get a loan of the amount I would need. I was told that I could file my application but that it would be a matter of two or three weeks before I would get an answer. I was rather badly disappointed at that. So I went to see an old white friend, Dr. Arthur Aimar, who kept a drugstore at the corner of King and Vanderhorst Street. I knew that he was a director of the Charleston Savings Institution, one of our Broad Street banks. So I asked him if he could secure a loan for me whereby I could buy the building where my business was conducted. I told him that the price asked for it was $3,500.00 and I need a loan of $2,500.00. And that if the loan was made, I would secure it with a first mortgage on the building and as added collateral, give a first mortgage on my home. He told me that he was pretty sure that it could be arranged but that the properties would have to be inspected and appraised before a reply could be given. A couple of days later, Mr. William Cohen, the President of the bank inspected the properties and told me that the loan had been granted and that I should have Mrs. Renken present her deeds to Mr. Barnwell, their attorney for examination and the drawing up of the papers.

On February 27th, 1914 the transfer was made. I shall never forget that day. The night before the weather had turned intensely cold and started snowing and sleeting. It was the first such weather we had had in Charleston for many years. I had arranged with a hackman to drive us down to the lawyer's office but when the time came to do so, he refused to risk his horse on the icy pavement. So Phenie and I took the streetcar down to Mr. Barnwell's office where we executed the papers.

When the executed deed was delivered to me, I was one happy mortal for not until then did I realize what my predicament might have been had someone else bought the property and then notified me to move out.

I told Thorne that I had bought the property and that if he was willing to move his office from Coming Street that I would erect an office for him to the rear of the drugstore. He heartily agreed with that idea. Three months later I had the small office completed and Thorne moved in.

I paid the mortgage off within two years. Business held up nicely and since I did not have to pay rent and instead was receiving rent from the upper floor of the building, I accomplished it without any privation.

The building was in very bad shape. In truth it was so bad that repairs were out of the question. So I started planning for a new structure and spent my spare moments drawing plans for what would be my model drug store. I searched the building and whatever in it that could be used in the new building, I noted and made a memoranda for its use in the proposed building. Eventually after much tearing up of plans and redrawing of plans I succeeded in producing what I wanted. While doing that I saved every penny I could. For much would be needed as not only was a new building to be erected but also was there to be new and modern fixtures for it. And I wanted to do it all on a cash basis.

THE EFFECTS OF WWI

When the European war broke out, I recalled what Dr. Baer had once told me about wars and the influence they produced on world markets and especially on such chemicals that went into the making of explosives. So I immediately went down to Geer's. Dr. Baer had since then died and his business had been sold to the Geer Drug Company, and placed an order for a large variety of chemicals and other drugs that came from Europe. I was joked at for appearing fearful that these supplies would vanish from the market because of the war situation. But I was insistent that the goods I wanted be sent to me without delay. I stocked up on quinine at 20¢ an ounce and saw the market reach $2.00 an ounce before what I had bought that day became exhausted. Carbolic acid which I bought at 18¢ a pound reached $2.40 and when the war ended, I still had some of what I had bought on hand. Of the heavier chemicals, the bromides and iodides, especially the potassium salts, I only bought an eight-months' supply and later wished that I had bought more. I could not bring myself to believe that any modern war could last longer than that time or that humans could be so stupid as to waste life and wealth in that way. My belief in that direction caused me to lose the opportunity to have become wealthy for had I followed my hunch to the limit I could have made contracts for future deliveries that would have brought me wealth. When it became apparent that the United States would be involved in the European conflict all of the activities of Charleston became centered around the Navy yard at North Charleston. The Navy yard had then been in existence for about fifteen years and consisted almost altogether of what Owen Wister had described it to be, in his book, *Lady Baltimore*, "a wide expense of marsh and petty politics." When the yard was first opened a large number of Negro mechanics, clerks, accountants and laborers were employed there. But as the years passed and the usefulness of the yard slackened their number diminished. As the certainty of America's entrance into the conflict became more apparent the activities at the yard increased and new facilities opened. One of these new facilities was the "clothing factory" where navy uniforms were made. All of operators in the factory were women. And at the time it opened all were white. A number of Negro women applied for work there but were all told that no Negro women would be employed and that the factory was only for white workers.

When I learned about this, I wrote a letter to the Labor Board at the yard, asking if Negro women, who were fully capable of doing the required type of work, would be employed in the clothing factory. A few days later my letter was returned to me with the penciled inscription—"No Negro women will be employed at the yard in any position." No one signed it but fortunately it had been stamped by the yard's receiving clock. Which proved that it had been received by the Labor Board.

I then called a group of my colleagues together and we discussed the situation. We decided to make an issue of the refusal by the yard to employ Negro women. We formulated a program of action, the first step of which, required that we induce as many competent Negro women as we could to apply for positions at the factory. We obtained a large number of applications blanks from the Post Office and distributed them among the women. Each blank required the execution of an oath of allegiance to the Government, before a notary public, before it would be complete.

Then we found out, just how much "petty politics" there was in the Navy yard. For the Governor had overnight revoked the commissions, as it was thought, of every Negro notary public within the county. We also found out that white notary publics were refusing to execute applications of Negro women. Which made it appear that some unknown power which was not a part of the federal government was using its force to defeat our plans. Fortunately for us, one Negro notary, Mr. Smith, a lawyer, had been overlooked in the liquidations. We arranged with him to meet all of the applicants on a given day at the Hospital and Training School where he could notary all of the blanks at the same sitting, so that none could be sent in until we had several hundred ready.

We had taken the precaution to see that only skilled workers made application for positions and were able to have over three hundred [or] so. We instructed them to take their applications in person to the Labor Board office and to present it to Taylor who was in charge of the office. But if they could not reach him to present it to whoever was in charge. And further that they should go in small groups. So that some of the group could serve as witnesses if affidavits of complaint had to be drawn up. The women did so and were bluntly told, that the positions were not open to Negro women.

I then drew up a letter for public distribution, which carried an open appeal that the policy in force at the Navy yard be abandoned and that Negro women be employed there. We mailed out 1,000 of these letters; sending them to State and city officials, the members of Congress and to merchants and other businessmen in the city. The letters evoked a near riot. The sheriff sent us word that he did not want any trouble from us. He received our assurances that we were not seeking to start trouble but only wanted work for our women. The Chamber of Commerce called us in for a conference on the subject. We sent a committee to the conference. I was appointed to make the presentation. We met in the Committee room at the Chamber and the conference began. Mr. King who was then the Secretary of the white Y.M.C.A. presided.

Mr. King opened the meeting by telling us that we should not insist on making our demands at that particular time and that was necessary that the restrictions made by the yard be carried out as they were all essential to the furtherance of preparedness. He asked that we sacrifice our desires for the good of the country and expressed the belief that we would not suffer doing so.

It was apparent to us that Mr. King was merely carrying out instructions that had been given him. As we kept his eyes centered upon a paper before him and never once, while speaking, looked us in the eye.

When he had finished with his remarks, I rose to reply. I prefaced my remarks by telling them that we knew only too well the needs for making sacrifice, even the supreme sacrifice, as one of the women who had applied at the yard for work and had been refused had already incurred a far greater sacrifice than anyone else in Charleston had, as her husband, Charleston's first casualty, a member of the Navy, had met death on an American ship in European waters. And that his widow, Mrs. Marshburn now needed work that she might live.[12] That she had applied at the yard for work and had been refused and that her situation was such that we would not sit idly or quietly by and see her suffer want and so would present the matter to Washington. Dr. Thorne followed me in a few words stated that we were not the only ones who should make sacrifices but that others should share equally with us in doing so. After which we left.

We decided to immediately take the matter to Washington. We got Mr. Archibald Grimke and Mr. Whitfield McKinlay to arrange an audience for us with Mr. Josephus Daniels, the Secretary of the Navy. And more than [illegible], to accompany our representative, Mr. Edward C. Mickey and assist him in making our presentation. We prepared a petition in which we prayed that opportunity be granted our women to work at the yard. We emphasized that they had been refused employment there solely because of their color. We attached, as exhibits, to the petition, my letter which had been returned to me when I inquired if Negro women would be given employment at the yard, affidavits by a number of women, setting forth, that they were competent to perform the work required at the yard and had made application for employment but were refused because they were Negroes. We also presented newspaper advertisements from

---

12 Death of Sergt. Julian C. Marshburn reported in "Three Americans Killed in Action Pershing Reports," *The Columbia Record*, 24 Feb 1918, p. 1 col. 5. "Died of natural causes." Died of disease was reported in American Soldiers of WW1, Vol. 3, p. 188; http://www.Ancestry.com : accessed 7 Feb. 2019).

out-of-town papers in which white workers were invited to come to Charleston to work in the clothing factory.

Mr. Daniels gave the committee a cordial hearing and his promise that the matter would receive early attention. A few weeks later we received word that a separate unit of the clothing factory would be established at the old Immigrant Station building with an entire corps of Negro workers.

In due time the unit opened and gave employment to over six hundred Negroes. Most of these were women. The men who were employed ranged from cutters down to repairmen and laborers. With the exception of a small white administrative force, the forewomen, and inspectors were all Negroes. We did not succeed in breaking up the restrictions at the Navy yard against Negro women but we did succeed in putting them on the government payroll where they earned from $3 to $6 a day. Our effort had a further effect as it brought a check to many of Taylor's methods in attempting to block the employment of Negro men at skilled work.

Local Politics

My belief about the origin of these efforts to bar Negroes from the yard is that they had their origin in the struggle which was then taking place between Mayor T.T. Hyde and ex-Mayor J.P. Grace to secure the political control of the city at the next coming election and that it was but a prelude to that contest.

So far as the influence of the Negroes was concerned, he was a nonentity in the struggle. But only so as a voting participant. Aside from that he then constituted a fairly large income-earning group which derived its income largely from sources which the Hyde administration could dominate. By diverting that income to those who were then or within a year more would be eligible to vote in the next coming primary, those who had the power to do so could by so doing be able to build up the voting strength of their contingent. So it came about that the economic privileges of the Negroes were being sacrificed, in much the same manner as are pawns in a chess game when it becomes necessary to save a more valuable piece. Which in this instance was the mayoralty of the city.

The events leading up to these efforts had their beginning several years earlier when John P. Grace became mayor. At the following election Mr. Grace, after an exceedingly bitter and controversial campaign was defeated by Mr. T.T. Hyde. It was known that Mr. Grace would seek reelection at the next coming election. So every possible effort was then being made by the Hyde faction to insure their continuation in power.

Mr. Grace's administration, the one proceeding Mr. Hyde's, had had been markedly successful in bringing into the city an additional railroad connection, the Seaboard Air Line and other major additions to its industrial life and promise of further improvements if he was continued in office. And as a matter of fact his was the first administration in many years through which the city derived material benefit.

It was not however against the material success which Mr. Grace had brought to the city that the opposition fought, but was altogether due to the fact that Mr. Grace had openly challenged the continuation of the older order of city government which Hyde's faction sought to maintain. Mr. Hyde's faction represented the big business interests in the city, especially those revolving about the Peoples National Bank and the Commercial National Bank. He had the support of the state government, the majority of the businessmen, the bulk of the Protestant church folks, especially those of the Baptist denomination, the Ku Klux Klan and the Junior Order of Mechanics. And in addition to those, included most of the remaining members of the old aristocratic families of the city.

Mr. Grace's following consisted largely of those of the Catholic faith, a majority of the Jews and the rank and file of whites, especially those of Irish descent. Mr. Grace was of Irish descent. He had started life in the "borough" section of the city, a poor boy who once had peddled milk on the city's streets. But who had the force and courage to rise far beyond his early environment. At the time of his political activities he had risen to one of Charleston's most prominent lawyers. He was an ardent believer in human rights, who never hesitated to use his official power to prevent impositions upon the weak.

But even more intense than was his desire that justice be done for all was his desire to have the city of Charleston become what it should be, and that was that it should become one of the nation's great seaports. He believed that the East Shore Terminal company should become a public utility and during his first term had accomplished that. After which had the docks improved and warehouse facilities installed so that ocean-going ships would have ample facilities for loading or unloading cargo.

He was a close associate of Mr. Bonzal, the President of the Seaboard Air Line, with whom he had arranged and consummated the entrance of that railroad system into the city. At the time Mr. Grace went out of office, he and Mr. Bonzal were planning the construction of a large dry dock and ship repair plant on the Cooper River just opposite to Calhoun Street.

Mr. Grace's plans for the creation of a big shipping industry made it easy for him to secure an additional industry for the city. Which was the manufacture of fuel oil and its byproducts. He succeeded in getting the Standard Oil Company to erect a refinery at a cost of $14,000,000.00 on the Meeting Street Road. Where gasoline, oils and asphalt were made. The entrance of the Standard Oil Company was quickly followed by the Texas Company and one or two other oil companies. And resulted in vastly increasing taxable property on the county's assessment roll. But of even greater value than these, was the amount of goodwill that came with it. And which was manifested, when the dam on Goose Creek cracked and saltwater from the Cooper River leaked into the settling basins at the water works and contaminated the city's water supply, by Mr. Bonzal who volunteered his services as supervising engineer to make the necessary repairs, without compensation, and so well was the work done, that at its completion, the dam was a much better one than it was when it was first constructed. The only cost the city bore was that paid for other labor and for material, which amounted to $60,000.00.

Perhaps some of Mr. Grace's conception of human rights had their stimulus from his earlier associations, when as a student he lived in New York. As on one occasion he told me that he and Ramon deValera, the great Irish liberator and statesman were fellow students and friends.

Though Mr. Grace had been defeated by the Hyde machine when he was up for reelection at the expiration of his first term, he yet retained considerable power in the executive committee of the city Democratic primary. A decided advantage to him in his subsequent race for the mayoralty. In addition to that advantage, Mr. Grace controlled and edited *The Charleston American*, a local daily newspaper, through the columns of which he could disseminate his views and intents. For very little in that direction could be done through the columns of the *News and Courier* or the *Evening Post*, the city's other two daily papers, except as paid advertising.

In the meanwhile the Hyde faction were not losing time in seeking to build up its voting strength. With the support of Senator Rhett, it dominated the Charleston Navy Yard and employment of all labor used there. And since the number of unfilled positions there could not be filled by the number of local unemployed whites they, instead of allowing unemployed local Negroes to fill those positions, sought to bring in white workers from other Southern areas with the expectation that they would in time become ardent supporters of Mr. Hyde.

This was largely the reason why Negro women were refused positions at the yard. We had substantiated the existence of the effort to import white workers to the yard when we made our presentation to Secretary Daniels by including therewith copies of Southern newspapers which carried advertisements for white workers wanted. Which also made it easy for us to establish that the local supply of white workers had been exhausted and that the giving or employment to unemployed Negroes would correct the local labor shortage.

We were not any too hopeful of a favorable [illegible] when we presented this situation fully understood the conditions in Washington were. Woodrow Wilson, the first Democratic President to be elected since Grover Cleveland won the election because of the splitting of the huge Republican vote through the formation of the "Bull Moose" party under the leadership of Theodore Roosevelt.

WILSON'S SEGREGATION POLICY

When Wilson assumed office he initiated a policy of racial segregation in all government offices in Washington. Even in that of the Registrar of the Treasury, where custom had established the position of Registrar as one to be filled by a Negro. Following that custom, Mr. Wilson appointed Dr. Tompkins, a Negro from Kansas City to the position. But Dr. Tompkins having knowledge that a "Jim Crow" set up had been established there, declined to accept the position. At which Wilson appointed an Indian to the position.

Wilson's intent to eliminate the Negro participation in the war efforts in any capacity except in the very lowest positions soon became apparent. For when the officers' training school at Fort Des Moines was opened all Negroes who went there were segregated. Three of our local men went there, E.C. Mickey, Thad Sasportas and Harleston. Only Harleston finished and received a commission. The other two were honorably discharged because of physical unfitness. Which I know was not the true condition of either Sasportas or Mickey. Which also happened to be the same reason by which Colonel Young, the top-ranking Negro army officer was deprived of the privilege of seeing active duty in Europe of being promoted to the rank of General and instead was retired from the service.

One could then easily see that many of the principles of democracy upon which the government had been founded were being thrown into the discard and that a new order of life was in the ascendency. One in which the "South was in the saddle" from where its likes and dislikes could all the more easily be directed where or when it chose.

The spirit of liberty which had prompted the Pilgrims, the Huguenots, William Penn and Roger Williams and his followers to seek asylum in a new land where religious liberty could be had, was seemingly forgotten. And likewise forgotten was the Boston Tea Party which had its culmination in the establishment of these United States and the acquirement of full political liberty and the even greater achievement under Abraham Lincoln by which slavery was destroyed and all mankind was made free. For all too brief a while America lived in conformity with the tenets on which its Declaration of Independence is founded—"That all men are created free and equal and are endowed by their Creator with certain inalienable rights—" but only for too short a while did that pertain.

It is needless to recite history which records the final acts of President Grant's administration but only to pick up where President Taft's left off and President Wilson's began. For in that short interval across much that is responsible for the nationwide anti-Negro attitude we find about us. And which in its growth gave birth to a new ideology, which in a few short years has almost entirely supplanted the true American national spirit—the spirit of liberty.

Free, White and 21

I am not so sure as to whether it is in reality an ideology or whether it is but a complex. But whichever it is there can be no doubt but that the present-day white American's ideal, "free white and twenty-one" has almost totally supplanted our true national spirit—the spirit of liberty—with that of its idea.

I am also sure that it has but little true ethnic significance but is on the whole only a psychological phenomenon that contaminates as it spreads. For when it is viewed from its ethnic aspect, one is compelled to wonder what became of the 250,000 people of mixed Negro and white blood who lived in the South at the end of the Civil War and who soon thereafter migrated to other parts of the United States. As practically all of them were so fair skinned that they could not be identified as Negroes and thus had opportunity to merge their blood with that of their newer neighbors. And so I for one, wonder if they and their descendants do not now constitute a large percentage of those who find it necessary to assert that they are among the "free, white and twenty-one." The impossibility of establishing a sound ethnic foundation for the "white" American was clearly understood in South Carolina when the question was debated by its Constitutional Convention in 1895. Moreover it raised a question about the extent to which the infusion of Negro blood with that of whites had already taken place and provoked the Convention to reconsider its action on Section 34 of the proposed Constitution, which read "The marriage of a white person with a Negro or mulatto or person who shall have any Negro blood, shall be unlawful, and the parties to such marriage, upon conviction shall be punished as the General Assembly may direct."

After two weeks of discussion, during which the Negro members from Beaufort found ample opportunity to inject their jeers about "the coons having a dog up the tree"—it was disposed of...

> on motion of Mr. W.D. Evans, sec. 34 was recurred to, and trouble began. Mr. Evans proposed to amend the section by providing that the miscegenation law shall not apply to persons of mixed blood, whose status is that of white people. Mr. George Tillman stated that he felt compelled to say something on this subject. For one he had felt ashamed when the delegate from Beaufort had clapped his hands, and declared that the coons had a dog up the tree. He was further mortified to see that the gentleman from Newberry (Mr. Sligh) and the gentleman from Edgefield (Mr. Ben Tillman) goaded and taunted into putting in the Constitution, that no person with any trace of Negro blood should intermarry with a white person and that for such marriage the Legislature should provide punishment even beyond bastardixing [bastardize] children and adulterizing marriage. Mr. George D. Tillman said the Mississippi law forbidding marriage between white people with those with more than one-eight[h] Negro blood is the old South Carolina law. If the law is made as it now stands, respectable families in Aiken, Barnwell, Colleton and Orangeburg will be denied the right to intermarry among the people with whom they are now associated and identified. At least one-hundred families would be affected, to his knowledge. They had sent good soldiers to the Confederate army, and are now land-owners and tax-payers. He asserted as a scientific fact that there was not a full-blooded Caucasian on the floor of the Convention who did not have in him a certain mixture of Mongolian, Arab, Indian or other colored blood _____.

The section as finally adopted stands:

> Art. III, Sec. 33, The marriage of a white person with a Negro or mulatto or person who shall have one-eight or more of Negro blood shall be unlawful and void.

The most patent reaction to its enactment came not from Negroes but from many who were "border line" whites who assumed belligerent attitude towards Negroes and towards whites of questioned status whereby they sought to emphasize that their ethnic status was that of white. Which became all the more noticeable in the Carnes Crossroads section, near Summerville, several years later when a large number of children, supposedly white, were denied entrance to the white public school by the burning down of the school building. It was currently rumored that the fire had been set by "brass ankles" but no arrests were made. The building was replaced. The "brass ankles" again sought to have their children enrolled but again were refused. At which the new building went up in smoke. While these people were denied a social relationship with whites, they yet held membership in the Democratic party and so were able to swing the balance of power in local elections. They resided mostly in the Summerville area though others of them lived as far away as Mt. Pleasant and Awendaw. Being refused the right to send their children to the white school they withheld from sending them to the Negro school. Eventually a compromise was reached under which an "Indian" school was opened where neither whites nor Negroes could attend.

Towards Negroes, they were intensely hostile and though usually much poorer, more ignorant, lazier and by far much filthier than Negroes, they never passed up an opportunity to impress upon all that they were white. And which perhaps brought them some economic value. For when they applied for work at the Navy yard and certified themselves to be white, they usually got a job. Ironically though, it also allowed a number of

Negroes who were no darker than they to get jobs there by doing the self-same thing.

I seriously question if there is much difference between the characteristic and methods employed by those of questionable ethnic origin in the North and that of his "bras[s] ankle" brother in the South. And though the Northern variety may be much lighter in skin color than is his Southern brother there is in both a similar degree of consciousness which assumes a more or less belligerent attitude when necessity requires.

Which makes me believe that much of the clamor about "free white and twenty-one" and the hue and cry for more segregation of Negroes have their origins or at least a good bit of its support from those who are not secure in their ethnic status and who hope that by championing segregation that their positions in society will be made secure.

Many of my former friends have "crossed the line." And I do not blame them one bit for having done it. As it has given them greater personal freedom and wider economic opportunity. All of them did not go north for some went south, one of whom went as far south as Texas.

This reminds me that my Uncle Edward who was by no means a flaxen-haired blond, by merely shaving his head and yammering some Mexican, spent two years "across the line" on the Pacific coast and only returned when the urge to see Martha, and the quest for the golden fleece proved a greater charm.

I think of another, a little girl who never did return. Her family once lived on Felix street. The father, one of Charleston's prominent white bachelors and a pharmacist of high repute, had died—so the family migrated to parts unknown. One day this little girl, then a woman, drove up to the Hospital and Training School in her limousine with its Irish liveried chauffer. She asked to see Mrs. Oliver the Head Nurse, and made herself known as a former patient who could never forget the kindly care that the nurses had shown her several years before when she underwent an appendectomy in the Hospital. She wanted to express her gratitude for what the institution had done for her when she was a child. She had married a wealthy Northerner and the two of them were spending the winter at the Pine Forest Inn at Summerville.

It seems to me that section 33 of the South Carolina code had largely only served to foster the development of an intermediate strata in American life. One that lies midway between those who are accepted as white and those who are accepted as Negroes. Beyond doing that it has accomplished but little since its power does not extend beyond the boundaries of the state. Neither does it control individual choice which ofttimes refuses to be bound by either tradition or by statutory act.

This intermediate strata is America's common melting pot. Into it goes the life blood of all peoples, even that of the Negro. And as they emerge, they rise as if from a baptismal font, "white as snow." True it is that ethnic purity has in the meanwhile been dissolved away. But what of that if its cleansing power can bring its neophyte to the open door where opportunity stands to shower him with economic, social and political privileges. Would it not be far better for the preservation of ethnic purity to allow every American irrespective of race or creed to acquire whatever his aspiration and his ability warrants than to have him wear the mask of white and from the psychological phenomena through which he passes to go forth to spread the venom of racial hatred far and wide and to contaminate with it all whom he could contact. The contamination, like a contagion, quickly infected all of white America. Reaching even into those areas where Negroes had never lived.

It cannot be said that either economic or political necessity induced it. For how could the 4,000,000 Negro workers then living in the forty highest of our more progressive states affect either the economic or political status of those states. In the deep South where economic and political control were secure to the whites, there certainly could be no change—only the greater certainty that Negroes could be reenslaved. But despite these facts the contamination took root and thrived. Largely within the ranks of labor unions and among the masses of the poorer whites, who in their poverty found consolation by enriching their egos with ideals of superiority over Negroes, through color.

There was a time in Charleston when white people knew their status so well and were so securely entrenched within their social positions that they never found it necessary to advertise the fact. But even they became infected with the ego superiority complex—sometimes to their own embarrassment but oftener to the annoyance of their Negro fellowmen.

One day I noted the change when young Allen, a white lawyer called at the drugstore. I met him and he stated, in a rather haughty, pompous manner, "You are McFall? I am Mr. Allen. I want to know something about—" when I interrupted him and said "Mr. Allen, I do not know who you are nor what your mission is but must inform you that I do not allow myself to engage in any way with anyone, who finds it necessary to address me as 'McFall' while referring to himself as Mister. So good day sir." He flew out in a huff. A couple of days later, Robbie Ingliss, the barber, told me that several of Allen's associates discussed the matter in his shop and that he gleaned from what he overheard, that Allen had proposed to them that they should come and get me and give me a whipping so that I would know my place as a "nigger." But that after some discussion one of them had said "suppose we look after it from another angle—here is McFall, a man of education, of respectability and with a good business—how would one of us feel if we were in his position?" So they dropped the matter, for after all it was only their ego and my self-respect that was in question.

As segregation extended itself in Charleston—streetcars were now included—the ego attitude of whites increased. White folks who were congenial with their Negro neighbors began to pass them on the streets without the former customary "howdy do" but would turn their heads away as if they had not seen them. And on the streetcars would assume a haughty air of indifference in the place of their former friendly nod—and so the ego magnified itself.

The interracial relationship in Charleston grew tense. Not so much because of friction for as yet none of that had occurred. But rather was it from the psychological resentment by Negroes against the newly ordained proscriptions. Most of which had only come into effect within the previous fifteen years. These proscriptions had caused many Negro families to leave the city, when they were first started. But it was not until 1912 that the migration assumed the proportion of a small-sized exodus.

As far back as the beginning of the Wade Hampton regime Negro families were migrating from the city. And even before then, as a number of families had moved to the North shortly after the emancipation. When the downfall of the Republican state administration happened a very large number of those who had enjoyed positions under those administrations moved away. And was next followed by a quieter though far more numerous migration of the near whites. While the latter movement was under way an even larger number of other Negro families moved away. With some it was the entire family which migrated and with others only their children went. By 1912 the neighborhood about the drugstore had been so depleted by the migration of many of its former residents that it presented an entirely different appearance—one approaching that of a slum. It would be an impossibility for me to attempt to name all who left the city but I shall mention some of those who lived within a distance of two blocks from the drug store. From Smith Street there went the Westons, the Reeses, the Saxons, Walter Mischeau, the Wiggens, the Carrs, the Manigault children, the Merchants, Rev. Sterret's children, the Smiths who lived over the drugstore, the Sanders family who kept the grocery store opposite to me and the Jones who lived with them. From off of Morris Street went the Davis boys, the Poyas, Rev. Dandridge and the Humes. And from Felix Street, the Deignans, the Jerveys, the Treadwells, the Vanderhorsts, the Smalls, one of whom, Edmund, is the owner of Small's Paradise in New York City, Jasper and Marion Streets sent the Pollards, the Hollings, the Jones and the Wheelers.

The loss could be extended but it would only consume paper. Nor have I included the lesser folks who left and at intervals would return for a brief visit and would boast that "they would rather be a lamppost in New York than be the Mayor in Charleston." And on their return to New York, take along a further group of migrants with them.

The census may not show a reduction in the Negro population of Charleston for these years because while Negroes were leaving the city others were moving in from the nearby islands. It was this influx that was largely responsible for the changing aspect of our neighborhood. For its newer residents were not like the former who largely were homeowners.

The psychological impacts which the Negroes had suffered while undergoing these changing conditions altered many of their earlier concepts of what American's democracy meant. So far as he could see its benefits and its privileges were all beyond his grasp, and that not because of any unworthiness on his part but altogether because of the color of his skin. Which made him all the more bitter and caused him to lose faith in America and his patriotism to wane.

Helping Others and Helping the Nation

FOOD CONSERVATION DRIVE

When I was called upon to take charge of the Food Conservation drive among the Negroes at the beginning of the First World War, I quickly learned the extent to which our national spirit dwindled, not only within Negroes but within whites as well and realized that except America's spirit of liberty could be rekindled within the beings of its people that the task of achieving victory would become hard and difficult.

I have no delusions about America or about its peoples. Whatever its faults have been, and they have been many, have been far outweighed by that ever-present intangible force which somehow or other steps in at the right moment to protect its weak. It is a force which is so definitely present in all of its people when catastrophes happen that it has caused me to wonder if after all—may it not be America's true spirit.

The attitude of the American Negro towards the American white man is by far a more generous one than is ordinarily to be expected under the existing conditions and is largely so because the Negro is not unmindful of the fostering care which has been bestowed upon his race by white philanthropists—some who gave in money and the many who gave in service. He is grateful for the educational, technical and professional training they have given him. And his gratitude for these knows no bounds. He knows that through these bounteous gifts that he has been privileged to scale the heights of human endeavor and to demonstrate through virtuous living his fitness for a place in American life.

Knowing that I had shared in the distribution of these bounties and that I had profited from them in a material way, I could not do otherwise than to promise to give my full service for war effort work, when the call came to me from Mr. James O'Hear, the Chairman of the County Defense Committee. But even more impelling than the knowledge of my material benefits was the knowledge that America was my country and that it was my duty to do whatever became necessary to do on its homefront so that victory could come to it.

Following Mr. O'Hear's instructions I called at the Chamber of Commerce to receive the material for the Food Conservation drive, which was to be my first command, and which from the conversation I had had with Mr. O'Hear was to be entirely under my direction. When I asked the Secretary at the Chamber for supplies he told me, that it was his understanding that Mrs. Visanska was in charge of the Negro group and that I was only her worker and that I was supposed to follow her instructions. I told him that either he or I had been misinformed. That my understanding was that I should have full charge of the drive among Negroes and that in accordance with that belief I had arranged all of the details for my drive and was only awaiting the delivery of my supplies. But that if Mrs. Visanska was in charge of it that I would withdraw and allow her to take full charge. Then he told me that he did not know what the arrangements were and that he would phone Mr. O'Hear. I suggested that he do so at once as I was in hurry to leave. He did so and after speaking with Mr. O'Hear told me that I was right and Mr. O'Hear had directed him to let me have all material I needed. Later I got in touch with Mr. O'Hear and arranged with him that the Negro group should have full charge of its activities.

My plan for the drive included the making of a citywide canvass of Negro heads of families and to receive from them their written pledge to support the conservation program. I districted the city into twenty-two divisions. Placing over each district, a captain, two lieutenants and from eight to twelve canvassers, according to the size of the districts. Each captain was supplied with pledge cards, window stickers and information circulars. We held one instruction meeting, for the captains and lieutenants—who in turn held separate district meetings with their canvassers. I sent circular letters to all of the Negro churches requesting that full publicity be given the drive so that it could proceed smoothly. I prepared a news release for insertion in daily papers, in which detailed instructions were given together with the roster of my workers. All of the names of the ladies who served had their status attached. When I presented that to the *News and Courier*, I took the precaution to tell the City news manager there that I did not want any deletions of "Mrs. or Miss" from their names. He replied that it was not the policy of the *News and Courier* to print Mrs. or Miss to names of Negroes and that the deletions would have to stand if it went in as news item. I told him that I was not concerned with the *News and Courier's* attitude but only seeing to it that the legal status of each of my women workers appeared before each name. And further that it was going to be printed in his newspaper and since it would not be received as a news item that I was presenting it as an advertisement and I wanted it to appear in the following morning's edition. I told him to make the bill out to the Government and I would see that his paper would be paid for the insertion if that was the only way by which Negro women could be saved from being embarrassed. The advertisement was published in the morning's issue but I never received a bill for it. For I intended if the bill was presented, to have it become an issue before its payment was made.

I arranged it so that my drive started a couple of days after the whites started theirs—so that the daily newspaper publicity would be build up for ours. It took my workers three days—working only in the afternoons—to complete the canvass. And required two more days in which to tabulate the report. My report went in the day following that on which theirs appeared and by comparison to theirs, which carried with it an expense charge for over $100, became a truly patriotic effort, as ours had "no expenses."

The Food Conservation drive furnished a couple of amusing incidents. The first happened when one of my canvassers reported that a family on Nunan Street had refused to sign the pledge. The lieutenants in charge of that section had tried to persuade the wife to do so but to no avail. So they brought the matter to me. I went out and asked the lady why was it that she would not sign. She replied, "Now see here Doctor, if I sign that, there is to be no waste of food, and if there is no waste food there won't be any garbage and if there ain't no garbage, there won't be any work for the garbage man and I ain't signing to put no man of[f] his job." Which was somewhat logical but I found out that her husband was a garbage collector and did succeed in getting her to sign the pledge by assuring her that the garbage collector would still have work and that we only wanted her to avoid unnecessary waste of food.

Several months after the drive was completed the rumor spread among the Negroes that only those who had signed the pledge would be allowed to purchase food. One night a crowd came to the drugstore and lined themselves. I wondered just what had brought so many patrons into the store at once, I had never before seen so many in the store at any one time. When I approached the first one and asked what was wanted, I was met with an apology by the lady, who assured me that she was sorry that she was not at home when the canvassers called but wouldn't I give her sticker for her window and let her sign a card so that she could get food should it become scarce. When I had issued all of the cards I had I was compelled to tell those who had not received one, that I would see that they got food but just how much that impressed them I never knew—only that their eyes showed mistrust in my promise, and which could not be hung in a window.

The purpose of the Food Conservation program was to impress the American people with the fact, that by avoiding wastage of food, that they could stretch the same amount of food through a longer period of use without diminishing their nutritional health. And that their compliance with its terms would release a portion of the country's transportation facilities—that required for the distribution of food—so that it could be used for the transportation of troops and other war necessities. The extent to which the government's request was complied with is not known. Neither is the extent to which it served its intent known. All that we do know is that it stimulated an inflationary rise in the cost price of most foods and even worse, the hoarding of foods both by consumers and by sellers in the anticipation of even higher prices to come despite the fact that an ample local supply was available. Just one example may be shown—sugar which sold at 3½¢ a pound when the drive was held, sold at 35¢ a pound twelve months later.

And since the government did not exercise any compulsory or restrictive measures over prices or over commodities prices soared to unheard of levels.

NATIONAL WAR SAVINGS COMMITTEE

Every effort to coordinate the daily activities of the people with those concerned in carrying on the war was based largely upon a patriotic appeal which often fell upon deaf ears and even oftener got only lip service in return. This condition became all the more evident to me when I was requested to set up a "National War Savings Committee." After the completion of the Food Conservation drive, I was called in to sit with the County Committee for National Defense. The Committee consisted of Mr. James O'Hear, Chairman, Mr. Montague Triest, Mr. Paul M. Macmillan, Mr. King McDowell, Mr. Sidney Rittenberg and two others whose names I have now forgotten. The functions of this committee consisted of the initiation and coordination of all activities which the local people were called upon to perform. Much of which was to be done along lines in which racial separation was the pattern. The Committee held its meetings at the Chamber of Commerce. It was altogether free from racial separation—for it is impossible to segregate a single individual, only to throw him out. And since that was not done we got along splendidly.

Under the Congressional war measure, the power of the "draft" was extended to all committees or agencies doing war service work to "draft" individuals for service. The County committee vested me with that power and instructed me to call upon such as I would require for the carrying out of the programs under way. This procedure made it possible for me to "set up" committees and not to wait for volunteers. Headquarters were established at the S.W. Cor. Smith and Morris Streets in rear room to the drugstore with Miss Sadie E. Conyers as Executive Secretary. I was allowed an operating budget and was also given a mailing "frank" privilege by being provided with U.S. Treasury department envelopes.

The duties imposed upon me were at first the sale of war stamps through a house canvass—the sale of Liberty bonds through bond drives and subsequently these were added to by my becoming to an extent, a mediator in labor conflicts at the Navy yard.

The greatest difficulty I met with in carrying out these programs came from the paucity of patriotism which was so evident on every side. I believe that I have told sufficiently how the Negroes' patriotism wanted and that he had ample reason for being bitter towards America. But when I saw the quality and quantity of the patriotism displayed by the whites I was shocked, for it evidenced but very little of true patriotism and was largely evident when it paid to be patriotic or when it could be used for the persecution of others, or to avoid being persecuted as it was from the German-Americans, who in a rush, changed the name of their Germania Bank to the Atlantic Bank, their insurance company to the American Insurance company—the Schutzenplatz to the Ashley Rifle Club Park. Closed the school in which the German language was taught and discontinued the publication of the *Deutsche Zeitung* when the German steamer, the *Leibenfels* was scuttled in the harbor.

John Grace was making capital and telling news accounts about the "patrioteers" who were profiting from the sale of land near the Navy yard. So it became necessary on both sides of the fence to inject patriotism into our folks. We did this through many "pep talks" to our workers and at church meetings where our "five-minute" speakers made the rounds. I was asked to arrange a mass meeting where Senator R.G. Rhett could speak. I agreed to do so provided as I said, the speaker will give the same courtesy to my audience as is usually given a white audience— and reminded them that on many occasions where white speakers address Negro audiences, that they usually arrive when the meeting had been started and leave when they have finished speaking instead of leaving when the program is over. I told them that Negroes did not consider that a courtesy, but that if Mr. Rhett and the others of his party would observe these courtesies that the meeting would be arranged. I secured the use of Morris Brown A.M.E. Church and we had a big meeting. I presided and introduced Judge Macmillan, who in turn presented Senator Rhett. The Senator made a splendid plea for national unity and when the meeting was adjourned remained to receive introductions to the officers of the church and to many of the gathering. Mr. Dubose Heyward, the author of *Porgy and Bess*, was another of my speakers, who on one occasion gave a very interesting talk at Plymouth Church.

I also had the National Bureau of Information send me a Negro speaker. I presented him to a huge audience at the Morris Street Baptist church on a Sunday afternoon. He was "Judge Harrison, a lawyer from Oklahoma and later of Chicago." He was a gifted orator and knew his mission.

The patriotic build up from these meetings made it possible for the "war savings stamps" sales to go over the top—in number of purchasers at least if not by the total amount sold. For it seems that very few Negroes viewed their purchase as an investment but largely as a contribution to the war effort. For as one old lady was reported to have said "Yes honey, I will give the government 25¢ and you can come back again and I will give some more."

LIBERTY BONDS

As an introductory meeting for the sale of Liberty bonds— we held one at the Chamber of Commerce and I presided. I think that that was the first and last time a Negro presided at a meeting there. My principal speakers were Mr. E.H. Pringle, the President of the Bank of Charleston and the Reverend D.J. Jenkins, founder of the Jenkins Orphanage. While the meeting was a success I became somewhat puzzled as certain of my Colored audience sneaked out. The next morning I saw one who had left before the meeting was over and asked him why he had left. It was Robbie Ingliss and he frankly told me that he was getting scared because he had never before seen a colored man presiding over white people as I did and that too in the Chamber of Commerce where I presented everyone as "Mister" and he knew that the whites who were there did not like it. However we sold $26,000.00 worth of bonds that night and foresaw for the drive a full success.

The Navy Yard and Charleston's Growth

NAVY YARD: TRANSPORTATION FACILITIES

The transportation facilities to and from the Navy yard were inadequate to meet the needs of the workers there. And as usual the Negroes had to wait until all of the whites had been cared for. I had a number of complaints about the manner in which street-car conductors acted. I took the matter up with the Department of Labor which was then under the direction of Secretary Wilson and asked if some relief could not be given as under the existing circumstances Negro workers had to leave their homes at 6 a.m. to reach the yard by 8 a.m. and when they ceased work at 4 p.m. could not get passage on the cars until 6 p.m. Mr. Wilson sent President Jones of the Southern Federation of Labor to investigate the matter. Mr. Jones called to see me before investigating the matter. We discussed it at length and then I suggested that since it was not generally known that he was in the city, that he immediately go to the yard and note the conditions there. He did so and a few hours later returned to the drugstore and told me that it was even worse that what I had reported it to be. And that he would recommend that alternate cars be used by each race and that a shuttle train service be started by the Sea

Board. These changes were put into quick effect and brought the relief we sought. When the war was over I received from Secretary Wilson a letter in which he expressed his appreciation for my service.

Just before the above happened another labor complication arose in which Negro common labor became a target for police [interference]. A rather peculiar situation had arisen in the difference between the amount of wages paid for common labor at the Navy yard and what was paid for similar work in the city—somewhat peculiar since the usual rate of pay at the yard was always higher than what was paid in the city. Moreover since no efforts had been made to import white workers for these jobs in the yard, the scarcity there of such labor became acute and plans were being formulated to correct the situation, by the Chamber of Commerce and Captain Brown, the Commandant at the yard. I was called into conference to suggest what could be done to alleviate the situation and much to my surprise found that the police department was about to initiate a program of arresting all Negroes found on the streets during working hours and especially those who loitered about the Tradd Street docks. I expressed surprise at that proposal and told the conference that it could not be done, since the men who were seen loitering at the docks were not vagrants but were farmers from the adjacent islands who came to the city early in the mornings with their produce and after disposing of it, were at the docks awaiting the departure of their boats back to the islands. I further stated that in my opinion the reason why Negroes preferred working in the city rather than at the yard was due altogether to the existing wage differential and that if the scale of wages paid at the yard was increased so that it would include transportation cost and a part of the extra time required in going to and from the yard that an adequate labor supply would be had. My suggestions were accepted. And it was decided to have me send circular announcements to the Negro churches calling for additional laborers at the yard. Newspaper announcements were also suggested and carried out.

While we were in conference a message was brought to the Secretary telling him that a white man, who was not an American citizen was in the building and had applied for a "note" to take to the yard recommending him for a position there. The applicant was a German national and though he had applied a year before for American citizenship had not as yet taken it. The Secretary was about to direct the issuance of a letter of recommendation when Captain Brown interrupted him and said, "Let me see that man before you give him a letter." All of which allowed me to see that the possession of a white skin was of greater value than was that of national safety. For a saboteur within the Navy yard could do much to weaken it.

When it was seen that the local supply of common labor was insufficient to meet the requirements at the yard the government imported five thousand Negro laborers from the Bahamas in the West Indies and housed them in barracks near the Port Terminal. Where they lived in a most pitiable way. The majority of them were totally ignorant of the "American way of life" and so were easy victims for "short-changing" at the commissary. When the flu epidemic struck them their death rate was appalling since they were neither physically fit nor sufficiently intelligent to understand the nature of the epidemic.

CHARLESTON'S GROWTH DURING WWI

The city no longer was the quaint staid old place it formerly was. Less than two years had elapsed since Germany declared war and during that short space of time the population of the city had almost doubled itself. Thousands of workers—the majority of whom were whites had moved into the city and so had hundreds of Negroes, not including those from the Bahamas. Every store building on King Street was occupied and business was booming. The Navy yard had been extended and about it several other projects were under construction. Of which the Port Terminal was the biggest and next smaller to it, the Remount station where horses and mules were conditioned for overseas service. Nearby was the Ordnance depot where ammunition was collected and stored while awaiting shipment overseas. Other ammunition dumps stood on Hog Island in the Cooper River. One of the ammunition inspectors was a Colored man who for a while boarded with Mrs. Emma Carr. The Charleston dry dock at the foot of Calhoun Street had been enlarged. That company employed a larger percentage of skilled Negroes than any other local industry at the time. Jack Dorsel, the electrician was in charge of its electric cranes. The harbor was alive with shipping—naval vessels, freighters and transports—all of them camouflaged in the most vivid colors.

Of all of these activities, the Port Terminals or as it was more commonly known—"Mason and Hanger" (the name of the construction company which built it) was by far the biggest and at the same time the most talked about thing that Charleston had ever witnessed. Its area was as great if not greater than that occupied by the Navy yard. While the extent to which it occupied the minds of the people of Charleston and the extent to which it influenced both overshadowed that which the yard did. As the yard's influence was mostly of a political nature while that which came from Mason and Hanger disrupted, by first inflating and then deflating its economic life.

The terminals were constructed under a percentage charge on time and material which created the most profligate waste imaginable. It was necessary to construct a causeway from a little beyond the General Asbestos plant to reach the southern boundary of the terminals. The causeway ran through water and mud and was constructed by dumping into water thousands of tons of building material until it would no longer sink. Upon which earth was dumped and over it the surfacing concrete pavement. The wage scale at Mason and Hangers was the highest paid in Charleston at the time and totally disrupted the wage system of the city. Anyone who wanted work could get it there as it seems that the company derived a ten percent commission on all of the wages it paid. One story that circulated in the city told how sick Bahaman laborers were compelled to get out of bed to go to work, only to punch the time clock after which they could return to their barracks and remain there until it was time to punch the clock at the midday return hour. And though they did no work they were paid that the company could draw its commission. Since the company employed hundreds of boys 12 to 13 years of age as water boys paying them $12.00 a week for that work my delivery service had to be discontinued as I could not afford to meet that scale of pay. I also found it necessary to close the soda fountain down since the margin of profit derived from it did not allow me to hire soda clerks and pay them a wage equaling what Mason and Hanger paid.

Our local money (currency) supply was inadequate to meet the demand and so in lieu of currency bearer checks were used, in twenty-dollar denominations which no one would cash except when the holder spent a goodly portion of it. It was currently known that at the commissary store where the Bahamans traded that when they made their purchases, usually averaging about 90¢—they would be shortchanged for an average of $4 to $5—by giving them their change in fractional silver coin, and since they could not count American money quickly they were easily fleeced.

The Negroes spent their earnings as fast as they made it. Very few of them saved anything. The wearing of silk shirts which cost them $15.00 a piece, with a tie to match at $5.00 and sleeve garters at $1.00 became the rage with the Negroes. After work hours and on Sundays the neighborhood about Smith and Morris streets would be a flaming panorama of vivid colors which flowed back and forth according to the amount of moonshine the wearer held.

The neighborhood reacted to this by becoming even more of a slum than it previously was. The well-behaved and respectable families who lived in Dereef Court, Pine Court and Palmetto Court moved away and in their place came some of the worst characters that Charleston possessed.

In the meanwhile the city had been made the base for a flotilla of U.S. destroyers which increased our population, by the added presence of nearly six thousand sailors, to something like 120,000 people. Almost double the number in Charleston of those who were there when the war started.

Felix Street had also undergone a change for the worse. As a few years before two Negro women had moved into the street where they opened a couple of "respectable" bawdy houses for white patronage only. When the police department under order from the Navy department closed the vice district in the lower section of the city, a number of white women who had houses there moved up to Felix Street and established [their] businesses there. And very soon thereafter the neighborhood became a menace to peace, as frequently, a drunken sailor would stray around to Pine Court and would be "rolled" for every penny he carried. I became fearful that the conditions might provoke serious trouble there and to avoid that happening, I wrote a letter to the Commandant at the Navy yard and requested to have the entire area made an "out of bound" area for sailors and for marines. In my letter to him, I stressed the possibility of riots occurring if enlisted men were allowed to congregate in a solidly Negro area and that he, perhaps more than anyone else, had the power to prevent it.

The Commandant gave immediate attention to my letter. Within twenty-four hours he placed the area under Marine guard and in cooperation with the police department ordered every "house" within the area closed and that the white women on the street move elsewhere within twenty four hours. Not a single white man was allowed to pass through Felix Street during the period it was under guard and within twenty-four hours the street became cleaner that it had ever been before.

Struggle and Strife
in Charleston

GREAT INFLUENZA EPIDEMIC

Shortly thereafter the great influenza epidemic reached us. During my previous business experience in Charleston, I had seen two epidemics, one of typhoid and the other the smallpox. But neither of these took life in such numbers nor incapacitated so great a number of the people as did the "flu." As the epidemic, in its southward march, approached our community, one could feel the fear which it conveyed to communities yet unreached by it by the awesome news reports of its ravages. These reports made me recall some of the anxieties Charleston experienced in the 1880s when the first epidemic of a similar type, the "la grippe" reached New York from Europe and the high death rate it caused in that city.

When the epidemic reached us, Miller my pharmacist took ill and remained at home. Not that he was really sick but because he was too badly frightened by the epidemic to meet patients who may be suffering from it. So the task of meeting the demands for medicines, which had multiplied many times over that of the normal demand, fell upon me with only Tommie to assist me. I persuaded Mary Lou [Saunders] to work with us in the drugstore. Since we had to discontinue the sale of cigars and other sundries to allow us to devote our entire time to prescription dispensing, Mary Lou became very helpful, as she could receive all prescriptions, write the patients names on them, and as they accumulated in batches of tens, bring them to me to be compounded. Then to wrap and deliver to the patients the one we had completed. Mary Lou quickly became even more useful to us for she could wrap powders as fast as I could, divide them and in addition allowed none to sit in the store but made everyone go in the street and stay there until she called them to receive their medicines.

One day I filled four-hundred-and-eighty prescriptions by myself. And for a period of over three weeks did not find time to record narcotic prescriptions for we were too busily occupied with prescriptions to do so. I had to abandon my usual hours–– and though Tommie and Mary Lou would leave at about 11 p.m. I would remain and work until 3 and 4 o'clock each morning and be back on the job at 8 a.m.

I was fortunate in having bought a large supply of essential chemicals and drugs when the war had first started since many of them, such as phenacetin, quinine, antipyrine etc. could not then be obtained and so since mine was one of the few drugstores with a complete stock on hand we received prescriptions from all over town.

I saw some very tragic happenings during the epidemic. I remember one—young man named Dukes who was employed as a cutter at the clothing factory—left home in the morning for work, leaving his wife and two children in apparently good health and on his return at 4 o'clock in the afternoon, found all of them ill. He got his family physician to see them at seven that evening. Brought the prescriptions to the drugstore and had them filled. He returned to his home at 8 o'clock only to find the three of them dead. Such was the rapidity with which the flu could kill.

The greatest toll however was among the Bahaman laborers at the Navy yard, where from five to fifteen were found dead in their bunks each morning. None of whom had received any medical care whatsoever.

We were fortunate in escaping flu as none of us caught it. I doubt if the nightly administration of five grains of quinine and ten grains of aspirin which all of us, Thorne included, took protected us against it and so believe that it was altogether our good fortune in escaping it.

CHARLESTON RACE RIOT

The fear which enveloped us when the flu came to Charleston was but an insignificant dread compared with that which struck on Saturday afternoon when we learned that a "race riot"[13] was taking place in the city and was rapidly extending itself from the Market Street section where it had started to the upper portion of the city. Very few of us could believe that the rumors were true as we knew of no reasons or causes through which rioting could start. By 8 o'clock that night the riot was a reality and was rapidly spreading itself throughout the city. Moreover it was getting beyond the control of the police. Fortunately for us the Commandant at the Navy yard sent the Marines down to restore order and by 12 o'clock that night order was restored. About twenty-one people lost their lives in it and an even larger number suffered injury. Perhaps the most significant thing about a race riot is that it is the only true means through which we can evaluate the quantity and quality of racial stamina and learn in what strata of Negro life it really exists. That Saturday evening when so many of our "best folks" were seeking safety behind the barred doors of their homes or were running to cover, my friends from Pine Court, from Dereef Court and

13 Event started on 10 May 1919. "Charleston Has Race Riot," *Keowee [South Carolina] Courier,* 14 May 1919, p.1, col. 3. also [Charleston] *News and Courier* 11 May 1919.

from Palmetto Court were arming themselves and arranging an ambush and a counterattack against the whites. Every roof on Morris Street and from behind every fence from St. Philip Street to beyond Smith held Negroes who had agreed among themselves to fight and die fighting if need be. I knew that a very similar action had been followed on Calhoun Street, east of Meeting, where when the white mob saw the number of Negroes awaiting its coming, it retreated back to King and Calhoun Street. Several of my friends were in the drugstore when the rioting had reached Vanderhorst Street and were urging me to close and go home as they were doing. But I chose to stay and remained there until quiet was restored—with my gun and my neighbors.

From the investigations we made—the riot could hardly be classified as a race riot although it was a clash between whites and Negroes it was one in which local whites did not participate. Neither did they have any part in causing it or by adding to its violence. If it is possible to use the term "decency" in connection with a mob of whites when bent on killing Negroes, it may be said that the mob was a somewhat "decent" mob as they refrained from molesting Negro women. For not a single Negro woman on the streets that evening was molested. And they [there] were many such, especially on King Street, doing their Saturday evening shopping.

The trouble had its start on Market Street near Charles, when three Marines approached several Negro boys and inquired of them where could they find some Negro women, at which the boys cursed them and told them to hunt "white whores." One of the Marines slapped one of the boys. The boys ran a little way off and gathered rocks with which they attacked the Marines. The Marines gave chase and the boys ran into a house on Charleston Street where an uncle lived and who when he saw the Marines chasing the boys, got his pistol and ordered them away. The Marines insisted on getting the boys at which their uncle fired one shot in their direction and they left. Only however, to go to the Marine barracks on Market Street between King and Meeting where they got three other Marines to join with them for an invasion of the Market and Charles Street section. The six of them went into Black's Pool Room on Market Street where a number of Negroes were playing pool and demanded them to tell which of them fired the shot. A free for all fight ensued in which the Negroes used cue sticks and billiard balls and with such telling that the Marines, most of them badly hurt ran off, returning to their barracks to spread the news that they had been attacked and injured by Negroes. As the news spread, a mob of sailors and Marines raided a shooting gallery a couple of doors from their barracks and seized the rifles and cartridges there and so armed started down Market towards Charles. On the way they fired at every Negro within sight. One Negro was killed in the gateway opposite to the stage entrance of the Academy of Music and two others were injured, one of whom died later. When the mob reached Charleston Street it turned south and entered Beaufain Street where it met a mob of Negroes who had gathered near Harry Gomez's restaurant. A general melee followed which lasted for almost an hour before the sailors and Marines retreated back to King and Market Streets. Where they were subsequently joined by a large number of sailors from the destroyer fleet that lay at anchor in the harbor.

We never learned how word of the riot reached the men on the ships or why nearly two thousand sailors were permitted to leave the ships at that hour as it was then far beyond the hour when "shore leave" is given. Moreover those who came were all dressed in dungarees and not in the regulation dress uniforms usually worn when on leave. We stressed this fact in our presentation to the Navy department since it made us believe that the men who came ashore after the rioting had started had been allowed to do so by those in charge of the ships from which they came. Which to us, seemed all the more probable since the men had to use the ships' launches for reaching shore. The mob, consisting mostly of sailors, and augmented by others who were on leave, numbering more than three thousand started up King Street beating up every Negro man they could catch. They paused for a few minutes at Fridie's Barbershop, a Negro-owned shop operated for whites, and wrecked it. The barbers escaped injury by fleeing through the rear and over the back fences.

When it reached Marion Square and Calhoun Street, the mob spread, a portion going east on Calhoun Street and a portion continuing northward on King. The number going down Calhoun stopped at Meeting Street beyond which was seen a large number of Negroes who had gathered there to meet the mob. At which the mob reversed it[s] direction and returned towards King Street. Near which several Negroes were caught and dragged over to the "green" and beaten. Mary Ann was passing through this area as the rioting was under way. She saw the crowd but thought that it was merely a crowd of drunken sailors fighting with each other. Neither she nor any of several other Negro women whom she saw passing through the mob were molested.

By the time the mob going northward on King Street reached the corner of Radcliffe Street word of the riot had reached the Navy yard and several companies of Marines were dispatched to [the] scene of trouble to quiet it. In a short while the majority of the sailors had been returned to the yard. It was after the rioting had been quelled that most of the fatalities among Negroes occurred for with the exception of the 22 caliber rifles which had been taken from the Market Street shooting gallery, the mob was an unarmed mob.

When the Marines took over the task of quelling the riot they started by stopping every Negro on the street and searching him for arms and by shooting those who ran when they ordered them to halt. Since the Negroes could not distinguish Marine guardians of the peace from those who were disturbers of the peace, they took no chance by stopping except when they came face to face with one. But even worse than that was the rifling of the pockets of Negroes by these "examining Marines" who after they had robbed their victims ordered them to go on and emphasized their orders by shooting after them.

In retaliation the Negroes started sniping—by shooting into the streetcars that were taking the sailors up to the Navy yard and also at those who had been wounded and were on their way to Roper Hospital. One Negro I knew, "Sweet," he was a constable for Magistrate Whaley, who used his forty four with telling effect from his hiding place in the vacant lot at the corner of Lucas and Calhoun Streets by firing into the patrol wagons as they went to Roper with wounded whites. And who when a squad came to hunt him moved on to another vacant lot at the corner of Huger and Meeting Streets where he took part with those who were shooting into passing cars.

The most daring of all retaliatory acts came from a young Negro named Ladson. Who formerly served as civilian chauffeur for Major General Leonard Wood when the General was in charge of the Southeastern Division of the Army. A few months before the riot happened General Wood, who was then the top ranking American General as well as the presidential timber and had been railroaded to the far West so that Pershing could be advanced, had sold or given his old Lozier automobile to Ladson. Ladson was using it as a public taxi. The night of the riot Ladson got some of his friends together, saw that they were armed, took them in his car and sped up St. Philip Street to the police station where a large number of policemen and Marines were stationed on the sidewalk. When he reached the station his friends opened fire on the policemen and Marines who made it post haste into the building without pausing to open its screen doors and in their hurry wrecked it completely. Fortunately for them and for the policemen and the Marines, Ladson's speed was such that the bullets from his car struck beyond where the men stood and so none were injured.

I am convinced that the action of Ladson and his group and that of "Sweet" and his friends did more than anything else to bring the riot to a halt. They were not the fearful ones who wanted to go home and lock themselves in but were the ones who were willing to fight it out and cared not whether they lived or died.

The *News and Courier* in its early morning edition gave a full account of the fatalities but in the city edition omitted to do so. I got a copy of the early edition which we used in our presentation to the Navy department. In that account about fourteen were listed as killed, seven of whom were Negroes. From other sources, we learned that fourteen dead, all white, were in the morgue at the Navy yard hospital.

The executive committee of the local (Charleston) N.A.A.C.P. made the investigation and presented a protest to the Navy Department. Our investigation showed that the rioting had been incited by members of the Navy only. And was not joined in by local whites. That there was an apparent collusion between the officers in charge of the ships in the harbor and the enlisted men whereby the enlisted men were allowed to leave their ships to join with the rioters; which in our opinion largely contributed to the violence inflicted upon Negroes. And further that the elapsed time which followed the initial break out of the trouble was sufficiently long a time in which to have stopped the rioting before it reached dangerous proportions as that was not attempted until nearly five hours had elapsed. And further that the majority of casualties were inflicted by the armed Marines who were sent down to quell the riot. We presented affidavits from Negroes testifying that they had been robbed at the point of the gun by Marines. One affidavit established the identity of one Marine, who was known to the operator of a pressing club who was his victim, as the Marine for whom he had cleaned a suit on the day of the riot and while on his way home the night of the riot was held up and robbed. In addition to those affidavits we presented a number of others from victims who were shot but not robbed.

City Council expressed regrets over the happening and the intent to reimburse Fridie with the amount of his loss. Which however was never done. The police department did not prosecute any Negroes. Even Ladson who had been recognized was not prosecuted. Beyond that nothing was done by the city officials to compensate those who suffered from the riot.

The Navy Department ordered an investigation at the Navy yard. A Court of Investigation was held there and a number of Negroes were called before it to testify. All of whom were told not to divulge to any one the nature of the testimony they gave or any of the happenings at the hearing, for if such was done they would be subjected to penalties. Dr. Thorne spent the greater part of one day before the Court where his testimony as attending physician to several of the wounded, established them to be victims of the Marine's gun fire. The hearings dragged along for more than three months. And that was all that came out of it.

NEGRO DRAFTEES GO ON STRIKE

Not long after the riot had taken place, a small size revolt broke out at the "labor battalion" camp on the Meeting Street Road just above the Standard Oil Company's plant. Where about five hundred Negro draftees were used for loading ships with coal. These men, though they had been drafted for military service, had been segregated into work battalions which operated under army direction. They enjoyed none of the privileges accorded to members of the armed forces. Nor were they not permitted to wear its uniform but only the blue dungaree. They worked seven days a week with a military guard surrounding their camp—more like convicts on a chain gang—than as members of the armed forces. But one day they tired of the treatment they received and went on a strike. The exact nature of their complaints we never knew—only that they were made to work more hours a day than others did and that the compensation they received for doing that work was far less than what civilians received for doing similar work. However since they maintained a solid front and insisted upon getting their grievances listened to before they would return to work, there was nothing left for the army to do but to grant them a hearing as nothing could be gained by putting them in confinement for then all work which they did would cease. So a new group of officers were placed over them under whom the men enjoyed more privileges than they formerly had.

A few months later I attended the annual convention of the National Medical Association of which I was then one of its Vice-Presidents in Philadelphia. At its opening session Dr. Joseph Cannon of Jersey City in response [to] one of the welcome addresses took the occasion as an opportunity to bring to the attention of the Association some of the later rulings of the Secretary of War and especially one which announced that all Negroes drafted into the armed forces, irrespective of their training and education would be assigned to "labor battalions" except such as were required for replacements in the then existing combat units and that no further combat units would be established for Negroes. Being familiar with what had happened to the "labor battalion" at Charleston I could easily understand the gravity of the situation and could foresee how destructive it would be to the training and skill of Negro professional men. But even worse than that would be the mental frustration that would surely follow. I had previously conversed with several young physicians about the matter and more than one had assured me that they would refuse to take the oath of allegiance and would welcome a term at Leavenworth prison rather than enter the United States Army.

The matter was discussed in an executive session of the Executive Committee and Officers. A committee, of which I was a member, was appointed to take such steps as may be necessary to abort the functioning of that order. Dr. Cannon was named the Chairman of the Committee.

We immediately sought to have a hearing on the Order before Secretary Baker (in whose Department and by whom the order was issued) at which we would request its cancellation or at least have it so modified that its carrying out would not impair the morale nor the technical, professional and educational acquirements of future Negro draftees.

Senator Frelinghuysen (I think I spell his name correctly) of New Jersey succeeded in arranging a conference with Secretary Baker at which the matter would be presented. The date of the conference could not be readily fixed. However it was believed that it would be held within a month. The members of the committee were instructed to keep in touch with Dr. Dumas in Washington and be prepared to come to Washington on notice. I remained in the North for ten days, so that I could be nearer Washington when the call came, after which I returned to Charleston. I had advised Dr. Dumas of my return to the south and that he should wire me at Charleston when the date of the conference had been decided upon. I was informed that Secretary Baker had gone to Europe and on his return would receive us.

A few weeks later the armistice was signed, bringing to an end to the war with Germany and for a while at least, the end of the vilest of all threats from Wilson's administration against the wellbeing of America's Negro minority.

With the advent of peace came a reduction in war activity work. The Bahamans were returned to their home in the West Indies as they were no longer needed at the Terminals. Many of the whites who had come to the city to work when the war started, and had been dismissed from the yards immediately left the city.

So did many Negroes who had come from other areas to work in Charleston. Within the short space of sixty days, following the armistice the population of the city had fallen from its mid-war number of approximately 120,000 down to 100,000 and folks were still leaving.

Building a New Store

Business however continued good as most of the folks, especially the provident ones, had saved their money. Only my friends with the silk shirts, now dirty and ragged, seemed lost for what to do—as many of the provident ones were buying homes or repairing theirs. Which brought about a smaller and more necessary boom to the city in which local property was receiving a much-needed improvement.

I, who also had sought to be provident, got out my old plans for the "model drugstore" and started revamping them again. In all of the previous plans, I had contemplated a single building—and intended during the while it was under construction to rent temporary quarters for the store elsewhere. In the meanwhile conditions had changed and it was no longer possible to find a nearby location in which I could operate by business while the new building was being erected. So I decided to continue business on the corner and at the same time to erect the new store building. In doing so it became necessary to plan for two buildings—both of which should face on Morris Street, where the available frontage was seventy-five feet. By which I could down the rear portion of the old building, and by removing the stock to the front and using upstairs for storage, erect a building to its west, and when that was enclosed, to move the drugstore

there, and then raze the remaining portion of the old building and erect the drugstore at the corner. Each building would
have two rental apartments on the second floor and would be
modernly equipped with all convenience even with gas cooking stoves. Which I lived to regret, as within five years, the tenants wore them out using them as ice boxes—by wrapping ice
in crocus sacks and storing it in the ovens. The lower floor of the
westerly building was planned to provide two store buildings.
I engaged Tom Pinckney to do the work and were waiting the
arrival of material with which to begin work, when Tommie read
a sales advertisement in the newspaper in which No. 150 Ashley Avenue was offered for sale. Gus Purvis was in the store at
the time and knowing that he was in search of a home—she told
him about it and suggested that he should buy it. But he wanted
none of it—it was entirely too large he said. So she bothered me
to buy it. She phoned Jac [sic] D. Leseman, the agent who had
it in charge and asked the price. He told her that it was held for
$7,000.00. Which caused her to pester me all the more. She asked
if I would take her down to one of the dry goods shops. Which I
did and as she got out of the car she again asked me to go down
and buy the place. So to appease her, I told her that I would go
but that I would not offer to pay $7,000.00 for it. I went to Lese-
man's and told him that I had seen the ad and would make an
offer of $6,500.00 for the place payable $500.00 on the signing of
the contract and the balance within 30 days or when the titles
were passed. He said that the owner, Mr. Reeves had insisted
on $7,000.00 but that he would go upstairs and speak with him.
A few minutes later he came back and told me that Mr. Reeves
had accepted my offer and that he would [deliver] the contracts
up to the drugstore at 2 o'clock. I was caught and caught with
something that in later years caused me more annoyance than
anything else has ever done.

While the construction work at Smith and Morris Street
was under way, I placed my order for new fixtures so that they

could be installed when the building was complete. And when installed would be the fourth refitting of my store in its twenty years existence. I found a buyer for my soda water fountain and so happy was I to get rid of it, that I sold the entire equipment on which I was carrying $2,900.00 of fire insurance for $600.00. Three hundred cash and the balance payable in monthly installments of $50.00.

Business was not interrupted for a single minute during the time the buildings were under construction. Neither did we suffer delay—for I had taken the precaution to have every item of stock so placed when moving back and forth that it could be quickly found. The new building was occupied when it was completed and ready for occupancy. When I drew the plans, I arranged the floor level should be four inches above the flood water level of the 1911 storm. Two weeks after we moved in a heavy rainstorm flooded the neighborhood and the store was inundated with four inches of flood water—which merely goes to prove that neither time nor tide conforms to the wishes of man.

Negro Teachers and Charleston Schools

For many years our school system had been deteriorating into one in which the Negro schools were becoming fields for indoctrinating their pupils with the most vicious forms of inferiority complex—the inferiority of Negroes to whites. With the exception of two Negro teachers at the Shaw School all of the teachers in the Negro schools were whites. None of whom held ideas towards Negroes as did those who taught in Negro schools twenty-five years earlier. With the later teachers, their contacts with their pupils, was always conditioned upon the supposed superiority of white to Negroes and eventually led to the punishment of Negro pupils for speaking to their teachers when they happened to meet on the streets. In addition to these attitudes the white teachers refrained from participating with their pupils in any extra curricula activities whatsoever. Neither could Parent-Teachers Associations be formed in any Negro school for that under the "code" would be an abomination unto them. Even the customary school closing exhibitions where parents formerly attended in large numbers had undergone a radical change from what it formerly was. We knew that the majority of white teachers in the Negro schools only accepted their positions because they brought them an income and not because they wished to teach Negroes. Hence there was the total absence in our schools of all of the necessary relationships between teacher, pupil and parents through which a worthwhile education could be imparted.

On several occasions, we had sought to have Negro teachers placed in our schools but invariably these efforts met with opposition from the school board. Who never offered explanation for its refusal to employ Negro teachers in Negro schools which made it all the more evident that it was based largely on the determination to continue the employment of whites who needed the salaries and the further opportunity to deprave [sic] the quality of the education it taught there.

The first request for Negro teachers was made under the leadership of Rev. J.L. Dart who got up a petition and had it signed by a large number of the more outstanding Negroes in the city. It was presented to the Board of Commissioners but was refused. A few years later, when Blease was governor, Rev. Coit sought his aid, and the Fortner bill, which made it mandatory that Negro teachers be employed in public schools throughout the state, was presented in the state legislature. But there it met opposition from the Charleston delegation with such effect that when it was passed it carried an amendment which exempted the city of Charleston from any of its provisions.

Two years before I tore down the old drugstore building, the Executive Committee of the local N.A.A.C.P. discussed ways and means for correcting the conditions in our schools. At a meeting held at Mickey's office on Calhoun Street, a tentative plan was offered and discussed. Mr. Thomas E. Miller, Sr. proposed that an effort be made to have a measure (bill) introduced in the state legislature whereunder it would be illegal for whites to teach Negroes in the city of Charleston and stated that he had friends there who would sponsor the bill. I suggested that any method used be supported by a citywide petition from Negroes, especially its free holders and those who were parents of children attending the public schools as that would be very necessary in substantiating that the majority of Negroes in Charleston wanted it so.

A majority of the Committee felt that my ideas were unnecessary and that it would entail too much effort and that it would only be necessary to have about six men sign a petition on behalf of the community and that that would be sufficient.

In my judgement it was not and I so expressed it. I also suggested that any effort made through the legislature be initiated as coming from a "citizens" committee and not from the N.A.A.C.P. Since the general attitude of animosity against that Association would alone be sufficient to kill the bill. My suggestion for the "citizens" committee was accepted. And the following men were appointed as the Committee—Mr. Thomas E. Miller, Sr., Rev. C.C. Jacobs, Dr. J.M. Thompson, Dr. W.M. Thorne, Teddy Harleston and I think E.C. Mickey and Dr. W.H. Johnson.

Mr. Miller made rapid headway with his plans. The measure was introduced in both houses of the legislature and had passed its first reading, when it became known that that it would be bitterly fought by the Board of School Commissioners. Mr. Miller who was constantly present in Columbia had taken the precaution to keep himself fully informed on the progress of the bill. For a while it seemed that the measure would not be opposed, especially in the house but in the senate it was much different as in that body it had only two supporters. Entirely too few to make us hopeful for its passage. As the session neared its close the bill was sent to a joint committee (composed of committees from both houses) for public hearing, out of which it could be reported either favorably or unfavorably. With the certainty that whichever report was attached to it, that report would determine the action of the legislature.

Mr. Miller had information that the measure would be hotly contested before the committee and that representatives from the Board of School Commissioners would appear at the hearing to protest against its passage. In addition to that he had also learned that the authority by representation, claimed by our petitioners, would also be questioned. But even of more vital importance than that was the knowledge he had that the School Board were in possession of a petition signed by nearly 280 Negroes protesting against any change in the teaching personnel of Negro schools.

Mr. Miller telephoned to Charleston and requested that a meeting of the Executive be held at Dr. Johnson's office on Saturday evening "and to be sure to have McFall there for it is absolutely necessary to the successful passage of the bill, to do the things he suggested" —I went to the meeting and listened to Mr. Miller's report on the progress of the bill and what should now be done. When Mr. Miller had finished, I rose and told the committee that what was required was an enormous task—with only four days in which to do it. But that I would accept it because there was not another member of the committee who could do it and that it was only through the experience I had received in the several war drives which made me feel that I could do it.

I outlined the procedures to be followed—there was first the formation of a canvassing committee, to make a house to house canvass of the city for signatures to a petition—public notices to be given in all Negro churches—the enlistment of every Negro minister in support of the measure—and lastly, the printing of petition cards, circulars and directions for canvassers. I impressed upon the committee that I could only promise a successful effort in putting over the drive if I received the full support and assistance of the Committee in doing whatever I assigned them to do. After which the meeting adjourned.

That night I had Mr. Miller prepare the form for the petition cards. I got in touch with John Harlee, a printer and he promised me that if I got my forms ready by 6 o'clock Sunday morning that he would start printing them at that hour. Teddy Harleston met me at the drugstore at 12 o'clock that night and we remained there until 4 o'clock the next morning, arranging districts and assigning captains, lieutenants and canvassers for each. In much the same manner as I had done in my former war drives.

I contacted B.F. Cox the principal at Avery and got his cooperation and through him, that of the pupils in the upper grades of the normal department, for them to serve as canvassers.

By 10 o'clock Sunday morning, Mr. Harlee had finished circulars and had them to me at the drugstore. These circulars told how necessary it was, if Negro teachers were wanted in Negro schools, to sign the petition cards when the canvassers called and that everyone should inform their friends to do likewise. I personally delivered these circulars to every Negro church in Charleston in time for their morning services and in addition urged every preacher I met to emphasize the importance of doing what was asked of them.

A little later during the day, Mr. Harlee brought me the petition cards. And having in the meanwhile contacted my captains and lieutenants was then able to deliver to them their supply of cards and circulars—with instructions that they start canvassing on Monday morning as early as they possibly could and to continue until they had canvassed every Negro home in their districts.

Realizing that it would be necessary to get the moral support of white citizens if our success meant the displacement of white teachers from the positions in Negro schools, I called on Mr. John P. Grace, the editor of the *Charleston American* and asked would he support our cause. I explained to him in detail why our action had become necessary and that I felt that he alone could present our cause to the white people of Charleston in such manner that they could see the justice of our cause.

Mr. Grace's support exceeded my anticipation. For not only did he publish daily editorials in our behalf and local news items about the drive but he also gave me some very practical suggestions which enabled me to check if not to entirely quiet one who was a bitter opponent to Negro teachers. But that particular bit of information was given under the seal of secrecy and so must be kept.

On Monday morning I attended the weekly meeting of the Minister's Union to urge their collective support of the drive and to get their endorsement for the change of teachers. But much to my surprise found that I had become the center of a storm of discussion in which Revered N.B. Sterret led the attack insisting that the petition was presented "under false colors" as it was not presented by a "citizens committee" but by a committee from the N.A.A.C.P. which I admitted was correct but which I explained was done for expediency. For by so doing we would avoid the usual form of opposition that came to everything the N.A.A.C.P. did. And we did not want that to happen. I told them that in addition to what Rev. Sterret claimed, that the local N.A.A.C.P. was defraying the expense of the movement. Rev. M.M. Hollins came to my rescue by bluntly asking "Whoever heard of any one grabbing a bull by the horns—you grab him by the tail if you want to play safe" and "McFall is right." With which the Ministers Union came in line with the movement.

I had told my teams to bring their reports in at the end of each day as they had to be tabulated and filed and made ready for presentation before the joint Committee of the legislature on Thursday. Mrs. Susie Dart Butler and Mr. E.C. Mickey brought their typewriters to the drugstore on Tuesday and that evening joined with me in typing, in duplicate, the names and addresses of those who had signed the petition cards. The canvass was completed by Wednesday afternoon. Over five thousand Negro heads of families had signed the petition cards. I prepared an affidavit setting forth that I supervised the canvass and that the name and addresses attached thereto were all from Negroes who were petitioners to the General Assembly and who numbered more than five thousand heads of families and included free holders and parents of pupils attending the free public schools of Charleston, all of whom were residents of the city of Charleston and constituted more than two-thirds of the Negro population of that city, and who pray that the petition they have presented be granted through the enactment by the General Assembly of the Act which provides that only Negro teachers be employed in the public schools of Charleston.

All of which were immediately sent to Mr. Miller in Columbia so that they could be ready when the joint committee met. About fifteen men from Charleston went to Columbia to be present at the hearing. We met at Butler Nance's home and discussed the situation. Mr. Miller told us that Mr. Lee, the sponsor of our bill, had advised him to be the only speaker from our group as he felt that Mr. Miller's experience as a former member of the legislature would permit him to more clearly present our case than what could by one who was unfamiliar with the procedures. While we agreed with that suggestion, it yet could be seen that one of the group, the Rev. C.C. Jacobs, who had prepared an address, was not in hearty accord with it and was much chagrined by the suggestion. We went in a body to the Capitol and sat in the Senate chamber where the hearing was held.

Mr. Neils Christensen, the Senator from Beaufort County presided. Mr. Christensen opened the hearing by asking if the bill before the Committee would affect the Penn School at St. Helena Island, where said he, a number of white ladies had been teaching for many years and had done splendid work in training the Negroes and if this bill interrupted their service at the Penn School he would be opposed to it. Mr. Miller replied by telling him that the bill before the committee applied only to the free public schools in the city of Charleston and had no statewide application. At which Mr. Christensen replied, "I am glad of that for it inclines me to favor the bill"—round one in favor. The hearing was restricted to thirty minutes, fifteen of which were allowed to each side. Mr. Miller requested the Chairman to permit him to divide his allotted time into five minutes for his presentation, five for rebuttal and five for closing, which was granted. Mr. Miller proceeded with his presentation and told why it was necessary that the measure be passed and that the time had come when it was impossible for young white ladies to teach Negroes or to enter into that close degree of friendship with their pupils as is requisite in good teaching. He said that on one occasion, on a bond rally parade, that the Negro pupils were the only school children in the parade who were not under the immediate direction of their teachers, and to the embarrassment of onlookers, the only ones who were committing nuisances on the street. And that it was to correct these conditions that we now found it necessary to apply to the legislature for aid. That we had requested the School Board to make the changes and had been refused by them—and that this was the only method by which the two free public schools of Charleston could be made efficient schools.

State Senator Young presented the position of the School Board. He merely stated that the Board opposed the passage of the measure and that Mr. Rhett, the Superintendent, and Mr. Smith, a member of the Board were present and desired to be heard.

Mr. Rhett spoke and in his opening remarks said that Mr. Miller misrepresented the facts when he stated that Charleston had but two public schools. And that it was his belief that Mr. Miller knew that the city had three such schools. Mr. Rhett continued by telling the committee that the set up in the school system at that particular time was such that it was not feasible to make change for if that was done it would be necessary for them to dismiss some sixty-odd white teachers from the service, because the Board could not place them elsewhere.

As Mr. Rhett finished, Mr. Miller asked permission to question him—It was he said, about the number of free Negro public schools in Charleston, which he claimed to be two and not three as was stated by Mr. Rhett. And then Mr. Miller tied him up by reviewing the history of Charleston's Negro public schools. He said that the Shaw School was a memorial to Colonel Shaw of the 54th Massachusetts Regiment and though it was operated as a school by the Board that it was the property of the Shaw Memorial Association, and could not be considered as being a public school facility. The Burke School, said he, came largely through the bequest from Mrs. Grimke and was in part provided for with public funds, leaving the Simonton School the only one that was in fact a public school building.

The fun really began when Mr. Smith, a member of the School Board, spoke. On many occasions I have heard Negroes, when pushed to the wall cry out that "the reason you do this, is because I am a Negro." But it was the first time in my life that I ever heard a white man cry out, as Mr. Smith did when he stated, "The reason they are doing this is because the teachers are white." At which a member of the Legislature, but not one of the committee, rose and asked "If I should promise to offer a bill in the legislature to pension such white teachers who under this bill would be removed from their present positions and not be able to receive other teaching positions, would you grant these people their request?" To which Mr. Smith yelled "No we would not accept that." The gentleman who made the offer nodded his head and said, "I thank you."

Though Mr. Miller had presented our petition cards at the opening of the hearing, Mr. Christensen did not ask to have them brought to the table. But that night the joint committee sent for them and as I afterwards learned, verified the lists of names by comparing them with the names and addresses of Negroes listed in the Charleston city directory.

Before leaving the Capitol that afternoon, I noticed that there was a very definite trend in our favor, for though it had been a hearing before a joint committee, it yet had attracted the presence of a very large number of the members of both the house and the senate and who when the hearing had closed were discussing it. So I told several of our party to remain in the Capitol and let us see if we can't do some lobbying for the bill. But only Teddy Harleston remained. The others were anxious to get away and did so. Not that they had anything else to do or that they could not stay but all too apparently because they were afraid to stay.

Harleston and I soon had a group of legislators about us, with whom we discussed the pros and cons of the situation. One of them said to me "If what you are telling is true I may be able to help you." I assured him that it was true and that it could not be contradicted. To which he said, "I am a member of the House and I promise you that when the bill comes up that I will move its adoption, and more over, I have a friend in the Senate whose influence is wide and I shall get him to do the same when the measure comes up in the Senate." We thanked him and left and as we left we knew that we had won a majority on both the Senate and in the House.

That night the Governor took a hand in the matter. He told Mr. Lee, that he had followed the measure in its course before the joint committee and had decided to allow the School Board of Charleston the privilege of granting the demands of the Negroes and would allow them twenty-four hours in which to do so, and should the Board comply, that he, Mr. Lee, should have the bill withdrawn from the calendar, for if it was not and was passed that he would veto it when it came before him. And in the event the School Board should refuse to grant the demands, that he, the Governor, would send a special message to the Legislature requesting the immediate enactment of the bill.

The Governor's ultimatum had the desired effect, as the School Board immediately passed a resolution to the effect that from and after the scholastic year beginning in September of that year, that only Negro teachers be employed to teach Negro pupils in the free public schools provided for Negroes.

Mr. Miller was immediately notified about the Board's action. So was Mr. Lee, who withdrew the bill from the calendar. I received an attested copy of the resolution and now have it in my possession. That one is the single notice which was given to us by the School Board, and with the list of petitioners and some of the petition cards is now stored in the drugstore.

I was glad to see the measure take the course it did as I did not care to see another "segregation law" enacted by South Carolina. The resolution adopted by the School Board carried with it the full effect of law. Since in the withdrawal of the bill, a copy of the School Board's resolution was inscribed hereon and a record thereof setting forth the conditions under which the bill was withdrawn, printed in the Journal of the House.

One member of the committee did not take kindly to the method by which the matter was settled and even though it had brought us victory and allowed us to secure our aims, this member, the Rev. C.C. Jacobs objected to it. He wanted to have the bill passed and since it had not been passed, had phoned Mr. Miller and told him, that "You and McFall have sold us out." Mr. Miller immediately got in touch with me and with tears in his eyes, told me what Jacobs had said and how he had cursed him out for saying so. I told Mr. Miller not to worry over it and that the matter would be handled at a meeting of the Committee which was scheduled for that afternoon.

It was easy for me to understand some of Jacob's actions, as I knew that he had taken umbrage when he was told in Columbia that he would not be allowed to speak at the hearing before the Joint Committee. But despite that I could hardly understand how one with his intelligence could so completely overlook the fact that we were not members of the Legislature but only the representatives of the Negroes of Charleston who had appeared before the Joint Committee in support of the proposed Act, and that the power to dispose of the Act in the way saw fit was altogether one which could only be exercised by the governing authority of the State.

Mr. Miller informed me that he would not attend the meeting of the Committee that afternoon but I persuaded him to do so. When the committee convened, Mr. Miller made a report of his activities and notified the committee that the aims and purposes delegated to him by the Association had been successfully achieved. Mr. Jacobs took the floor and in a tirade attacked the methods Mr. Miller had followed. When he had finished I rose and offered a resolution attesting to the high confidence and appreciation which the Committee held for Mr. Miller and for the manner in which he had so successfully managed and directed the campaign in Columbia and which would result in our having Negro teachers in our public schools and that a rising vote of thanks be given him. My motion was adopted by the vote of all present, save that of Jacobs—who refrained from voting.

The financial report showed that $237.00 had been expended by the Association in carrying on the fight. That amount however did not include all that was spent in bringing us victory for each of us assumed our own individual expenses on the Columbia trip or otherwise. In return for this outlay we got a variety of responses, some were gratifying as were the results of our victory and the entrance that year of about sixty Negro teachers into the City School system. And a little later by an increase in the membership of the N.A.A.C.P. from the ranks of our newly created group of teachers, and some were not and these came from some of the newly appointed teachers who refused to take membership in the Association because the Association had not gotten them their jobs "for they had received their positions by passing examinations."

Several months later, and much to my surprise and amazement I saw an article in *The Crisis* which described the change in the teaching personnel corps at the Negro schools in Charleston. It was accompanied with a photograph of the committee and was written by one of its members, who in it claimed, on his own behalf and on behalf of the other members of the committee all of the credit attached to the placement of Negro teachers in Charleston schools. Needless to say, that since I did not appear in the photograph nor was even mentioned in the article, that I had no previous knowledge about its publication, as I had none.

As I said the article surprised me very much, as it was difficult for me to understand why this particular group of men, the same group, who when they were told by Mr. Miller at that if success was wanted, that it was absolutely necessary for them to abandon their methods and procedures and to immediately do the things which I had previously advised them to do, who then and there placed everything under my direction and accepted service as my assistants, doing only the things which I directed them to do, should seek to claim all of the credit for the achievement.

And moreover, with the exception of Mr. Harleston who rendered valuable service in many ways, the others who did serve acted only as canvassers getting signatures to our petitions. As a matter of fact the committee had no meetings between the one held at Dr. Johnson's office and the one held at Harleston's when it received Mr. Miller's final report. During the interim between these meetings, which was the period in which public sentiment was aroused through Mr. Grace's editorials on behalf of our cause, and in which there also was carried on a campaign among the Negroes to acquaint them fully with what was going on and why it was taking place, for the masses of the Negroes knew nothing about it until the petitions were circulated, everything which was accomplished was by either Mr. Miller in Columbia or me in Charleston. None of which was directed by the Committee or of which they had preknowledge. During that interval Mr. Miller and I were in constant communication and through that means were able to coordinate our efforts.

The members of the committee had full knowledge of what I had done to make the fight a successful one. Not only from their personal experience but also from Mr. Miller's final report where he emphasized that it was largely through my efforts and my directions that the Negro teachers had gotten into the public schools. Hence I was surprised when I saw the article in *The Crisis* in which the committee claimed all the credit for doing what was done.

But even more surprising than the action of the committee, was the action of a large number of Negroes, some two-hundred and eighty of whom presented a petition to the School Board in which they prayed that white teachers be retained in the schools. But since many of these were employed as domestics in the homes of whites, who desired to have the status quo remain, it made me feel that they signed the petition under duress—and which perhaps made their action somewhat excusable. But I could see no excuse whatsoever for the many, some of them prominent Negro families, who refused to sign our petition. Though strange to say some of them were among the first to seek employment for their children in the schools when they were opened to Negro teachers.

It is a question if the committee ever sought to fathom the possible effects which could have arisen from the petition which the School Board received, and that had that petition been presented in evidence at the Joint Committee's hearing, I could in the absence of a contradicting petition, have such weight with the Joint Committee that it might have defeated our aims.

Despite the fact that the existence of that petition was generally known nothing was done by the committee to offset its possible ill effects or to circumvent it until I undertook the circulation of our petition. And since the number who signed ours so far outnumbered those who had signed the petition to the School Board, praying that white teachers be retained, their petition was not presented at the Joint Committee hearing in

Columbia. For had that been done it would have strengthened our case.

Neither do I believe that the committee ever realized what force there was in our petition and that it held sufficient potential power which could be used in bringing the issue before the courts, had it not been otherwise settled. Which was pointed out by Mr. Grace in one of his editorials in the *Charleston American* at the time in which he asserted that the results of our petition was tantamount to a vote since it expressed the desire of the majority of Charleston's Negroes.

And now closing this part of my narrative which tells how Negro teachers got into the public schools of Charleston, I must add that the article in *The Crisis* did not create any rancor within me. Neither did I feel embarrassed by what it left unsaid—as the personal satisfaction I derived from doing what I could to bring about the change was altogether ample for me.

Edith having completed the high school course at Avery was now ready to enter college. I had visited Nashville a few years previously and while there had investigated Fisk University with the idea of sending her there and being much impressed with the atmosphere which then surrounded the school—the quiet cultured demeanor displayed by the girls as they strolled about the campus at the rear of Jubilee Hall, all of them clad in blue uniform dresses and black sailor straw hats, separated from all contacts with Jefferson street by a huge iron gate and from their male coeds by a distance of nearly two blocks and an insurmountable barricade of teacher chaperones—did so. Perhaps had I the opportunity then, which I later had by seeing the inside of the basement floor of Jubilee Hall with its myriads of roaches as I did when she graduated or knew that the front gate had been removed, I may have changed my mind. But being ignorant of these and also because my sister Lottie was then attending Fisk and the insistent praises Maud Smith that Fisk was the very best school for her, I reached my decision and sent her application in.

On August 20th, 1919 the stork paid us another visit. This time it was "Buddy" who came. He was a splendidly formed baby who remained with us but a few hours. We named him William Thompson, after our two friends—Dr. William M. Thorne and Dr. John M. Thompson. The passing of "Buddy" came as a shock to us as none of us had the slightest idea that such could happen. But it did, leaving us a memory that we never like to recall.

Buddy's passing brought us an awakening—an awakening to the realization that Edith had passed from girlhood into young womanhood. By the capable and thoughtful manner in which she assumed the duty and making of all of the arrangement for "Buddy's" funeral.

The back room of the old drugstore once again became the scene in which our group undertook its first step in the field of banking. As it was there that the Charleston Mutual Savings Bank came into existence. But since there is so much to be told about the Bank and about its origin, its existence and its ending—they shall be told later on.

150 Ashley Avenue

When I bought 150 Ashley Avenue, I had acquired it under a tenancy lease which did not expire until January 1, 1921. Until then it continued as a rental property. When I got possession of it on that date, I immediately had Tom Pinckney begin the work of remodeling it. As I intended moving there and making it our future home. Before the repairs were completed, a real estate broker from the firm of W.T. Thompson & Co. offered to buy the place, offering me $14,000.00 and the assumption of all bills so far contracted for the repair work. I declined the offer and shortly thereafter moved our home there.

A few months after we were installed there, Montague Triest, a real estate broker called on me and stated that he wanted to buy the place and would offer me $12,000.00 for it. I told him that I was not interested in selling it as I intended to live in it. He then said that the High School of Charleston wanted it as part of the site which the[y] had chosen for a new high school building and that if I did not accept his offer that the school would condemn the property and take it anyhow. I told him that I did not think they could do so and that I would stand on my rights.

I soon learned that the high school plans were. And that they had already purchased the "Moose Home" building on Rutledge Avenue at the rear of my place and the Barkerding property next to it. Paying $32,000.00 for the Barkerding Place and $30,000.00 for the Moose Home. They had also bought the two places on Ashley Avenue, south from the Smith's home, leaving only my place and those belonging to Dr. Johnson at the north of me yet unacquired for the completion of their plans. A few days after these properties had been bought, the Trustees for the High School advertised for bids for the removal of the buildings and clearing of the land. I became interested in the Moose Home and acquiring it if possible. So I got Tom Pinckney to go with me to examine it and see if it could be rolled over to the southern part of my lot. As it would make a very desirable apartment building. We did so but found that its dimensions and construction was such that it could not be rolled across my lot. Otherwise I would have bought it and done so.

The construction of the new high school building quickly got under way when the ground had been cleared. When the rear foundations were placed I found that they had encroached upon Dr. Johnson's rear line by six inches. In fact it was beneath one of his houses. I went to see Johnson and told him what had been done and advised him to notify the school and also the builders about their encroachment and to make them withdraw to their property line. I pointed out to him that by doing so at once, what he could sell his property to them at a more advantageous price then, than he could do at a later time, for if he should knowingly allow them to continue construction that it would only cause him future trouble.

But it was not Dr. Johnson who was in for future trouble, and did not know it—it was I who was going to have it and a plenty at that. And that became apparent a few days later when I saw an account in the newspapers that the Charleston County Delegation to the General Assembly had introduced a bill in the Legislature in which the right of eminent domain would be conferred upon the High School of Charleston through which they could condemn and acquire property desired for its use.

The measure prescribed the methods by which the condemnation value would be determined—by having the property appraised by a jury of six men who would set its price. Which if it was not acceptable could be appealed against, only however to be referred to a second jury of six men, whose appraisal price would be final.

When I learned of this, I quickly realized the meaning behind Montague Triest's threat that "they would condemn it and take it away from me." And perhaps do that with an award which would not exceed the $12,000.00 offer which Triest had made. I immediately conferred with my attorney, Thad Sasportas, who had recently come to Charleston, and decided to present a protest to the County Delegation against the measure. Also that we attempt to secure the services of a local white attorney who possessed sufficient political power to cope with the situation. Sasportas suggested that I see Mr. Joseph Barnwell. I knew him as he was the attorney who examined the titles for the drugstore building when I bought it. I called on him and stated my case. He listened to me and when I had finished said, "I am sorry that I cannot take your case. But sit down a while longer I want to tell you some things." He started by telling me that he had had considerable experience with condemnation proceedings while serving as attorney for several of the railroads operating in South Carolina and that he was considered by many of his colleagues as being an authority on the "right of eminent domain" and that he wanted me to know what some of the most difficult conditions were when it became necessary to determine the compensation. One of these he said involved the inclusion in the compensation of the full amount of any exist[ing] liens against the property as it was very difficult to depreciate the value of a negotiable interest by a condemnation verdict. I saw the point and on leaving thanked Mr. Barnwell and told him that I regretted very much that he could not help me.

I immediately returned to Sasportas' office and told him of my conversation with Mr. Barnwell. He considered the mention about an existing lien a very good suggestion and that we could consider that at a later time. But for the present, it would be best for me to see a member of the County Delegation and seek to have the measure withdrawn or to have it referred to Committee before whom we could appear to protest its enactment.

I went to see Representative Thomas McMillan and told him what the proposed act would do to me. I said that I was convinced that it was not so much for the purpose of obtaining my property as it was for obtaining it at the price which Mr. Triest had offered. And that that would cause me much loss. And also, that previously to any knowledge by me about the bill, that I had offered to sell the property to the high school for the sum of $30,000.00 which I did not consider an exorbitant price.

I explained that Mr. Triest's offer of $12,000.00 was less than what I had spent in remodeling the building and for [furnishings] which would become worthless for use elsewhere than in my present home and that I had refused an offer of $14,000.00 several months before Mr. Triest made his. Mr. McMillan promised me that he would present the matter to the Delegation as he felt that it was not their intent to cause me any loss and that he would let me know what their attitude was by the following morning.

I was there on the following morning and much to my surprise found Mr. McMillan somewhat agitated. He told me that he had presented by case to the Delegation and in reply had been warned not to interfere—and also that Mr. Rutledge Rivers, the Chairman of the Trustee Board of the High School, had threatened him with political extinction if he dared to take the part of a Negro against a white high school. I told Mr. McMillan that I appreciated what he had done in my behalf. But that I could not think of accepting any further help from him if such would jeopardize his political career. And that I would continue to use every possible method to avert the harm which the bill would impose upon me, even though it meant going before the United States Supreme Court as the matter had now become more than one of values for it now involved that of principle and that I would spend my last penny and exhaust every avenue before I would submit to its impositions.

I saw Sasportas at once and told him what McMillan had said. We knew that the measure would soon be ready for its second reading in the Legislature and perhaps would receive final action within the next few days. But when the day, we did not know. Neither could we learn. Moreover since the County Delegation had refused to present the bill to Committee for public hearing, that barred me from the opportunity to appear before that Committee to protest its enactment. We knew that the usual procedure required all bills to pass through the appropriate committee and that this particular measure should have gone before the Judiciary Committee that the question of its constitutionality could be passed upon before it got its second reading. We therefore decided to write the Judiciary Committee and to petition it to grant me a hearing. And which was done on Jan. 19th, 1922 in the following letter:

> To the Judiciary Committee of the Senate State of South Carolina, Columbia Gentlemen:
> I am asking the privilege of being permitted to appear before your Body at the hearing on the Bill to grant to The High School of Charleston, the right to confiscate or condemn property in the city of Charleston.
> This Bill if enacted into law will inflict a hardship upon me by forcing me to sell, without my consent or the right to state a compensation, my home and to accept whatever price a jury might award.
> The occasion for this Bill lies in the purchase, by The Charleston High School, of property on Rutledge Avenue, for purpose of erecting a new school building. Before construction was begun, Mr. Montague Triest, representing the Board, notified me that the Board desired to buy my home which is situated at the rear of

264 | RESISTING JIM CROW

the Rutledge Avenue property. I told Mr. Triest that I did not care to dispose of my home unless it was absolutely necessary to the school because it was not an easy matter for me to purchase a desirable home. I signified my willingness to give the Board an option on my home if they in turn would secure me an option on an equally desirable property in a neighborhood which would have no antipathies to a Negro. Mr. Triest intimated that a refusal would only result in condemnation proceedings and the taking over of my home by the school. I made an offer to him of the property, which however, he considered exorbitant. My price was based on what it would cost to duplicate my home, the costs of securing another home (not the purchase price), the costs of moving and for furnishing which would become useless. I suggested that the Board have its Architect inspect my home and confirm the valuation I placed upon it. This was declined and instead, I find through the newspapers that power is being sought from the Legislature to confiscate or condemn and which if granted will place me in jeopardy of having my home taken over by the Board without my consent or the right to state a compensation.

I am not opposing the program for better educational facilities but seeking protection from the wrongs which the proposed act will inflict. I am willing to sell the Board my home and made an offer to that effect several months ago. No reply has been made to it nor has the suggestion of an Architect's appraisal been followed. If this Bill should [pass] it would create an authority which could work to my detriment."

I signed the letter and mailed it that day. Before a reply could be received I learned that the Bill had been given its second reading. Which was somewhat unusual as it was only seldom that a bill got so far along the calendar during the first three weeks of any session. From all appearances it seemed that the measure was being "steamrolled" through the Legislature and being as it was a local measure that through "legislative courtesy" received no opposition. And as a matter of fact was being enacted by the "courtesy vote" of members who were altogether ignorant of its intent or were indifferent to it. For such was the customary attitude towards all bills of local import only when they were unanimously supported by a County Delegation.

Sasportas advised that I go to Columbia at once and seek to have the bill sent to Committee for a public hearing at which we could present our protest. I prepared and had printed an open letter addressed to the members of the General Assembly in which I stated my case. It recited how I had sought to have the members of the Charleston County Delegation allow me the privilege of appearing before the Delegation to plead my case and how one of its members who was impressed with the justice of my contention had sought to obtain that privilege for me and who had been threatened with political ostracism if he insisted that I be given that privilege. In addition to that I included all of the other pertinent facts as they affected me and closed the letter with a request that a hearing be granted me.

Armed with these letters I took the night train for Columbia arriving there early on the following morning. I went immediately to the Capitol where I found the janitors at work doing their morning cleaning under the supervision of a sergeant-at-arms. I spoke with him and requested him to allow me to place a copy of my letters upon the desks of every member and in the committee rooms. He said that he would do it for me. I thanked him and shook hands with him and left something in his hand.

I then left the Capitol and went in quest of Mr. Butler Nance a Colored attorney. I found him and we met at his office at 7 a.m. that morning to discuss my further plans. He suggested that we see Mr. Cooper who was a member of the Richland County Delegation and seek to obtain his help to have the measure referred to Committee. We met Mr. Cooper at 9 a.m. and told him about our mission. When I mentioned that Mr. McMillan was the member who had sought to have me accorded a hearing—he halted me and said "Tom McMillan is the only honest man on the Charleston County delegation, I know him. He and I were roommates at college. And if he wanted you to have a hearing, I'll see that you get it and get a fair one at that.

While at the Capitol that morning, I went over to the Association Press Bureau and gave the attendant a copy of my letter and told him to "release." It was somewhat dark at the time and the attendant seemed sleepy but however he managed to say "Yes sir" and that was that. After leaving Mr. Cooper's office, Mr. Nance took me over to the office of the Columbia State, where I asked that they publish the contents of my letter. Which they did. I did these things because I wanted the public to be fully informed about what was taking place and if possible to create in my behalf some degree of public sentiment, if not in Charleston then perhaps elsewhere. But especially among the members of the Legislature for it was in their power to mete out justice.

I then returned to the Capitol to see if my letters had been distributed in keeping with the promise given me. And found that it had been carried to an even greater extent than what I had anticipated as copies had been placed on the Speaker's and in the Lieutenant Governor's office. Also a goodly number had [been] placed in the Judiciary Committee room. I got several of the messengers to point out to me the more prominent members of the Legislature as they entered the building so that I could address them. In that way I was able to approach Mr. Christensen, the Senator from Beaufort. I did so and told him why I was there. I gave him one of my letters and asked him to support me. After he replied—"Why if this measure goes through then nobody's property in South Carolina will be safe. I will look into it." I remained there for about an hour and contacted a number of members, one of whom was Senator Edgar Brown whose support I also asked.

Before leaving the Capitol, I discussed my situation with one of the messengers. One who served in the committee room where Mr. Edgar Brown presided. He said that Mr. Brown had secured him his appointment and that he was from his hometown. He advised me to proceed as I was doing but that if things got bad, to have him speak with Mr. Brown and that he was sure that he could get Mr. Brown to represent me as my attorney, and who being a member of the Senate could oppose the measure when it came before that body.

I then returned to Nance's office but was there not more than fifteen minutes when the telephone rang. I was called to the phone and was told to come to the Capitol at once. I did so and found that it was the Speaker who wanted me. Mr. McMillan met me and took me in to the Speaker. Who told me that a public hearing had been granted and that it would be held on the following afternoon at 4 o'clock in the Judiciary Committee room. That representatives from the high school would be there and that each side would be allowed fifteen minutes in which to present their case.

While at the Capitol I learned that my letters had created a furor and that a heated argument had ensued in which Mr. McMillan took part and said that "Everything which McFall has said is true and he should have his hearing."

Lieutenant Governor Harvey G. Wilson called me to his office and upbraided me for the statements I had made in my letter. He said that the members of the Charleston Delegation intended doing the right thing by me but that my letter had alienated them and that they would now do nothing to help me. I told him that what I had written was true and that if there was any doubt about it that the Legislature could subpoena me and I would testify under oath to what I claimed had been done to me. And that while I regretted to learn what the attitude of the Delegation was, I would yet continue to fight against the enactment of the bill and if it was passed that I would fight it up to the United States Supreme Court.

I returned to Nance's office and phoned Sasportas, telling him to come to Columbia at once to be with me at the hearing on the following afternoon. But to try to be there early so that we could plan our presentation. While I was in Columbia, Sasportas had not been idle. He had had Tom Pinckney to execute an affidavit in which he described No. 150 Ashley Avenue, its original construction and the changes and repairs that were made by him for me and the cost of doing that. And in addition, an estimate of what it would cost to duplicate the buildings. He brought these with him so that they could be placed in evidence should it be necessary to do so.

That night the weather became intensely cold and a blizzard came. Columbia was covered with a heavy snowfall. I was never before so numbed with cold as I was that night. I was compelled to get up during the night and put on my flannel underwear but even then when I got back in bed I could not sleep as it was too cold to sleep. When I arose I was unable to find water with which to bathe as everything was frozen hard. Finally I got some and took a "canary" [bath] and after eating breakfast went to Mr. Nance's office where Mr. Sasportas met us.

We decided to restrict our presentation to only the issues involved and to avoid any generalities, especially such that could inject the question of race into the discussion. Which reduced our scope of opposition to the bill to those matters in which ownership rights, the valuation of property, and the lack of assurance in the bill that justice would be meted out.

I told my attorneys that we would divide our fifteen minutes into three periods of five minutes each. Mr. Sasportas to take the first and make the opening. That I would follow him and review the entire matter from its incipiency up to the present. That the closing period should be used by either Mr. Sasportas or by me. While Mr. Nance was to carefully observe and note everything that should be either corrected or injected at the closing. I impressed upon them to "soft pedal" and leave it to me to do otherwise. Should I deem it necessary.

The hearing was held in the Judiciary Committee room. When it convened I found that it was a joint hearing in which both the House and Senate committees participated. The Chairman read the bill and introduced Mr. Young, the Senator from Charleston County who explained why the measure had been presented and why its passage was necessary. For said he, it is necessary that the Trustees acquire sufficient land that the building now under construction can be completed and put into use.

Mr. Sasportas followed Mr. Young. Mr. Sasportas entered a protest against the bill and stated that the measure was in all reality but a "sword of Damocles" held over McFall, and which should it be allowed to pass would through its passing fall on him alone, since it was devoid of any other intent, except against him. He emphasized the possibility of injustice arising against me at the hands of a jury who may or may not be qualified to pass upon real estate values. Since the jury designated in the bill were not required to be "six men" of special qualifications but merely "six men" who may or may not possess the necessary qualifications that would enable them to impartially and to accurately determine the value of my home. But worse that this said he, is the provision in the measure whereby an appeal against a first verdict must be made, not to any court of competent jurisdiction but to a second jury only, one similar to the first, from whose verdict there is no appeal. He assured them that I was not seeking to prevent the Trustees from attaining what they wanted but that I only wanted to be made secure in the holding of what belonged to me. And that under the bill there was no guarantee that justice would be done. And that in my behalf, he asked that the bill be reported unfavorably.

Mr. Daniel Sinkler, a real estate broker from Charleston was the next speaker for the Trustees. He opened with telling about the plans of the Trustees to provide additional high- school facilities for the white youth of Charleston and about the purchases the Trustees had already made. That so far it bought only from whites and that McFall was not the only Negro they expected to buy from as the expected to buy some places from Dr. Johnson and that they intended to treat them fairly. That it was not the intention of the Board to seek any advantage over them because they were Negroes. At which I interrupted by asking the Chairman to request Mr. Sinkler to avoid the injection of race into the hearing, as the matter before the Committee involved only values and ownership rights. Mr. Sinkler granted my request after making a few more remarks sat down.

When I was with Mr. Miller at the Joint Committee hearing in the school-teacher fight, I had observed how he managed to stretch his time allowance by questioning his opponents. So when I arose, I did likewise by asking the Chairman's permission to ask Mr. Sinkler a few questions. At which he glanced towards Mr. Sinkler who nodded in acquiescence. I began by asking him "What was the price the Trustees paid for Mr. Barkerding's home?" He replied $32,000.00 "And for the Moose home?" I asked. $30,000.00 he answered. Then I asked "What was the combined frontage of these two places?" "About 175 feet," he replied.

I then asked if he knew what the frontage of my lot was; he said it was about 160 feet (in reality it was only 112 feet). I then asked him what in his opinion was the relative value of my home to that of the Moose Home. He said that in his opinion the Moose Home was worth about two and two and a half times, the value of mine. So I asked him had he ever made an examination of my home for the purpose of appraising its value. He countered by saying that he knew the property well. That years before while Mr. Reeves resided there that he was a frequent visitor there and had the opportunity of going through it. He knew that it was a splendidly constructed building but that it was now an old building. I asked him had he visited the place after I had repaired and remodeled it. To which he said "No." So then I asked, "Mr. Sinkler since you have never inspected my home since I remodeled it, your opinion about its value is only arrived at from what your recollection of what it was when Mr. Reeves resided there, many

years before I bought it and is altogether based upon that recollection and is without any knowledge of what it now is?" He
answered "Yes."

I noticed that several of the committee were smiling but I
went on asking Mr. Sinkler what was the price paid by the Trustees for the Moose Home. He said that it was $30,000.00. I next
asked, "How much did the Moose Home pay Mr. Marks for it?"
Then Sinkler got rattled. He said it was like this, that Mr. Marks
was a very old gentleman who had retired from active work and
who wanted to get rid of his home and for that reason had sold it
to the Moose Lodge for $10,000.00 but that is was worth far more
than that. I then asked, had not the Mark's lot, with a frontage
about half that of mine, in its purchase by the school, acquired a
three-fold increase in value within the two-year period in which
the Moose Lodge held it. And again he answered "Yes."

The Judiciary Committee room was entirely too small to
allow seating accommodations for all who were there. For in
addition to the Committee and those who appeared for their
respective sides there were a number of legislators present. Most
of whom were standing. Mr. Cooper was one of them and I had
offered him my seat. But he declined and was now squatting
on the floor. When Mr. Sinkler replied to my last question, Mr.
Cooper leaned forward and in a whisper said to me, "You people in Charleston don't seem to know that a financial crisis is
approaching." I said, "No but if this bill goes through it will bring
me one."

I then addressed the Committee (my time had now only
started). I explained that I was willing to sell my home to the
Trustees and had so informed Mr. Triest. But since the price
he offered me was only $12,000.00 I could not accept it as I had
already spent over $11,000.00 in remodeling, repairing and fur-
nishing it. Not to mention its purchase price. That I did not consider the price I asked an exorbitant one. As it certainly did not
reflect the possibility of yielding a profit to anything approaching

that which the Mark's home did. That I had offered the Trustees the privilege of having their architect examine my property and estimate what it would cost to duplicate it. But that that offer was never accepted. For had it been then the Trustees could have easily informed themselves as to the correctness of my asking price.

Continuing, I said, if this measure is enacted and a jury should award me $6,000.00 or any amount which to them was deemed sufficient, The Trustees could deposit whatever that amount was with the court, and evict me and take my home away from me. I cannot see any other application of the proposed act, except against me and since all of these possibilities are couched in the act, I must ask the Committee to save me from the injustice it may inflict by recommending that the bill be not passed.

Mr. Frank Frost, one of the Trustees then rose and said, that he had had no previous knowledge about the bill and that this was his first information about the matter and that he wanted it known that so long as he was a Trustee of the School that he would not allow that injustice to happen. And moreover that he did not know if the school had the money to buy my place at that time.

Mr. Sasportas in closing asked that since the school had no intention of buying at that time, that the measure be reported unfavorably. Since its enactment would in all reality make it a sword of Damocles which would continue to hang over my head and would become a force that would impair the value of my property.

The Chairman announced the hearing at an end and we left. On my way out I spoke with Mr. Frost and told him that if the high school wanted the place and did not have the money to pay cash with at the time, that I would sell to them on terms and that the only security I would require would be the bond of the Trustees supported with a mortgage of the property.

Though we were confident that our presentation had been effective we nevertheless could not feel assured that the measure would be killed as it was still on the calendar. On our way back to Charleston that night Mr. Sasportas and I discussed our future program. As we neared Charleston we could see that the blizzard which had struck Columbia the night before had visited Charleston. For when we got there we found the city covered with several inches of frozen sleet. Only the trolley cars were running and it was dangerous to walk on the streets. However I did manage to get home safely.

Our future plans required me to make a trip to New York where I would seek to obtain the services of the N.A.A.C.P. in getting for me the very best legal advice that could be obtained. And in addition to put into effect a "prior lien" against my home. Mr. Sasportas had already prepared a mortgage for $25,000.00 which I was to take with me for the negotiation of a loan in that amount. It may sound somewhat funny for me to say that I intended borrowing $25,000.00 in New York. Not that I needed any money or even expected to receive any—as I only intended to borrow that amount and attach it all as added collateral to my loan. And to pay the interest separately and in advance. In this way any bank would be absolutely safe as it would have the full amount borrowed in their possession at all times and the right to use it for the settlement of my debt at any time after its due date. In fact it would be making money (its interest charge) by merely recording my loan. And since Mr. Barnwell had said that the existence of a lien was always a difficulty. We decided to create one.

I started for New York that night, overtaking the blizzard, which had now taken a northerly course. When we neared Richmond, my train became snowbound and was halted. Eventually, we got started again and made it to Washington. Where I found everything halted by the heavy snowfall. The night before the Knickerbocker Theater roof had collapsed [28 January 1922] under the heavy weight of snow upon it killing a large number of people. The snow about the Union Station was about six feet deep and all railroad traffic was in a tangle. I had bought reservations only to Washington but after leaving Richmond I got reservation in the New York coach. When we reached Washington I had the porter transfer my bags to the New York coach. The food supply in the diner had been exhausted by the time we reached Richmond. I had had breakfast but that was many hours before. So I looked up the conductor and asked him how long would it be in Washington and if I would have time to get a meal in the restaurant. He told me that we would pull out at 11 p.m. It was then about 9 p.m. So I went to the restaurant and got supper, returning to where my train had been at 10 o'clock, only to see it disappearing in the distance.

I got after the train master and told him that I had been misinformed about my train's departure and that by bags were on it. He directed me to the Pullman headquarters where I was given an exchange of berths on a later train. The Pullman agent telegraphed Baltimore and had my bags placed in the custody of the conductor from whom I received the following morning when I arrived in New York. I was somewhat perturbed that night for the executed mortgage was in my lost bag and had it gotten into the hands of an unscrupulous person could have been negotiated to my loss. I had notified the Pullman agent that the bag contained valuable papers and if they were lost that I would institute suit for damages. Which perhaps accounted for the promptness with which they located and took charge of my luggage.

On arriving in New York I immediately went to the offices of the N.A.A.C.P. where I met Mr. Walter White. I told him what my mission was and that I wanted the Association to help me by putting me in touch with an attorney in whom I could place implicit confidence. And that I was not seeking to have the Association take up my fight, as that was altogether my private affair for which I expected to pay the full cost. But since the matter would perhaps reach the United States Supreme Court I wanted to be prepared for that emergency by having at my disposal the best obtainable legal counsel.

Mr. White assured me that he knew such a firm of attorneys and that he would take me to them at once. And that it was the firm of Studin and Springarn, both of whom were officers of the N.A.A.C.P. as well as its principal legal advisers. We went to their office at once where I was introduced to them. I told them what my mission was and that I wanted to obtain their services to aid me in freeing myself from the predicament in which I had been placed.

I explained that the High School of Charleston was not a public school. But was altogether a quasi-public corporation which operated a high school for white boys in Charleston. That the corporation was non-profit sharing and was without capital stock. And had been in existence for more than seventy-five years. During most of which period its pupils paid a tuition fee. Which fee was largely determined by the amount of public funds contributed towards its operation and towards the payment of interest accruing on certain of its bonds. Neither was it a part of the free public school system of the city but was altogether a private institution which operated under the direction of its Board of Trustees in whose names its properties were vested. It was to this Board of Trustees, I said, that the right of eminent domain would be granted under the bill which I was opposing and which if enacted into law would enable them to take my home away from me and to use it for such purposes which it saw fit, by merely filing notice with the court of common pleas of that intent, and the further appointment of not more than two juries who would determine what award should be given me. And against which I could make no appeal whatsoever.

I told them about my conversations with Montague Triest, who as the representative of the Trustees had offered me $12,000.0 for my property. Which I refused and in reply had offered to sell it to them for $30,000.00. And that it was in reply to that proffer that the Trustees had had the County Delegation to the General Assembly introduce the bill there.

I next explained the transactions which surrounded the sale of the "Moose Home" property on Rutledge Avenue to the Trustees for $30,000.00. And which was supposedly the property of the Moose Lodge but which in reality belonged to the "Home Corporation"—a holding company of which Montague Triest, Thomas Stoney, Leo Kanapaux and seven others, most of them political figures in the community, were the Corporators and who had bought the property from Mr. Marks for $10,000.00 and later sold it to the Trustees for $30,000.00. All of which I had verified from the records at the R.M.C. office. And I having knowledge that Montague Triest was a partner in the Home Corporation was impelled to the belief that his offer was made with the intent of securing my home at the price he offered me and then selling it later at a profit. And that when I refused to do so, that it caused him to seek to carry out his threat to have my home condemned and taken away from me.

I then told them, that I had invested over $19,000.00 in the property and that my proffer at $30,000.00 did not appear to me to be exorbitant when compared with the prices which had been paid for other property that had been bought as the site for the new school building. All of which averaged a one-hundred percent profit. While what was asked by me was slightly under sixty percent and which had it been obtained would have been diminished by what it would cost to find another home.

I showed Mr. Studin the mortgage I had brought with me and asked his advice about placing it with a bank. I told him that the idea which prompted me to make it, had come from a conversation with Mr. Barnwell, a very eminent lawyer in Charleston who had declined to serve as my attorney. Both he and Mr. Springarn advanced the opinion that by placing the mortgage at so late a date as it then was, would perhaps prejudice my case. So they advised me against doing it. Which I followed.

They expressed the opinion that I had already done all that was necessary in preparing the way to take the matter before the courts, even to the United States Supreme Court if that was necessary. Both of them assured me that they would do all within their power to help me and that I could consider them as my counsel. They said that they could not then advise me what further actions to take. Since that could not be decided upon until after the Legislature had acted on the bill. For if the measure was defeated or if it was withdrawn, then that would end it. But that if it was enacted that the procedure would be to seek a restraining injunction. I expressed my gratitude to them and to Mr. White, who had remained with us during our conference and that night returned to Charleston.

I was never able to learn just what did happen to the bill. But about ten days after my return from New York, Mr. Rutledge Rivers the Chairman of the Trustee Board called and told me that the Trustees would not need to buy my home and that the incident was settled. I thanked him for that and told him that it was not altogether a matter of selling with me but the even more difficult one of securing a desirable home location as that was a very difficult matter for Negroes. He said that he knew it and then he told me what had been done to Dr. Seabrook, who had taken an option and had paid a part of the purchase price on the property at the S.W. corner of Ashley and Cannon Streets, by several members of the Holy Communion Church who objected to a Negro living near their church.

I told Mr. Rivers that I thought it would be necessary for the Trustees to secure a portion of my rear lot so that they would have a communicating passage between the northern and southern portions of their lot. He wanted to see what I had reference to. So we went to the rear where I showed him what they needed. I then offered to make a donation of not more than twenty feet or less than ten feet of my rear lot for that purpose. Mr. Rivers was amazed at my offer. He told me that I was magnanimous and that he would call a meeting of the Trustees that evening and present my offer to them.

I felt that my offer would partake of the characteristics of a hot potato in the mouth when it reached the Trustees. As perhaps if a bequest given by a Negro was accepted might it not serve as an entering wedge whereby Negro pupils could gain admission to its school. So I was not surprised the next day, when Nick Sottile, one of the Trustees came to and said "Doctor the Board want[s] you to set a price on the lot." I replied that my offer to donate the land had been given and that I could not refute it. He replied "Don't mind that the Board has got money and is willing to pay what you ask. So don't be bashful—take the money."

I smiled as I said to him "Perhaps it was the Board did not care to accept a bequest from a Negro." To which he gave sheepish grin. So I told him to tell the Board that I would convey a portion of the lot to them if they would reimburse me what it would cost to move my garage to another portion of my lot. And that I would have my contractor give me an estimate for doing it. His estimate was $500 and was accepted by them. A few days later Mr. Rivers phoned me and asked me to call at his office with my wife to sign the deed. We did so and after signing it and delivering it to Mr. Rivers found that Mr. Rivers had forgotten to get the check. He was much embarrassed and asked me to take the deed with me and to deliver it when I received payment. But I told him to keep the deed and that they could mail me the check. Which was done the next day. I made that concession because I wanted to live there and I believed that by doing so that I would be able to enjoy a more peaceful residency there than I otherwise could. For by doing this I knew that I had created some friendships on the Board.

Several days later, Nick Sottile came to see me and showed me a contract, signed by Dr. Johnson, in which he had agreed to sell all of his places, consisting of a sixty-foot frontage on Ashley Avenue with two-hundred-and-forty feet in depth, with five two-story buildings thereon for $5,000.00. I told him that he should be ashamed of that. That they were gyping the doctor. I asked how had he done it. He said that he had asked the doctor what would he take for the places, and that he said $6,000.00. At which he said, he expressed surprise and told Dr. Johnson "that he knew him to be a public-spirited citizen" and that the property had not cost him that much and in addition that the rents he had received from it had already reimbursed him for his investment. So would he let the school have it for $5,000.00. At which Johnson swallowed the bait and signed an agreement by which he conveyed to the high school $8,5000.00 worth of real estate for $5,000.00.

Sometime after that incident I had another conversation with Sottile. It took place at the bank and we were talking about our line fences. We had never before discussed the bill which had been introduced in the Legislature. But that day our conversation involved some of it—and just to see what his reaction would be, I said, "Now we have been talking "Moose Home" all along let's now call it by its real name, "Home Corporation." He smiled broadly and rose and said "Goodbye McFall."

But that was not all that I learned from Sottile as there was also that in which he told me that Mr. Grace, who was then the mayor, had planned the erection of a modern high school building for Negroes. And knowing Mr. Grace as I did, I had every reason to believe that had he continued in office longer that it would have come to pass.

Since I was now assured of the possession of my home, I wrote Mr. Spingarn and told him the matter had been satisfactorily settled and would he let me have a bill for his services. I was surprised when I got it. For it was for only $25.00. Which I quickly and thankfully paid. But even more welcome than was his bill was the very kind letter he wrote me in commendation of the manner in which I had carried my fight through.

Of course the whole thing was far from being a pleasant experience as at times it became definitely threatening. For once I received a threat that my home would be burned down. I replied to that by announcing that I had a gun and a plenty of ammunition and that there would be some shooting first—and also by placing an additional amount of fire insurance on the buildings.

What has so far been told about 150 Ashley Avenue would be incomplete if I did not include with it my acknowledgement for the valuable experience I acquired while observing the tactics which Mr. Miller used when he appeared before the Joint Committee in support of the bill to supplant white teachers in the Negro public schools of Charleston with Negro teachers. As it was largely through the use of similar tactics that we were able to expose the true nature of the intent behind the high school bill.

During the while that fight was taking place, the construction of the two new buildings, that on the corner to house the drugstore and the other for renting, had been completed, and their fixtures installed. The fixtures in the front shop of the drugstore, with the exception of the wrapping counter, were all new. And even that exception, the wrapping counter had been so modernized that others could not identify it. I kept it for sentimental reasons—for it had been with me from the beginning of my business career and was linked with too many memories of bygone days to permit me to discard it.

Persecution Leads to an Exodus

THE KLAN IN CHARLESTON

Some of these memories recalled the kindly relationships that once prevailed between the races in Charleston and which now was rapidly disappearing. And what a difference there now was. What pertained during the early 1890s no longer existed and even the more strained relationships of twenty years later were being ruthlessly destroyed by the forces which sought to make racial hatred its chief means to political ascendency.

John P. Grace, recently reelected to the mayoralty, had achieved his victory by defeating the old conservative faction and their newer allies in one of the most bitter and vicious political campaigns the city had ever witnessed. And in which T.T. Hyde and Senator Rhett were made the chief target of attack and with such telling effect that their faction was well-nigh destroyed. Their new allies, the Klan, fared better however for when the campaign had ended it had increased its membership and had embarked upon a drive for an even greater membership. Much knowledge of which could be had by seeing the extensive use they made of the mail for distributing pamphlets which carried an open invitation to membership. So indiscriminately were they sent forth that it could be seen that they were being sent to all persons whose names were listed in public directories. Even I got one. Needless to say, that I was perturbed by it. For I was. As I realized fully what the spread of that organization and its purposes meant for Negroes. So I sent my pamphlets to Mr. Walter White of the N.A.A.C.P. that he would have some information on what was taking place.

At first there was little more to excite our attention to the Klan. But one night when it held a public ceremony on nearby John's Island it created consternation among the Negroes who lived there. For when their huge wood cross was burned, the reflection from its burning could be seen for miles around, which so alarmed the Negroes that they became panicky. I afterwards talked with some and found that it was not so much the fear of the hooded riders that they dreaded as it was a premonition that further living on John's Island would be neither pleasant nor safe.

The majority of these Negroes were farmworkers or tenant farmers. Many of them were employed on farms owned by whites. The ceremony took place at the time when the crops were ready for harvesting. And so frightened these workers that hundreds of them immediately left the island without pausing to harvest their crops or to help with the harvesting of their employer's crops. And since these Negroes were the only available workers to do it, the farm owners were faced with a dilemma. Which was not so much one that was created by the Negroes but by one which was created by the Klan. The resultant labor famine brought the farm owners face to face with the realization that they and not the Negroes would be the principal financial sufferers from the coming of the Klansmen. And that unless the exodus was stopped they would face financial loss.

Several of the farmers wrote letters to the newspapers asking that the appearance of the Klan in rural areas be stopped and so insistent were these pleas that they succeeded in stopping the public appearance of the order.

It did not however stop the increasing hostility trend towards Negroes. Not by overt acts so much as it was by the changing attitudes of whites who formerly were more friendlier disposed towards Negroes. But who now had become less so.

One night a group of hooded whites visited a premises on Nassau Street near the corner of Columbus. They walked into the yard and looked around but did not molest the residents. After which they went away. The police department was notified. They sent an officer to investigate the matter but nothing came from it—except that the Negroes who lived there and their friends, experienced a greater sense of insecurity than they formerly did.

One night shortly after that incident, Thad Sasportas came to the drugstore and told me to come outside, that he wanted to speak with me but did not care to have those in the store overhear what was said. I did so and took a seat in his car where he told me about an incident which had happened that afternoon in which Dr. A.G. Purvis was involved. The incident had its beginning that afternoon while Purvis was driving his car down Meeting Street. Where when he had reached the corner of Broad the traffic light signaled the stop command. When the car in front of his came to a sudden stop and his being so close behind it bumped into it doing no damage whatsoever. Upon which one of the occupants of the front car, turned and cursed him. To which he replied, only to have one of them (both were white) come towards him with an automobile crank handle in his hand, threatening to beat him with it. And that Purvis said to the man "You start hitting and I will start cutting." That Purvis then drove away but was followed by the others in their car who overtook him some distance away from the scene of the trouble. Where one of the men, Michael by name, threatened to beat him up for cursing them. After an argument in which no blows were struck, Purvis went to his office.

That night while he was at home, a woman, who was rather heavily veiled, came and told Mrs. Purvis that Dr. Purvis' life was in danger and that she had come to warn him. She said that she was employed as maid at the Huguenin home on Legare Street and that that night a group of men had met there and that she had overheard them talking about what Dr. Purvis had done to one of their number and what they were going to do in retaliation.

From how she described those who had gathered there, it could be seen that they were all men of local prominence. As some were lawyers and some held high financial position in the city. None of them could in any way be considered as being a part of the rabble. For they were not. But yet they had all met and though versed in the law, they had decided to administer condign punishment upon Dr. Purvis, not so much because of what he had done. But only because it was a Negro who had done it. Which I am sure would never had been done had all parties to the incident been white.

Their plan, she said, was to have constables from Magistrate Whaley's office serve a warrant on him early the following morning, if possible before he arose, and under the pretense of "resisting arrest" to set upon him and beat him up unmercifully.

She would not disclose her identity even though Mrs. Purvis begged her to do so. She left the house immediately after giving her warning and was never again heard of or seen.

My advice was to get Dr. Purvis away at once. And if not out of town, then to my home for the present at least. We conveyed that message to him and told him to pack a handbag so that he could be ready to leave at once. I suggested to Sasportas that we call upon Mayor Grace and tell him about the trouble and seek to have him give Dr. Purvis protection. While we were discussing that, we received word that an automobile filled with white men had driven slowly by Dr. Purvis' home and had carefully looked it over.

I phoned Mr. Grace and told him that I would like to have a talk with him about a very urgent matter. He was at his office at the *Charleston American* and told me to come down at once. Sasportas and I went together. We told Mr. Grace what had happened and that we had planned to secretly take Dr. Purvis out of the city. Mr. Grace said "No, that must not be done, for if Dr. Purvis had to leave the city to avoid mob violence, that it would be the same as if he had been lynched and so long as I am mayor of Charleston, nothing like that shall ever happen." He immediately phoned the Chief of Police, Mr. [illegible] and told him what had happened, and that he must send a squad of policemen, armed with rifles, to Dr. Purvis residence, with orders to shoot any who should attempt to invade his home.

Mr. Grace then said, "I cannot ask any favors of Magistrate Whaley as we are of different political complections [complexions] but I can tell him what he cannot do in Charleston while I am Mayor." I then asked Mr. Grace if he would undertake Dr. Purvis defense, should he be prosecuted. He replied, that he had made it a rule not to appear in any courts, while serving as Mayor. But that he would have his law partner, Mr. John I. Cosgrove, do so and further, that in the event that Dr. Purvis should be threatened with conviction, that he, himself, would enter the case as his attorney, before he would allow him to be convicted. He told us to go home and to have Dr. Purvis remain in his home, with his assurance that nothing would happen. In spite of that assurance Sasportas spent the night on Purvis' front porch, with his gun in his hand, waiting to meet any who should seek to enter there.

I do not know what Mr. Grace said to Magistrate Whaley. Only that Magistrate Whaley phoned Dr. Purvis and told him that a warrant had been issued for his arrest and that he must appear before him at 2 o'clock that day. And that he should have his attorney and bondsman with him.

We held a conference at Sasportas' office that noon where we discussed what our action should be. Sasportas advised that we waive the preliminary and allow the charges to go before the Grand Jury. For by doing so it would restrict the Magistrate's action to only what was covered in the warrant and in addition would exclude all verbal testimony. Leaving it only the formality of giving bond for Dr. Purvis appearance at the next term of court.

Lawyer Smith, one of the bravest Negro men I have ever known sat in with us at the conference. Mr. Smith advised us not to take our pistols with us. For we were then armed, but to leave them in the office. He said that he would be with us and that he had his pistol, showing us his fully loaded forty-four, and that if any trouble started he would shoot, as it didn't matter much with him whether he died or not as he was an old man and did not mind dying if that would stop the whites from doing their dirt.

When we reached Whaley's office on Church Street, we found Michel [sic], "Doc" Huguenin and another white man there. Whaley read the warrant under which Purvis was charged and Sasportas answering for him, replied that Dr. Purvis waived a preliminary hearing. Whaley then announced the amount of the bond and prepared it. I signed the bond, after which we left.

During the hearing I noticed "Sweet," Magistrate Whaley's Negro constable, the same one who had done some shooting during the riot, sitting at the rear of the room, across from Mr. Smith and that the holster to his gun was open. A little later that day, I met him and he told me that he had intended killing that bunch of whites had one of them started any trouble. For he knew that the "whole thing" was a dirty trick. I have since wondered if Mr. Smith had talked with "Sweet" about the hearing— for it seemed strange to me, that these two should be found sitting on opposite sides of the room.

Mr. Cosgrove appeared before the Grand Jury when the bill of indictment came before it where it was thrown out. And so it ended but only in so far as Dr. Purvis was concerned. For beyond that there was then present in the community a definite though intangible something which created unrest among the Negroes. Some of it had come through unemployment for we were then approaching the beginning of the "Great Depression." The Navy yard had already dismissed many of its workers. The fertilizer mills had reduced their operating time. The construction boom which had followed the close of the war had ended. All of which resulted in the unemployment of many Negroes. While these conditions had come about largely because of the economic dilemma into which we were heading, they were also becoming intensified by the machinations of the "Board of Trade," a recently organized white employment agency which operated under the slogan that "no job should be given to a Negro if a white man wanted it." Naturally then, since unemployment was rife, only white men got the jobs. I do not know whether this was an adopted plan of action which had its conception within the confines of the Klan and of those of the white labor unions, or not. But I do know that we sensed its presence and that it created an atmosphere of unrest among the Negroes which persuaded many of them to that belief. And though it was not as openly seen as was the Klan's demonstration on John's Island it yet had a somewhat similar result as that one did, by causing an exodus of the Negroes.

MIGRATION

I have told how previous migrations got under way and what induced them. Also that the majority of those who had gone in these earlier migrations were mostly those who lived the higher walks of life—who had largely been "pushed" out of Charleston by the pressure of Jim Crowism. But this one differed from those for it partook of a "push-pull" nature in which could be seen not only the "push" from social and labor restrictions but the even more compelling "pull" which *The Chicago Defender* gave. I do not mean by this that Editor Abbott was in any ways concerned with Charleston or with what was then taking place there or that he even knew about it. But some-how or other, this man who perhaps was unaware of the magnitude of his accomplishment—had become a Moses, a newer prototype of the original, who by his beck and call had persuaded thousands of Negroes to leave "Egypt land" and go where life would be more bountiful.

They went from Charleston and when the exodus had slackened its Negro population had dwindled from its sixty thousand 1918 number down to less than thirty thousand. The movement took with it Negroes of every class. The well-to-do and the poverty-stricken ones. Many of whom had only their passage money and hope, that once in Harlem—the land of mythical plenty—their troubles would be ended.

Although our economic condition had become worse there was a slight amelioration of "police pressure." For when Mr. Grace became Mayor several of the more "brutal to Negroes only" policemen were dismissed. Their dismissal however was not because of their inhumanity to Negroes but altogether because of their party affiliation. However it helped us immeasurably. Which made it an improvement over what had previously existed. Not only among the police but also from white streetcar conductors who were vested with police power. And whose brutality was responsible for the murder of two Negro passengers a short while earlier. One of these was a Negro man. A Mr. Ferguson, a man of unquestioned reputation and standing, who was callously killed on a car near the corner of King and Calhoun Streets. The other was a young prizefighter. His name was Grant. He was a popular favorite with many and was far from being uncouth or disorderly. He was on a Spring Street car and had run the bell to get off at the corner of Ashley. Some slight altercation arose and the conductor without any warning shot him as he was leaving the car. Grant fell in the street just in front of Seignious' drugstore. A few minutes later Dr. Seignious came out and exhibited a pistol which he claimed the dead man had. It was strange that none of the other onlookers saw it. While one girl who was directly behind Grant swore that Grant did not have a gun. However, the usual plea of "self defense" was set up and the case set for trial.

The local N.A.A.C.P. made an issue of it as it was the second such killing within six months. Thad Sasportas was engaged to cooperate with the Solicitor in prosecuting the case. The Solicitor at first declined to have him associated with the case—claiming that he would do everything possible to bring about a conviction. But later he allowed Sasportas to come [?] in and to gather evidence. Mr. Sasportas took part in the prosecution and did everything that could possibly be done to bring about a conviction. The trial ended in an acquittal. Which came about largely through the jury's acceptance of a "white man's word" Dr. Seignious'. But even though we had lost a verdict—our determination in prosecuting the murderer had a good effect —for it put all on notice that indiscriminate killing of innocent Negroes would be prosecuted to the limit. Which together with the improved conditions in the police force made life a little more secure.

Mr. Grace was still intent upon having Charleston become a great city and not to remain as it was then, a dirty little town with unpaved streets and bad sidewalks. He believed these could be improved. For we had easy access to asphalt, which then was manufactured at the Standard Oil Company's plant on Meeting Street. And a fairly adequate supply of rock—by cracking up our cobble stones and Belgian blocks—and to do the job at a very nominal cost. He had me to call a meeting with several of our Negro citizens at Dart's Hall where he presented the details of his program. He first told that in most Southern cities it was customary to provide street improvements in only white areas where the rich folks lived. And to pay for it by taxing all property with the amount of cost. His plan, he explained would call for an abutment tax levy which would be assessed against only the property which was so improved and so would not become a burden to those who did not share in its benefits. Under his plan the city would issue paving bonds with ten-year maturities and would allow the taxpayers ten years in which to retire their paving indebtedness with the privilege of making annual installment payments on it. Mr. Grace said that he wanted to see the Negroes have clean, well-paved streets as well as anyone else and in addition not made to pay for the pavements and streets on which they did not live.

If we wanted to have improved streets under the arrangement he proposed then we must join with him in putting the program over. And in which we could assist by telling our people about it and advising them to sign the free holders petition when it was presented. Since we were all in hearty accord with his program we did so. And thus it is that most of the streets where Negroes lived are well-paved streets.

I was sorry to see Eugene Noisette who lived at the corner of Marion and Jasper Streets circulate a petition among his neighbors in opposition to the paving of those two streets. As it was altogether through his petition that these streets have not been paved. Needless to say the City Board of School Commissioners were in full accord with his petition since it relieved them from the necessity of paying the amount it would have cost them for the paving of the two blocks which Simonton School abuts. But I am sure that if Simonton had been a white school and not a Negro school, his protest would have gone unheeded.

Mr. Grace's term of office expired before his program could get well underway. But that did not prevent his successors from continuing it. For he made that mandatory upon them by the simple process of tearing up every street that was to be paved.

Continued Advocacy for Negro Education in Charleston

AVERY INSTITUTE

One Sunday afternoon a meeting was called and which, as we thought, was intended as an opportunity for the parents of pupils at Avery and their friends to meet with and to felicitate the members of the Trustee Board of the American Missionary Association. That Association is the operating sponsor for Avery and though it had been visited at times by individual members from the Trustee Board it was the first time so far as any of us knew that the Board as a whole had ever visited the school. So the occasion became one on which the school's chapel was filled to its capacity. And it may be said with happy faces, who evidenced by their expression every anticipation for an interesting meeting. After a brief preliminary program, the Rev. Doctor Beard who was the Chairman of the Board of Trustees, was introduced to the gathering. Dr. Beard after a few pleasant remarks proceeded to tell us about the work which the Association was doing—its work in carrying on colleges and schools in the mountain areas and what the cost of doing that amounted to. Then he told about the Association's funds and that these were inadequate to meet the cost of an expanding program and that it now had become necessary that the Association curtail some of its activities. Continuing he said that the only way in which these activities could be curtailed was by discontinuing their support of high schools. Especially those located where the schools could or should be merged with local school systems. And that this had become all the more necessary because several of their high schools were annually being operated at a deficit. He told that it had been necessary to close the nearby school at Brunswick, Georgia that year and that several other schools of like type would be closed in the near future. He regretted very much, said he, to tell us that the Association had decided to close Avery, as it was now operating with an annual deficit and which he said would amount to about $800.00 for the current year. For it was impossible for the Association to continue its operation under these circumstances.

When Mr. Beard had finished, I rose and asked permission to speak. I told the Trustees what Avery meant to our community. That it was the only available high school for Negroes along the entire coastal area of South Carolina and that the nearest high school to it was that at Orangeburg. I said that should the school close, it meant that no child from Charleston, except that child was from a family which could afford to send it elsewhere for high school training, could ever hope to enter college, and that it would close the only door they had to enter a fuller life or to be prepared for leadership. I then asked, "If I would agree to reimburse the Association the amount of deficit it had suffered that year within thirty days and to annually thereafter raise an amount which would guarantee the operation of the school on a balanced budget, would it not rescind its action and allow the school to continue?"

Dr. Beard smiled and called the Trustee together. They went into a "huddle" at one end of the rostrum and after a short deliberation, announced that if we did so, that the Association would continue the operation of the school. But that that was conditioned upon the community raising $1,200.00 in addition to the present year's deficit. And that in future the annual contribution expected from the community would increase each year beyond that sum.

I thanked Dr. Beard and the Trustees for what they had done. When the meeting adjourned, I received the assurance from a very large number of those present that they would give their services and money towards meeting the conditional requirements which the Trustees had stated. And though it was a big job which I had undertaken, I knew that it could be done because I had the full support of those who were interested in Avery behind me.

That night I planned the formation of an organization which in its preliminary task would join with me in raising the amount of the deficit. We accomplished that task within the allotted time of thirty days and remitted the amount to the Association. A temporary organization, which we termed "Avery School" was created. From which we appointed several committees, the principal one being the "Drive Committee" whose duty it was to raise the sum of $1,200.00 and to have that amount in hand when the school year commenced in the coming September. The Drive Committee accomplished its task within the allotted time and the amount was paid over to the Principal, Mr. Cox, in keeping with the Association's instructions. And thus the school was enabled to continue its operation.

But these were only the immediate necessities, the greater needs was [were] the formation of a permanent organization that would be so all embracing and so thoroughly imbued with its purpose that the continued operation of the school would be insured.

The methods through which these objectives were to be clarified and determined had been placed in the hands of other committees—one on permanent organization—one on membership and one on finance. Rev. C.S. Ledbetter was the President of the temporary "Avery School" organization. Mr. John Pinckney as Secretary and I as Treasurer.

The recommendation of the organization committee, was that the organization incorporate itself as "Avery Institute" and by the recommendation of the "Committee on Membership" that its membership shall consist of the representatives appointed by the American Missionary Association, the Alumni Association of Avery Institute, the Parent-Teachers Association of Avery Institute and all such other persons who would wish to join. It provided for a Board of Trustees consisting of four representatives from the American Missionary Association, three from the Avery Alumni Association, three from the Avery Parent-Teachers Association and three from the community at large, who would have charge of the directing of the affairs of the corporation.

All of this was communicated to the American Missionary Association for its approval and acceptance. Both of which we received. In conformity with the Association's directions the temporary organization "Avery School" went into permanent organization as "Avery Institute" and adopted a constitution and bylaws for its government.

At its regular meeting on July 1st, 1925 it adopted a resolution that the body be incorporated. And authorized Caesar S. Ledbetter, John A. McFall, Robert F. Morrison, Benj. F. Cox and John H. Pinckney as its agents to accomplish the same.

On July 2, 1925 the following notice was published in the *Charleston Evening Post:*

> Notice of Incorporation—Whereas, Avery Institute, a society for conducting a school in the City of Charleston, at a regular meeting held on the 1st day of July 1925, passed a resolution directing the undersigned as agents to apply to the Secretary of State of South Carolina for a Charter of Incorporation of said Body: Now; therefore pursuant to the said resolution and in conformity to the laws of the State of South Carolina, the undersigned will apply to the Hon. W.P. Blackwell, Secretary of State,

for the Incorporation of the said Avery Institute as an eleemosynary corporation. Caesar S. Ledbetter, John A. McFall Robert F. Morrison Benj. F. Cox, John H. Pinckney Dated July 2, 1925.

The date of the above cited resolution would be somewhat confusing if reference was made to the minute book of Avery Institute, as in it there would be found a record of an earlier resolution to the same effect and which directed Mr. John H. Pinckney, the Secretary to apply to the Secretary of State for the forms for so doing. Which Mr. Pinckney did. But it happened that when Mr. Pinckney received the forms that they included a copy of an Act which restricted the incorporation of eleemosynary and fraternal organization to only such applicants as could present a petition from not fewer than fifty freeholders in the county, and, the recommendation of *all county officials* that incorporation be granted. This particular section of South Carolina code had been enacted under the Tillman regime for the specific purpose of limiting the incorporation of Negro organizations as well as to acquaint all county officials with that information. In fact it was to all intent merely a restrictive measure contrived for the sole purpose of dominating Negroes. As shortly after its enactment, a second Act was passed under which much of the requirements in the earlier act had been eliminated. Notwithstanding which, the older Act was invariably used whenever Negroes applied for incorporation but never to my knowledge when whites did.

Mr. Pinckney quickly realized what complications, inconveniences and delays would ensue if that course had to be followed. He consulted Mr. Sasportas and showed him what the Secretary of State's office had sent him, and asked his opinion. Mr. Sasportas' opinion was to the effect that the requirements of that act had to be met. I saw Mr. Sasportas a few days later and learned from him what he had told Mr. Pinckney. I told Mr. Sasportas that I was sure of the existence of a later act which did not require all that the former did. And that it was my belief that the reason why the earlier act had not been repealed, when the later one was passed was to have it remain as a means for "bypassing" Negroes. And that it was this which the Secretary of State office was doing. I found a copy of the later act and that it only required—the publication of notice of intent to incorporate—the attachment of that notice to the application—and the payment of a fee of $3—upon of all of which, it became mandatory that the Secretary of State should grant and issue a charter of incorporation.

I presented this information to the society at its meeting on July 1, 1925. Which resulted in the adoption of a second resolution by the society for the same purpose. I was directed to complete the application and to present it to the Secretary of State. Which I did. A few days later I received the Charter and had the same recorded in the R.M.C. office for Charleston.

The Corporation of Avery Institute functioned through its Trustees for several more years. During which time it annually raised amounts, beginning with $1,200.00 the first year and then in increasing amounts which ultimately reached $3,500.00 in the year prior to its dormancy.

It conducted the annual drives for contributions and retained them until they were needed by the school. When I, as Treasurer, would on order by the President, pay Mr. Cox the stipulated amount. All of the financial records of the corporation were delivered over to Mr. Frank DeCosta when he was Principal with my request that they be filed with the other records of the school. Unfortunately, they have all been destroyed by the fire which recently damaged the school.

The duties which the trustees assumed, though centered about the raising of funds for the operation of the school, included the responsibility of directing the affairs of the schools under a system of guidance by the A.M.A., whereby the local trustees could acquire a fuller knowledge of their duties and at the same time enjoy the privilege of benefiting from the experience which the A.M.A.'s administrative office had acquired in its many years of operating the school. Mr. Fred M. Brownlee, Executive Secretary of the A.M.A. was a member of the board. He, Rev. Ledbetter, Mr. Cox, the Principal and Mr. Johnson from Savannah, Georgia. comprised the official representatives of the A.M.A. on Avery's trustee board, as well as the majority membership on the Executive Committee.

Mr. Brownlee usually attended the annual meetings of the Trustees where the budget for the ensuing year was determined. And what improvements, if any, could be made in the school. One year we had a surplus of $600.00 and at Mr. Brownlee's suggestion it was expended for additional equipment for the manual training department. In another year we found it possible to make further improvements—that time by equipping the chemical laboratory. In our last drive for funds we experienced much difficulty in obtaining contributions. As it seemed the community had lost much of its former interest in the school. And in addition was seeking to justify its attitudes by telling "that it was paying for what it got" or by telling canvasser that they had already contributed. Which many had not done. Before the campaign closed that year I published, at my personal expense, in the *Jenkins Messenger*, an itemized list of donors with the amounts they had contributed. Which caused a howl from many whose contributions averaged 25¢ apiece. However it did accomplish something as several of those sent in additional donations. And though we raised $3,500 that year we yet suffered a deficit of $800.

When the annual meeting was held, Mr. Brownlee informed us that the $800.00 deficit had to be met by the local members of the Trustee board. Which when allocated between us amounted to $100 each. Mr. Johnson, who was the President of the Wage Mariners Bank of Savannah, and an A.M.A. representative was present at that meeting. By virtue of his appointment, he was exempt from any liability for the deficit. He was fully aware of that but instead of doing otherwise, was the first to make payment of his proportionate share in the deficit. He gave us his check for $100. E.C. Mickey, A.J. Clement, E.B. Burroughs and myself (J.A. McFall) each did likewise. Robert F. Morrison sponsored a public recital by the Fisk Singers and contributed the proceeds therefrom as his share. Rev. C.S. Ledbetter who also was an A.M.A. representative raised a contribution. We cleared off the deficit. But getting back to that meeting—where we were then discussing how the school could be operated in the future without involving its trustee in debt. We also questioned if we could hope for a more generous contribution from the community in the coming year. After debating the pros and cons we reached the conclusion that the surest way of ensuring the continued operation of the school would only be by increasing its tuition fees, and to charge an admission fee to the annual commencement exercises. We authorized that these increases be made and by that means succeeded in effecting a balanced budget for the ensuing year.

As we neared the end of that year Mr. Cox informed me that a small deficit was likely to occur. As a large number of pupils had failed to pay their tuitions in full even though some of them were graduating that year. I knew that this condition had not arisen through any inability on the part of parents to pay but that it was largely only a reaction against the increased tuitions and a means by which some of them thought that they could get "even." As I well knew that many of these parents were anticipating expenditures which averaged $50.00 each for graduation—clothes, invitations, class pins, automobiles and flowers. Hence I could easily see that poverty was not one of the reasons for tuitions not being paid. So we decided to charge a 50¢ admission to the commencement exercises and that each graduate be allowed only two complimentary tickets. I assumed charge at the doors that night and personally collected for the tickets. A few of those who attended the exercises took umbrage because of the increased charge over that of the previous year. But that mattered little with us as we were able to close the school year with a surplus of about $62.

Like all trustees we had our trials and tribulations. Some of it came from parents and some from teachers. One family in particular I remember—the Browns on Coming Street. Mrs. Brown believed that the teachers who taught her children did not give them the marks they deserved and so she wanted me to compel Mr. Cox to dismiss a couple of teachers or if he did not that I should dismiss him. And when neither was done, I saw her withdraw her children from the school and send them to Augusta, Georgia to school.

That year we had some complaints from teachers, the most of which criticized the charges they paid for their noonday lunch. Which they thought was excessive. And so did I when I learned what it was. As it included a profit on both material and labor involved in preparing it. I felt that their lunches should be sold at actual cost of material only and that no part of the expense of preparing and serving should be added, as all of that was provided for in the school's budget. And also for the laundering of table linen which was likewise provided for.

The complaints were discussed by several of the local trustees just prior to the annual meeting. I was among them—we prepared a questionnaire which covered those problems and mailed it to Mr. Cox with a request that he come to the annual meeting prepared to help us solve them. When the meeting convened, Mr. Cox was absent from the city—doing summer school teaching, I believe, at Albany, Georgia—Mrs. Cox appeared and stated that Mr. Cox had given her his proxy and that she would represent him at the meeting. Rev. Ledbetter ruled that proxies could only be exercised by members of the Trustee board and since Mrs. Cox was not a member that she could not exercise that privilege.

The consensus of opinion was, that Mr. Cox did not care to reply to the questionnaire. After some discussion of the matter the Board directed its Secretary to communicate with Mr. Brownlee and seek to have him require Mr. Cox to answer the questionnaire, a copy of which was sent to Mr. Brownlee. After which a temporary adjournment was ordered, to meet again when Mr. Brownlee's reply was received.

A few days later we received his reply. Which curtly told that since the Trustees no longer raised an annual contribution that they had through that negligence lost all voice in the management of the school, and were without power to direct its affairs.

We were somewhat surprised at the tenor of Mr. Brownlee's letter and at its implications. For we knew well that our position as Trustees were in no wise ways [sic] conditioned upon the securing of contributions except when such were absolutely necessary for the conduct of the school. And since that had been provided for by increasing the tuition fees—with full knowledge to the A.M.A. when it was done and without objections from it—there was no necessity for going to the people for more money. Also that each member of the Corporation, and that included all of the trustees, save those who were the representatives of the A.M.A., paid an annual membership fee. Which was all that the constitution and bylaws required.

In view of the fact that our questionnaire was our first demand for a clarification of some of the Principal's methods of management, Mr. Brownlee's reply made us conclude that his office would not tolerate any action by the Trustees in that direction.

We had no inclination whatsoever to protest Mr. Brownlee's ruling. As we were only interested in retaining the educational facilities which Avery offered to the children of our community. So we agreed, that for the sake of retaining these facilities that we would let the matter rest there and not to seek to make an issue of it. This is why the Corporation became dormant.

About two years after that Mr. George White one of the assistant secretaries of the A.M.A. called on me at the bank. During our conversation he mentioned the Mr. Cox had been reported as being solely responsible for the raising of the funds and not the Trustees. I told him that he had been misinformed. And then I showed him the records of my office and how the monies had been collected by the Trustees and who in turn had ordered me to pay to Mr. Cox, as Principal, those as they were needed. Mr. White appeared somewhat non-plussed when I showed him President Ledbetter's orders for the payments of those amounts and my voucher-checks covering them.

When the Corporation became dormant it had a balance of about $62.00 in its treasury. For several years I sought to have the A.M.A. direct me what to do with it. Finally they did and then I was authorized to pay the amount to Avery that it could be used for the purchase of furniture for the training school department.

HOSPITAL AND TRAINING SCHOOL UNDER NEW LEADERSHIP

Returning now to the Hospital and Training School—several years had passed since I resigned my position there as Dean of the Training School. During those years I had little to do with the management of the Hospital although I had retained my membership in the Corporation. Dr. W.H. Johnson who was serving as Surgeon in chief when I resigned, soon tired of the arduous and exacting duties which were required for the proper professional care of the patients. He had rigidly adhered to his policy maintaining racial exclusiveness in that direction which resulted with practically all of the white physicians withdrawing their support. From the financial standpoint this was almost disastrous, as one of them, Dr. T.M. [Scharloock ?] who was company doctor for several of the fertilizer companies who patients formerly numbered a daily average of three, had practically discontinued his patronage and instead was sending his patients to Roper.

In addition to that, the hospital had lost two members from its staff—one of them, Dr. Ridley U. McClennan, the son of Dr. A.C. McClennan by death—and the other Dr. M.M. Edwards who had so suddenly left the city, that he did so without pausing to say farewell to any.

The finances of the institution were in bad shape. But in even worse shape than that was the physical condition of the plant. Which in need of much repair. The same could be said about its equipment as much of that required replacement and there was no money to do it with.

Such was the condition of the Hospital when Dr. Johnson persuaded Dr. H.U. Seabrook to take over and to carry on. Seabrook's undertaking was no easy one as many of those who were formerly staunch workers in the hospital's behalf had become indifferent for they were never in accord with Dr. Johnson's methods. The Lucy Brown Auxiliary had become dormant. The Corporation had not met for several years thus leaving all of its officer's as those holding their positions under the constitutional provision—"until their successors are elected and qualified"—and not by being elected for the periods in which they were serving. Mr. C.M. English then the acting President was also Chairman of the Executive committee. Neither he nor his committee had during their entire administration displayed any constructive efforts towards improving the conditions at the hospital. As a natural consequence to that community interest in the work waned.

Dr. Seabrook succeeded in reviving the Corporation. Which at an annual meeting elected Rev. Brooks, the pastor at Central Baptist Church, its president. Mrs. Susan Simmons Treasurer, and in the place of its former Executive Committee—a Board of Managers consisting of the President, the Treasurer and three members of the Corporation, the personnel of which were—Rev.

Brooks, Mrs. Susan Simmons, Dr. Seabrook, Dr. Thorne and myself.

The chief objective of the new Board was to obtain a more certain financial income for the hospital. Application was made to the Community chest for admission as one of its agencies, and was granted. That year the hospital received from the chest, double the amount which the Negro chest Committee canvassers collected. The following year, Mr. Harmon, the New York philanthropist, who spent his winter at Adam's Run, contributed $800.00 through the community chest, earmarking it for the salary of a head nurse. For some time Dr. Seabrook had been endeavoring to have the Duke Endowment, a recently established Trust, accept the hospital as one of its beneficiaries and at last succeeded in doing so. Public interest in the hospital was now being reawaken. More so from these public agencies than from any other sources. The following year Mr. Harmon increased his contribution to the chest, by adding to what was earmarked for our nurse's salary the sum of $800.00 for the purchase of equipment. But somehow or other that amount was never paid over to the hospital. Dr. Seabrook discussed the matter with Dr. Banov who then was County Health Officer. Dr. Banov advised him not to make any question about the money and that he would see that the hospital would not lose thereby. I believe that Mr. Harmon was aware of what had been done as one day while he was visiting the hospital, he told me in answer to my questions about making repairs to the building, that he considered repairs and remodeling a waste, as an old building could never be made into a modern one. But that we should continue as we were going improving our services and helping mankind. That he well knew what our problems were and that we did not get all that was coming to us then. But perhaps would raise friends who would see that our work would thrive. Mr. Harmon was a philanthropist in every sense of the word. One who looked beyond race and which was so clearly shown on an occasion when he said to me "I do not give to Negroes because they are Negroes but because they are men and women"—with emphasis on "men and women"—and "I recognize no racial bounds for the attainment of worthy aspirations by any." Mr. Harmon died suddenly a few weeks later. Perhaps had he lived the hospital would have benefitted more materially from him than it did.

I cannot help at this time avoid breaking off from the hospital's affairs by telling more about Mr. Harmon—He was the sponsor and donor of the annual Harmon Art Exhibit Awards and perhaps did more than anyone else to foster the advent of Negro artists to the world of art. And about the annual award which had been made the year before his death. Teddy Harleston had exhibited his "Old Servant" at that exhibit but in spite of the excellence of his work, the judges saw fit to give the award to another painting, which in my opinion and that was shared by Aaron Douglass, did in no way exceed the quality shown by Harleston's. Harleston died that spring and carried with him to his death, the belief that he had been unfairly treated. But Harleston was not the only one who thought as he did. For shortly after his death I received a letter from Mr. Harmon's secretary saying that it was the opinion of the Foundation that Mr. Harleston's painting had not received the appraisement it merited and that it was the desire of the Foundation to have a posthumous exhibit of his paintings at the next, and which would be the last, exhibit under the Harmon Foundation. These matters were left in Mrs. Harleston's hands.

It was while the exhibit in question was being shown at Fisk that I had Mr. Aaron Douglass, one of the most outstanding Negro artists, go with me to inspect the paintings and to pass upon them. The painting which had been given the award, was one done by a student in the art department at Howard University, and by no imaginable method of appraisement could be compared with that one done by Harleston. A few days later I saw Mr. Schomburg who was one of the judges and asked how did they arrive at their verdict. He very frankly told me, that of the five judges appointed to serve, two who were artists did not show up—which left him, the art teacher at Howard University and another judge to make the award. That he personally knew nothing about painting nor did the other judge—so they decided to leave it with the Howard University art teacher, and that it was he who picked out his student for the award.

A couple of years later, the art teacher, I have forgotten his name now, came to Charleston to see if a number of Harleston's painting could not be secured for a permanent exhibit at Howard University. He called at my home to inspect the ones I owned, and while there I told him what Mr. Schomburg had told me about the Harmon jury and its award. His reply was that "Schomburg lied. He was the one who urged that the award be given in the way it was."

But getting back to the Hospital—In the meanwhile Dr. Seabrook had succeeded in getting the Duke Foundation to accept the hospital as one of its beneficiaries. And whose annual contribution with that from the community chest did much to strengthen the hospital's financial structure. At the insistence of the Community Chest two white citizens were appointed on the Board of Managers. These two were Mr. Bates, the Superintendent at Roper Hospital and Mr. L [illegible], the President of the German-American Fire Insurance Company. These new members met with the Board but once, on which occasion they found that its agenda allowed them no room for even a suggestion. So they very frankly told us that they did not see where they could help us in any way as our methods left no room for suggestions. So they never came to another meeting of the Board although for the following three or four years they would sign our annual reports.

The only help we got from Mr. Bates, was on one occasion, when he learned that we were going to buy a couple of beds, on which he offered to buy them for us through Roper Hospital's purchasing office. We did that but found that the beds cost us about twice what we could have bought them for. A month later I bought four more beds at half the price of those he bought and invited him to see them. He came and expressed surprise at what we got and asked for the name of the company from which we had bought them. Beyond this, the management of the hospital has been altogether under its own people.

The Board of Managers had been reorganized and I became its Financial Secretary. We met weekly—verified all bills and made payment. We operated on a budget and authorized the purchase or contractual agreements for only what we had money then in hand to pay. In that way we avoided all danger of failure or embarrassment.

Dr. Banov made good on his promise to see that the hospital did not lose. As he had got the County delegation to appropriate a sum to defray the cost of remodeling the basement of the hospital for outdoor clinic purposes. The staff had heartedly concurred with the proposal to inaugurate a free outdoor clinic and I to operate the "free" dispensary—at 10¢ a prescription. Mr. Herbert DeCosta had agreed to make the repairs and plumbing installations for $750. He did so and gave us a very good job.

One of our graduates, Nurse Bell, was appointed clinic nurse. Her duties at the clinic were part time duties but were extended by outside visiting service under the direction of the Board of Health. The inauguration of the free clinic tied the hospital in with the County Board of Health and with the Charleston County Delegation to the General Assembly. The following year with Dr. Banov's help, we received a county appropriation of $1.00 a day for each indigent patient we cared for. And which amount and that from the Duke Endowment of $1.00 for each free patient allowed us to care for a considerable number of charity cases. As our total cost per day for each patient was then about $2.544 each or not quite 55¢ within its actual cost.

The county's annual appropriation for the drug dispensary took care of its purchases and allowed the retention of all of the drug room receipts to the hospital. These receipts averaged about $250 a year. Since they were altogether under my control, I exercised that privilege by expending it where I thought it would do most good. At the end of the year of operation of the clinic when I made my report to the County Delegation, I asked for an additional sum for needed equipment. I discussed the matter fully with Mr. Dan Huger, who was Chairman of the Committee on Health, and through his efforts, we received an additional $400.00. That year I bought with these monies—the new operating table and some other minor equipment. From then on through several more years, the drug room receipts and the special appropriation of equipment permitted me to repair the annex, putting down the acotile [?] floor covering—installing the operating room lamp—the anesthetic machine and additional instruments. The nurses' classroom was added, by enclosing the lower floor beneath the operating room and installing a complete equipment for chemical study and analysis. Dr. Purvis contributed a microscope—thus making our laboratory equipment [illegible] if not an elaborate one.

With the inauguration of the free clinic, I again took up my teaching work—Chemistry and Materia Medica. Mrs. Oliver our head nurse and superintendent, was a very capable and efficient worker under whom our nurses showed excellent progress.

But even more gratifying than these successes was that of having the white physicians once again cooperating with the hospital. Dr. Scharloock was again most cooperative both in bringing his patients into the hospital and by giving a special series of annual lectures to the nurses. And then a near tragedy happened—Dr. Purvis was taken suddenly ill with appendicitis. Thorne was out of the city or was ill I can't remember which—but whichever it was, he could not respond. Dr. Hoffman had been called in and pronounced the diagnosis. Mrs.

Purvis phoned me and asked me to come down at once. When I got there I found Dr. Purvis suffering from an acute attack—but worse, that he had taken a dose of castor oil the day before believing that his condition was but an upset intestinal condition. They were discussing the advisability of sending Dr. Purvis to Washington where Carson could operate. I advised against that for I was fearful that a rupture would occur before he could reach Washington. Dr. Purvis expressed a preference for either Dr. Cathcart or Dr. Buist as his surgeon if the trip to Washington could not be safely done. Dr. Cathcart was out of the city so Mrs. Purvis got in contact with Dr. Buist who responded at once. Dr. Buist concurred with Dr. Hoffman's diagnosis and said that the operation must be done without delay. Dr. Purvis asked him if he would operate at the Hospital and Training School. He said yes, if you are satisfied that the facilities there are adequate. I told them that I would go and see that everything would be prepared for his immediate entrance. Dr. Buist replied that he would be there to operate at 9 o'clock and would bring his son, Dr. Buist as his assistant and his nurse to administer the anesthetic.

It was then about 8 p.m. We got Harold Mazyck's ambulance to take him to the hospital. I got in touch with Mrs. Oliver and told her of the emergency and went to her home for her. I took her to the hospital and then went back to the drugstore for a supply of everything which I believed would be needed. When I returned to the Hospital the ambulance had arrived and Purvis was being prepared. I ran a urine test and found everything satisfactory with him. The operation was a complete success even though it was complicated with a rupture. Purvis made an uneventful recovery and as an expression of this gratitude gave the hospital his compound microscope, since it would not accept any compensation.

The need for immediate action in Purvis' case did not allow any time for me to acquaint Dr. Seabrook or anyone else about the operation and that caused some of the men to take umbrage.

But since none of them could openly come out and express just what they felt about it—it took a childish turn which expressed itself through one of them styling me "the surgeon in chief." But whether its intent was meant to be satirical or not mattered little—as a life was in the balance—and that alone was sufficient reason for the occasion not being made a "Roman holiday."

The incident was of value to the hospital—for not only had it brought Dr. Buist, both the elder and his son, young Dr. Buist in close contact with it. For the afterwards brought in many of their patients but it also served to make its facilities known to other white surgeons who subsequently brought their Negro patients in for operations.

The operation of a small community hospital is no simple task. And so was ours. Our average annual budget required between $11,000.00 and $12,000.00 a year to balance it. One can easily see the extent to which contributions and public grants enabled us to operate when its income from patients—which averaged only $4,200.00 is taken into consideration. Had it been necessary to depend upon the local group for operation it never could have lasted. For somehow or other Negroes, particularly the Charleston Negroes, are averse to giving financial support to welfare organizations even though those organizations function for them alone. They are always eager to benefit from these agencies but are seldom ever willing to give or to work to maintain them.

This fact became all the more noticeable to me when I put on a drive to raise money for the hospital. It was a two directional drive—one to whites, using the mails as a means of solicitation, to about 900 whites—Within one month we received over $900.00. The second direction included only Negroes—through a house-to-house canvas. Where we anticipated not less than 150 canvassers to volunteer their services—we got less than twenty-five. While the amount they brought in totaled only $327.00 of which $75.00 had been contributed by three members of the Board of Managers.

Dr. Seabrook justly deserves the credit for salvaging the hospital from the fate it faced when Dr. Johnson passed out of the picture, and for the vision through which it was able to reach an even higher plane that it formerly held. Many were the difficulties he had to overcome—and the least of these were not the financial ones—but the more biting and annoying ones which bred from jealousy and suspicion. But despite these he went forward doing the things which were necessary to do—no matter what they were. I have known him to get out of bed at 2 o'clock in the morning to fix the elevator at the hospital. I saw him cut and thread the iron pipes for curtains in the clinic room and to place them in position; that the hospital could be saved the cost of installing them. Whenever members of his family entered the hospital as patients they always paid the regular "full pay" fees. As it was always his insistence that no consideration be given him, not even the customary "professional courtesy" one.

I tell this because there were some who believed that Seabrook derived financial benefit through his position at the hospital. Those beliefs do him an injustice as they are supported by neither truth nor other basis of actual happenings. I can vouch for this as my position as Financial-Secretary and the added duties of the making of annual audits for the county and for the Duke Endowment gave me full opportunity to substantiate both the correctness and the propriety of every transaction by the hospital, whether by him or by its other employees.

Dr. Seabrook's duties centered chiefly around the professional care of patients, and mine with the financial operation of the institution. In matters pertaining to the care of patients, he and the staff were supreme. But in the expenditure of funds to provide for that care there was the rule, and it was adhered to, that all expenditures not provided for in the budget could only be made with the approval of the Board of Managers of which

Dr. Thorne was Chairman and I the Secretary and the deciding factor. Naturally there were times when we differed about what was to be bought or not. But in all of these I cannot recall a single instance where the ruling of Board was circumvented.

Improvements and replacements which I advised, especially those for which I had applied to the County for, and could supplement the appropriation so made with the amount accruing through the drug room, were only made under my direction. In doing these things I sought to have them conform with my ideals for a hospital. Most of which were based upon what other small hospitals similar to ours had done. I had visited some of them in other cities and it was from these that I learned what the basic requirements for a small hospital should be. I knew that our financial strength would not permit us to do all which I wanted done. That deficiency however did not prevent us from striving to do all which we could and so I started on a "piecemeal" job by doing that which was most needed first and others as funds would permit. The splendid cooperation which Mrs. Oliver, our head nurse, gave us, helped us immeasurably in putting our program over.

Only those who assume the task of carrying on community welfare projects can know how essential it is to maintain an adequate operating fund that the work may continue. For no matter how well-equipped a plant may be except there is the certainty of continued operation collapse will happen. In keeping with this fact I sought to build up the operating funds of the hospital to where it could successfully operate for at least one full year even should its receipts from patients fall below $2,000.00. In doing this it became absolutely necessary that the annual budget be adhered to.

The task of increasing our facilities was made a difficult one because the building we occupied was an old family mansion which had been built in 1807. Despite that we were able to put into it all of the essential requirements for the work of a modern hospital. We enlarged the operating room. Which with its new equipment—a new operating table an anesthetic machine, a new lamp and other accessories—made it all that was required. Two small additional rooms were erected at the sides of the passageway to the annex. One of these was reequipped with a new high-pressure steam sterilizer. While the other cared for a Fisher x-ray machine, fluoroscope, Bucky table and a film-development room. A fracture bed was installed in the annex. A new delivery table was provided for the obstetrical room. New bassinets and an incubator were installed in the nursery. We had an ample number of late-type hospital beds, mattresses and linen. A small two-room building was erected in the yard where patients who required isolation could be placed. I have mentioned that the laboratory provisions for chemical and microscopical examinations were ample. Most of this was accomplished within the short period of five years. But that was not all that was done. As the building had been thoroughly repaired and the grounds converted into a rather pretty garden.

It was inspiring to hear—on hospital celebration day—a visitor, one of the maids from Roper, say to her companion that though we did not have the things which Roper had, that we had a much "sweeter smell" and that our "beds were cleaner."

It was my delight to work for and with the hospital. To see it grow and prosper and to see the many indigent but always grateful ones benefited by its presence. And to have the pleasure of knowing and to have had a part in the training of, so many young women in the art of nursing. And later to see them embark upon a professional career and to make good at it. Even if these had been the sole activities of the hospital, they would have constituted a successful existence. But they were not. For in addition to that circumstances had made of it a community center where many community problems were handled. I have mentioned one—when the clothing factory fight at the Navy yard took place and how we had the women meet there for instructions. But there was another occasion, very early in its life. When an epidemic of typhoid fever invaded that section of Charleston south of Broad Street in the homes of the wealthy, its nurses went there, and by their skill saved many lives.

And its outdoor clinic service for the sick and for the syphilitic. Its well-baby clinic and the many women who received prenatal instructions there.

In times of crisis it responded to all demands—wars, storms and depression. Yes—depression. For when the hungry days came it participated in one of the P.W.A. projects and so relieved a number of sufferers. When the N.R.A.—the "blue eagle" of the "brain trust" sought to stabilize American life, the Negro group of Charleston gathered there, that they too could share in its benefits.

Both Seabrook and Thorne had passed into the great beyond—and I was tiring and feeling that the work should pass on to younger hands decided to retire—so I tendered my resignation to be effective at the end of 1942. More than forty years had passed since I first connected myself with the work. I had seen it grow from a feeble, impoverished thing into a strong and healthy, community-owned, non-profit sharing corporation whose entire assets were held for community service. All of which were free from debt on December 31, 1942 and consisted of plant and equipment valued at $22,000.00 and an operating fund of $3,7000.00, not counting the accrued free days of care given in 1942 for which the Duke Endowment would pay for later.

CHARLESTON NEGRO PUBLIC SCHOOLS

And now back to our public school, to pick up where I left off when I told that the Board of School Commissioners had finally agreed to the placement of Negro teachers in our Negro schools. And also a reminder that the agreement under which the change was made had only been reached after the Governor's "ultimatum," was issued. It was generally known that our insistence for the change had provoked some hostilities towards us. Which came not only from the Board but also from some others in the community. When the change was ordered I learned the Board had created a special salary scale for Negro teachers under which they would only pay Negroes about one-half of the pay which white teachers got for doing the same type of work. I knew that this combination of ill will and poor pay would not create an attractive atmosphere where the best prepared teachers would care to work. Also that it could become a force which could be used in a revengeful manner to penalize us for the fancied wrongs we were supposed to have committed when we insisted on having our schools manned by Negroes.

There was a probability that this could happen for we had absolutely no voice in weighing what qualifications should be required for our teachers. It was with a sense of trepidation that I awaited the Board's announcement which would tell us who our future principals and teachers would be. I was not surprised then, when I learned the names of the appointees to the principalships in our schools. For while they were all men of good repute, it yet could not be said that they possessed the required training necessary in efficient educators. For none of them did. There was Mr. W.S. Montgomery who was appointed to Simonton. Where he remained a short while and was succeeded by Rev. Felder. Neither of these men accomplished anything worthwhile during their incumbencies. With Rev. Jones, the principal at Burke, it was much the same. Mr. Berry the principal at Shaw was by far the most efficient of the original group of appointees, as he did good work there. I cannot overlook the splendid services which Mr. Wamsley, the Supervisor, contributed in seeking to overcome these handicaps. For handicaps they were and so evident were they, that I took occasion to speak about them at a meeting of the N.A.A.C.P. at which a large number of teachers were present and whom I made a special appeal, asking them to do all that was within their power to make our schools not merely successful ones but definitely outstanding ones. As it was largely upon them that the community relied for doing so. And not so much upon the directional ability or privilege of their principals. For much of this I believed was circumscribed. Some by regulations and some by a lack of experience. But that they the teachers through their efforts and the closer personal contact with pupils could do more to advance their educational progress than anyone else. And that they did. For whatever measure of success our schools attained in their first few years under Negro teachers is altogether due to the splendid services which its teachers gave.

For many years the physical condition of our Negro public schools had remained much the same. The only major improvement being the repairs made to the Simonton school. Which was done none too soon. For when the flooring in the "main rooms" were removed its floor joists had so shifted from their positions that less three inches thereof were resting on the center girder, with every possibility of falling and creating a catastrophe.

Neither had the accommodations for our children been increased although our population had. Our two elementary schools, Shaw and Simonton, still accommodated about 1,300 pupils, the same as they did in the 1870s. While the Burke School, the only addition since then, held room for 500 more. Making the total number of Negro children provided for about 1,800 out of a total number of about 4,000. Had it not been that Avery Institute, Wallingford Academy, St. Stephen's Mission, St. Peter's School and several other small private schools were then operating, our educational facilities would have been deplorable.

Against this set up could be seen what was provided for white children. Which consisted of the Craft, Bennett, Courtney and Mitchell elementary schools, the Memminger High School for girls and the quasi-public institutions, the Charleston High School and the College of Charleston, and the privately operated

Catholic schools—an altogether adequate accommodation for our 4,000 white school age children.

About two years after our new system was inaugurated, the city held an election to decide the issuance of $250,000.00 of school bonds, the proceeds from which was to be expended in making additional facilities for the school system. Newspaper accounts predicted that most of it would be spent on white schools, with no mention that any part of it would be expended on Negro schools.

I had recently seen how the Negroes in Atlanta had benefitted from a school bond issue there by solidly voting against the measure and thus defeating it when it was first voted on, and later when assured that if they voted for it, that they would get a modern high school building. Which they did at a subsequent election where the measure passed. That procedure appealed to me and caused me to get in touch with Robert Smith, who was then President of the Civic League, a Negro organization which sponsored a movement to encourage Negroes to register. His organization numbered over 700 Negro voters. Which made me believe that if I could get their cooperation, we could do a similar thing in Charleston as did the Negroes in Atlanta. Smith promised me that he would have his organization do that. But this they failed to do. As on the afternoon of the election he notified that none of his members had voted. I immediately got in touch with Dr. Thorne, Mr. T.E. Miller and Dr. Thompson and told them what had happened and urged them to go to the polls before they closed and vote for the measure. That I would do likewise. Also to get others to do the same. About seven of our group voted for the measure. The total number of votes cast in that election was under seven hundred. Of which number 107 opposed it. Had the Negroes voted and as they were asked to vote, the measure would have been defeated.

Within a few months after the election, the School Commissioners had contracted for $190,000.00 of repair and remodeling of white schools and made no mention of any such work on the Negro schools. When Mr. Miller, Dr. Thompson, Dr. Thorne and I addressed a joint letter to the School Commissioners in which we stated that we had learned from newspaper accounts that all but $60,000.00 from the bond issue had been expended on white schools and that we were uninformed if any provisions had been made for Negro schools. Also that the requirements of the compulsory education law made it mandatory that all children of school age attend school and that in the city of Charleston there then resided more than 2,000 Negro children, whose parents were amendable under the Act for their attendance at school. But who could not comply therewith because there were no facilities provided for them—and that we now wished to [know] what provisions, if any, have been made for Negro schools.

The following morning, I interviewed a white lawyer and asked what retainer would be required if we desired to engage his services to determine the validity of the Commissioner's acts should they expend the entire amount of the bond issue on white schools only. The inquiry went no further. For a few days later Mr. Miller was asked to create a committee to designate a site for a new Negro school. The only restriction being, that the selected site, be either east or west of King Street and south of the center of Calhoun Street.

The executive committee of the N.A.A.C.P. served as the committee. My suggestion was that the new school be placed in the Magazine Street area. Where a very large number of Negroes lived. But this was opposed by a majority on the grounds that the Jenkins School already provided for most of the children there, especially the smaller ones, while the area from Mary Street south to the Battery and east of King had no facilities whatever except what was given by St. Stephen's Mission. So we unanimously selected the site on Calhoun Street which is now occupied by the Buist School. In addition to this duty the committee was entrusted with the securing of option on the properties desired. Shortly thereafter the grounds were cleared and construction was begun on the Buist School. When it was finished it increased our accommodation for elementary pupils by 600.

The increase did much to relieve the pressure. Since it permitted many pupils to enter the public schools where the advantages and comforts were vastly superior to those found in some of the private schools.

But it also created another problem—that of maintaining an adequate supply of good teachers for the public schools. So far the majority of the teachers were graduates from Avery Institute. Some of them had finished the "teacher training course" but the majority were only graduates of its academic department. There were also some who had graduated from various colleges. And though they had the ability to pass the teachers entrance examination, they yet had but little specialized training for teaching. This made it imperative, of our public schools were ever to become effective forces for educating youth, that definite steps be undertaken whereby a constant supply of properly trained teachers would always be available.

Avery Institute had always been the main source from which our teachers came. As nearly ninety percent of the teachers in our city and county schools had graduated there. Its average annual number of graduates from the teacher-training school seldom exceeded four, which then, was entirely too few a number to meet the increasing demand for Negro teachers. Besides that, there was the effect from our low salary scale which made our teaching positions unattractive to college graduates in other areas. Both of which contributed towards the creating of a shortage in our local supply of well-trained teachers. All of which made it imperative for us to devise some new means by which we could increase our supply or face the alternative of having our schools suffer from a lack of good teachers.

I discussed the situation with Mr. Cox and asked him if it was feasible for Avery to undertake the task of providing us with more teachers each year than it formerly had. Mr. Cox said that he believed that Avery could do so but that it would require the services of two additional teachers for the training school department whose combined salaries would not be less than $2,000.00 annually. And if that could be guaranteed from some new source that the rest would be easy.

Believing that the School Board should be vitally interested in having its supply of Negro teachers increased, I interviewed one of its members, Mr. Moffett. To whom I explained my views about the situation and that we were interested and eager to extend the facilities at Avery so that it could relieve the situation. I told him that Avery could not do so except [if] it got financial assistance that would enable it to employ two additional teachers for the training school and which would amount to $2,000.00 annually. That if the Board would see fit to provide these salaries that we would undertake the training of not more than twenty graduates from Burke School each year from its current graduating class under scholarship awards.

Mr. Moffett said, "speaking for myself, I like the plan and think that it can be worked out" and that I should put it in the form of a proposal and when it was finished to bring it back for a final conference before presenting it to the Board.

My interview with Mr. Moffett brought to view a rather interesting side light on his conception of what was best for Negro education. As he expressed the belief that Charleston was doing more than any other Southern city for Negro education. For said he, "We have the finest school building of any Southern city for Negro pupils. For not where else in the South will you find such splendid brick building as we have." When I broached the question about the efficiency and capability of teachers and about an expanding curriculum he said, "All of that is left in the hands of the Superintendent."

We communicated with the American Missionary Association and got their concurrences. Mr. George White, its Assistant

Secretary, who had authority to act for the Association came to Charleston and accompanied me when I presented our proposal to Mr. Moffett. Mr. Moffett expressed satisfaction with what we offered and said that he would arrange for me to be present at the next meeting of the Board where I could present it in person. And where I would have every opportunity to answer questions if such was necessary. Mr. Moffett continued with telling us that he was in hearty accord with what Avery was doing but said he "you should know that a large number of white people here are opposed to the school because they believe that white and Colored teachers lived together in the Teachers' home." I told him that I was familiar with the situation at Avery for more than thirty years and that during that time, the only Colored person who resided in the teachers' home was Mrs. Cochran, the housekeeper who also did the cooking and cleaning. And that the Colored teachers lived elsewhere in the city.

I could have also told him that the reason why Avery then had a Negro principal and an all Negro faculty was because the principal who preceded Mr. Cox, a Mr. Stevens, had bluntly told Mr. Merton Lawrence, the Secretary of Avery Alumni Association, when that gentleman had called to discuss some alumni affairs with him, "Lawrence I can only speak with you on the street as I do not permit Negroes to enter my home." And that Mr. Lawrence immediately came to the drugstore and told me about it. But the incident did not stop there for in a few days a joint letter was sent to the American Missionary Association reciting the happening and requesting that Mr. Stevens be immediately recalled or that the school be closed. For we would rather have Avery closed than to have "Jim Crowism" in it. That summer the Association sent William Pickens, a recent graduate of Yale who had won some renown by winning the Ten Eyek prize that year, to inspect the plant and if he cared, to accept the principalship. Mr. Pickens declined the position. After which the Association sent us Mr. Cox, from the school at Albany, Georgia.

But I refrained from telling Mr. Moffett any of it. For it was something that I never cared to talk about.

Mr. White, however, took an entirely different view of Mr. Moffett's comment and immediately started an argument as to the propriety of believing that Negroes should not live in the same home with whites. And so what may have been a very pleasant conversation soon got to be a rough one—when "social morality [?]" became involved in it. But the joke in the matter was that Mr. Moffett did not know that Mr. White was a Negro. But believing him to be a white man sought to inject in him the "pride of race"—that of the white race. At this point I managed to get in a word, by asking when would the next meeting of the Board be held. And when this was answered, we left. Mr. Cox was with me when I went before the Board. It was my first appearance at a meeting of the City Board of School Commissioners and I was somewhat dubious as to the manner of the reception which would be accorded me. Mr. Rutledge Rivers, the Chairman of the Board presented me and told me that I had the privilege of the floor. I opened by, that my presence was for the purpose of submitting a proposal to the Board, the intent of which was to assist the Board in its operation of Negro schools by providing them with a more adequate supply of competently trained teachers than what our community then could. For we believed that except this could be done that the Board might find it increasingly more difficult each year to man our schools with capable well-trained teachers. I emphasized that Avery Institute had been the source from which came the majority of Negro teachers. Both those employed in the city schools as well as those employed in our county schools. And that it was my belief that these teachers had given satisfactory service. And further, since this had not been contradicted, it made us believe that the training given in the "teacher training" department was altogether satisfactory to the Board.

Unfortunately said I, the annual output of teachers from Avery Institute only averages four a year. Which is altogether too few a number to meet the demands from both our city and county schools. Moreover we seriously doubt whether experienced teachers from other areas would come to Charleston to teach or if they did might they not be merely transients who would leave at the earliest opportunity. These conditions, I said, create a problem which Avery Institute can help to solve, by increasing its output of teachers, and thereby providing its community with an adequate supply of teachers whose homes are in Charleston. Avery Institute desires to increase its output of teachers so that the difficulty may be removed but is unable to do so because it lacks the funds to do it with. As any effort to enlarge its teacher training school beyond its present size would require the addition of two teachers to its present faculty, whose combined salaries, would be not less than $2,000.00 annually, and which is beyond Avery's ability to pay.

But said I, should the School Board agree to underwrite these salaries Avery would agree to enlarge its training school and to award graduates of Burke School, in any number not exceeding twenty each year, free scholarships for the entire course. While I was speaking I could discern from the faces of some, that my proposal was agreeable to them. Especially so to Rabbi Raisin, who had interrupted me with several question, and who from his attitude appeared to be very enthusiastic over my proposal. However, Mr. Rivers soon put an end to all of it. For when I had finished, he announced that a teacher training course would be inaugurated at Burke School that coming September. I was astounded at the turn which the matter had taken. But perhaps no more so than several of the members of the Board. For by their facial expressions it became evident that this was their first knowledge of the establishment of a teacher training department at Burke.

Of course Mr. River's announcement put an end to our proposal. But it also did something else and that was to elevate the curriculum at Burke. Which in itself was something to welcome.

That summer the Board sent Mrs. Ethel Hoffman to Columbia University for a three months' course in education. And on her return to Charleston placed her in charge of the newly established "teacher training course" at Burke. I am sure that Mrs. Hoffman did all that was humanly possible for one individual to do to make eighth grade pupils, competent and efficient teachers in two additional years of study. Unfortunately she could not perform miracles. But despite that the product of her department were given the preference over other teachers when they applied for position, irrespective of their qualifications for teaching. A few of them made good but the majority were like boomerangs which failing to hit the mark quickly return to whence they came from. This experience impelled the Board to again give preference to Avery graduates.

With the exception of the "teacher training course" but little more was done to elevate the standards at Burke during the years in which Rev. Jones and his successor, Mr. David Hill held the principalship. Supposedly a high school, it was in reality a sub-standard junior high school. With classes ranging from the seventh grade through the tenth. It was devoid of any laboratory facilities for the study of sciences. Neither did it possess a library. It had been "labeled" an industrial school when it was first opened, where boys and girls would be taught useful trades. It had a carpenter shop where its head used most of his time making repairs to furniture and such like things for other school attaches. It also had a bricklaying department of which little was heard of. The domestic science department, for girls, consisted largely of a laundry, where the clothing of white teachers (this was before the change in teachers was made) were washed by the pupils—without charge of course. With the change in teaching corps, pupils were permitted to bring their own clothing for laundering. Beyond this the condition there remained much the same as it was in the time prior to when these two principals held office.

Conditions somewhat similar to these then prevailed in the Negro schools in District 4, the North Charleston area and its extension in Ladson and Lincolnville. So bad were they that Rev. Steward Anderson who pastored a Baptist church near Grant's Park sought my assistance to remedy the situation at the Four Mile School where a large number of children of his members attended. The school, he said was a small four-room one, in which more than four hundred children were crowded. It had no sanitary toilet facilities nor did it have ample playground facilities. Its drinking water came from an outdoor well where a single tin dipper was used in common by all. I learned from him that Mr. Mappus, a German grocer who kept his store nearby the school, was a member of the state legislature and that the majority of his members bought their supply of food from him. He also told me that he had organized a Parent-Teacher Association at the school and that that was as far as he had gotten.

I prepared a petition in which I set forth the improvements wanted, one of these an auditorium, I camouflaged by styling it an "assembly hall," for the very good reason, that a nearby white school did not have an auditorium, as I knew it would be inadvisable to ask for something which the white school did not have. I directed Rev. Anderson to have every member of his Parent-Teacher Association sign it and to get as many others as they could to do likewise. And when the signatures were complete, to have several of Mr. Mappus' best Negro customers take it to him and tell him that we are the people who have been dealing with you from the time you first started in business here and that we want you to in [illegible] in the county supply bill an appropriation for our school.

The county delegation appropriated $14,000 for that school. By which its size was increased, an "assembly hall" added,

modern plumbing fixtures installed, hygienic drinking foun-
tains placed and an automatic oil burning steam heating plant
installed. It had ample accommodations for six hundred children but even better than that was here it was formerly a "four
teacher" school, it emerged from its remodeling, a first class elementary school, with a principal and six teachers, a well-orga-
nized and active Parent-Teachers Association and a center for
community activity. At that time very few of our county schools
went beyond the seventh grade. The Liberty Hill School and the
Four Mile School were exceptions for these went through the
eighth grade. The whites however fared much better as they
were supplied with several modern high schools. Located at
North Charleston, St. Andrews Parish, Meggett's and Mt. Pleasant. With additional arrangements under which pupils from
other areas were transported by bus into Charleston for attendance at Memminger High School and at the Charleston High
School.

It was difficult to determine if this marked disparity between
the facilities provided for Negroes and that which was provided
for whites was altogether due to a fixed policy on the part of the
county officials or whether it was in part due to the absence of
any requests from the Negroes for improvement in their schools.
What had been done for the Four Mile School inclined me to the
belief that much more could be gotten had the Negroes asked
for it. Dr. A.G. Purvis, Mr. Thad Sasportas and I discussed this
matter and decided that we would try to do something to remedy the situation. We realized that it would be futile to attempt it
by making a public outcry against "discrimination" or unfairness
but that it would be best to seek cooperation of those who held
key positions in the public school system and thus be able to
work from within. We did not seek to diminish in anyway whatever what was being done for white schools but only to have
more done for Negro schools than what was formerly done.

Our first effort was through a conference with Mr. Garrett who was principal at the North Charleston High School and who also served as Superintendent of District 4, the North Charleston district. In which we told him that we were seeking his cooperation and assistance in improving the standards of the Negro schools in his district. He agreed with us in that the standards were much lower in Negro schools than in the white schools but that he was trying to improve them. And not only that but also to have the schools become a definite factor for improving the living conditions of his pupils so that it could be reflected in their homes. He told us that he was then seeking to get some sewing machines for the girls and wood-working tools for the boys, these to be installed in Negro schools, that the children could be taught some useful handicrafts. Not only for the purpose of having them become more manually dexterous but also because he believed that these things would stimulate their interests in school activities. He promised us that he would do all that was within his power to do, to improve these conditions and suggested that we confer with Mr. Strohecker who was a member of the County Board of Education and seek to enlist his services. As he knew that Mr. Strohecker was keenly interested in the improvement of all of the county schools. Mr. Garrett appeared to be quite enthused over our visit. But on parting he said to us, "I want you to do something for us. Recently we spent a good bit of money on the Four Mile School. But Negro vandals have been entering the building at night, gambling and committing nuisances there. Also destroying fixtures. We have tried to have the police stop it but they can't catch them. Won't you try to break it up?" I promised that I would. A few days later I got in touch with the chief crap shooter and told him that I wanted him to do me a favor. Which was this—to keep the fellows from gambling in the Four Mile School. "For," I said, "you know it is the best school we have where your sisters and brothers can go. I know that you have more influence with the fellows than anyone else. So won't you see that they go somewhere else to gamble and don't let them break into the school again? So I am going to depend on you to stop it." And he did. Shortly thereafter we held a conference with Mr. Strohecker at his office in the Charleston High School. Where he served as principal. We told Mr. Strohecker of our visit on Mr. Garrett and of the things we had asked for and that we were seeking his assistance for getting them. He replied that he also was interested in having Negro schools improved but that the authority for doing so as well as the funds with which to do it could only come through the County Board of Education, of which he was a member. "But," said he, "I will arrange for you to meet with the Board where you can make your presentation."

A few days later we met with the County Board in the office of Superintendent McCauley, in the Fireproof Building. Maier Triest and another member of the Charleston county delegation were present. Again did we present our plea for a more extended course of study in the county schools for Negroes than what existed. I urged that if it could all not be done at once that at least a beginning in that direction be made so that the many Negro boys and girls whose sole dependence for an education was upon public funds could benefit at least a little more than they then did.

We left the meeting with the assurance that the Board would do what it could to improve the Negro schools. And that they would do so as soon as possible. But to be perfectly frank in the matter I doubted just how much it could do. As I knew that the South Carolina system of school operation, in which its schools are distributed into the districts, each of which is controlled by a local board of trustees whose whims and prejudices usually dictated the management of our schools, and that this had to be taken into consideration.

Also that it was these local trustees who elected our teachers, fixed their compensation, prescribed the duration of the school term, kept the schoolhouse in repair or in the event it was uninhabitable, instead of repairing it, could rent a church or hall building for school use. In addition they were the ones who provided the schools with all of their supplies. Which in some instances allowed room for self benefit, as it did in the case I heard of, and that was when the trustee for a Negro school sent an opening supply of brooms, water pails and stove pipes and a week later sent that same school a duplication of the first delivery. On which the teachers sought to keep both deliveries but was told by the man who delivered it, "You can't do that because the trustee say I must get the one I left last week and take them to his house." And though it was petty, it yet depicts more clearly than words can tell, the type of authority which controls many of our Negro rural schools.

Fortunately for us, this does not apply to all of the schools in Charleston County. For in some of them their trustees are enthusiastic over their duties and seek to make their Negro schools as efficient as they can. This is noticeably so on Mt. Pleasant where the county school has been merged with the Lang [Laing] School—a Quaker charity, with headquarters in Philadelphia. And where I had an opportunity to observe the wholehearted and diligent concern which Mr. Moultrie Moore, one of its local trustees, displayed in its management and for the higher education of its pupils. Much of which prepared the way and was the early "spade work" for its new school plan—an $85,000.00 high school now under construction, largely through federal grant.

Much the same can be said for District No. 4—and where I believe our visit to Mr. Garrett has borne good fruit. For it is in that district that our Negro schools have been improved most. For there is now there, one junior high school for the district and seven nicely equipped elementary schools, three of which are new buildings. One of them being an eighteen-room school with a capacity exceeding that of all of the schools in the district when I drew up the petition for Rev. Steward Anderson.

But even more gratifying than the physical improvement has been that which has come through the broadening influences which these schools have created through their well organized and coordinated Parent-Teachers Association and which is now so clearly seen in greater interest which the Negro community manifest in their schools.

The rapid development in that district has made it necessary to employ a full-time Negro supervisor for Negro schools, and I am happy to say, that Mr. James Bonds, who fills the position is doing a splendid work, and is now not nearly so fearful of the might of authority, as he appeared to be when we had him with us before Mr. Garrett that he could tell of some of the things the old Four Mile School needed.

We did not restrict our activities to the county schools. For the three of us, Dr. Purvis,[14] Mr. Sasportas[15] and I also planned to make a similar appeal to the City Board of School Commissioners. But which would have as its main objective the extension of the Burke curriculum to that of a fully accredited high school.

We had written the Board that we would seek a hearing at its coming meeting. Dr. Purvis and Mr. Sasportas had agreed to meet me at the corner of Wentworth and St. Philip Streets five minutes to eight on the night of the meeting and that we would go as [a] body to the Board room. Neither of them appeared at the place of meeting at the appointed time. So I went in alone and was met by Mr. Rhett who told me that my letter had been received and had been delivered over to the Board. I thanked him for that information and asked to let the Board know that I was there. When the Board had finished with its routine business, I was called in and was told by Mr. Rivers that I could tell them what I wanted to say.

---

14 Augustus G. Purvis

15 Thaddeus Sasportas

I told the Commissioners that I was there in the interest of the many Negro children whose parents could not afford to pay tuitions at private schools where their children could receive high-school training and since the Burke School was the only school available to them, that the curriculum there be so extended that they could derive that benefit. I continued by saying that in my opinion, education beyond the elementary level made better citizens and more efficient workers, than it did when it was held at the elementary level. To illustrate which I said, the boy who is a brick mason and knows the chemistry of mortars and cements is by far a better mason than one who does not. The same parallel is true for the painter or for the girl who cooks or launders—for if she knows the chemistry involved in cooking or that involved in the use of soaps and washing powders that she could more efficiently perform her work as she was putting intelligence into it. I also told that they were many among the underprivileged of my race who had the potential quality for higher training and for usefulness in the professions and that those children should not be barred from attaining their full possibilities merely because their parents were unable to provide them with what other boys and girls in the community got. I urged that if these things could not be done all at once, that at least a beginning in that direction be made so that something could be done on behalf of the many Negro boys and girls whose sole dependence for education was their reliance on public sources.

I do not know if my appearance there accomplished any good purpose or not. Certainly I saw no immediate improvement at Burke. Whether it was that I was still persona non grata with the Board—because of my earlier participation in the movement to replace white teachers with Negroes and my other clash with the high school—I cannot say. I only know that the atmosphere in the Commissioner's board room was not quite as congenial as I had found it in our other conferences. However that mattered but little. Since the fight for better school for Negroes had to go on.

It was about this time that the Board appointed a newcomer to our community to the principalship at Simonton School, in place of Rev. Felder who had died.[16] He was Rev. Samuel R. Higgins.[17] Rev. Higgins was a graduate of Howard University, an M.A. from Columbia University and a graduate of Union Theological Seminary. He was a gentleman in every sense of the word. He possessed ability, intelligence and best of all, a mind of his own. His selection was in so marked a contrast when compared with the qualifications his predecessors had that it may well be termed the beginning of a new era in the history of our public schools. As it initiated the policy of using only well-prepared college trained men in the position of principals. For prior to Mr. Higgins entrance these positions had been filled by men of comparatively meager training and whose chief assets appeared to be a willingness to be subservient to the Board in all matters, irrespective of the right or wrong thereof.

Perhaps it may be, that this change of policy was induced by Mr. Higgins' quiet personality, his keen sense of propriety in all things and his insistence upon doing only what was right. But of even greater moment than this was his success in quickly coordinating his teachers into a cooperating, zealous working group through which the standards in Simonton were raised. And in addition through its extra curricula activities to become, what all schools should be, a force for good in the community.

When he tendered the principalship at Burke a few years later, he came to me and told me that he did not want to leave Simonton, even though it meant a promotion and an increase in salary, because, said he, "I have now got my school to where it is working splendidly and I don't want to leave it." I persuaded him

---

16 Maybe William M. Felder.

17 Samuel R. Higgins, Bishop of A.M.E. Church and President of Allen University.

to do so. "For there," I told him, "you will find opportunity to do an even bigger job, than you have done at Simonton."

Mr. Higgins went to Burke where he found a giant task awaiting him. He tackled that job with the same good judgement he had used at Simonton and quickly got his teachers organized into an efficient, harmonious group. Many an hour did we spend together in the back room at the drugstore planning how best the curriculum at the school could be improved. And when that was satisfactorily arranged, he would present it to the Superintendent and urge that he be allowed to institute it. And which was usually granted. In this way he quietly but persistently went forward in making the school a high school, though not as then, a fully accredited one. He favored all forms of extracurricular activities, especially athletics. Although he had given a surety bond to the School Board for the proper handling of monies collected from these activities, and so was personally responsible for it. He nevertheless allowed his teachers to assume full control of these funds and to advise how they should be expended. And so by placing explicit confidence in his teachers, he in turn received their full support and fealty.

His football team soon became the outstanding high school team in the entire state but yet, up to that time it had never played against the Avery team. And this was because there was a general feeling in the community that if such a game was played it might cause trouble. To clearly understand just why trouble could start, it is necessary to recall the age- old feeling of ill will which existed between the pupils at Avery and those in the public schools. In which a fancied superiority attached itself to the pupils at Avery much to the chagrin of those in the public schools. And which was almost certain to produce a near riot whenever groups from these schools met. The superiority idea had no foundation in fact. For as a matter of fact the majority of Avery's students were former Burke pupils. And who by merely enrolling at Avery became vested with that "quality."

But it caused us concern. For except it could be destroyed and totally eliminated from the minds of pupils it would remain, a complex capable of impairing the prestige of Burke.

Mr. Higgins and I talked over the matter and came to the conclusion that having the teams play against each other perhaps would do much to extinguish the feeling and to create in its place one of goodwill. So far as the pupils were concerned, we knew that order could be maintained. But the greater problem was how to control the attendance, especially the Burke fans, whose numbers would be largely augmented by the worst of our hoodlum group.

The game was played. Burke won by a margin of one point, which made the day not quite the nightmare it might have been. For in spite of extra police protection there was much disorder from the hoodlums who had gathered to cheer Burke on. Other than this the game was in every respect similar to any other interscholastic game. And more, for when it was over Burke had lost its "inferiority" complex and in its place it had acquired a new quality of consciousness, with which its standards could never have been definitely raised.

When Mr. Higgins tendered his resignation to accept the presidency at Allen University, our community lost the services of the most capable and constructive worker in our school system. For it was he, more than anyone else, who had persistently and courageously labored that our schools could become worthwhile schools.

I must now recount an incident which happened when Mr. Higgins was transferred from Simonton to Burke—and was the occasion when Mr. Wamsley, the Supervisor for Negro schools, called on me and said that the Board had instructed him to call on me, to get my recommendation as to which of three men, whose names were brought me, would be best suited for the principalship at Simonton. I could not refrain from smiling or to tell Mr. Wamsley, that his mission surprised me, as for many years I had been made to feel that I was persona non grata to the Board. But that I was now glad to learn that it was not so and that I would do my best to acquaint the Board with whatever knowledge I had about the applicants. As I read the list of names, I could see that they were all of them young college graduates, from good schools and in my opinion capable of carrying on as Higgins had.

And more than that, for it revealed to me that the Board was intent on getting the very best man it could find and perhaps one who could do things as Higgins had. From the three, I recommended J. Andrew Simmons for the position and I did not live to regret it. For he was one of the best principals our system had had. Mr. Simmons did not remain very long. As he and the Board had a difference in opinions over the propriety of a school principal giving political admonition. So he tendered his resignation rather than to accept the restrictions which the Board placed upon its employees. Several years later, Mr. Wamsley while speaking with me said "I was very sorry to lose Simmons for he was one of the best men we ever had."

William H. Grayson succeeded Mr. Simmons at Simonton. During his administration the attendance reached its highest peak. In truth all of our schools were overcrowded. The old Shaw School had been closed and a new school, the Archer, had been substituted in its place. And even though it had been enlarged under a federal grant, it yet could not accommodate the number who applied for entrance.

Portable school rooms had been placed in the Simonton schoolyard. But even this did not help. As a means of last resort, the Board secured the use of Salem Church on Smith Street near Morris where it placed several classes. There were no toilet accommodations there for the children so it became necessary for them to run the distance of nearly a block to reach the toilets in the Simonton School. In addition to this the church building was poorly heated. Its benches though suitable for adults were altogether uncomfortable ones for small children. Imagine then what the condition was when these discomforts were only added ones to the confusion produced by having several different classes meet in a single room.

The conditions at Simonton were bad and Grayson knew them better than anyone else. Whether he had ever made an official report to the Board on the matter or had refrained from doing so, I do not know. Neither do I know who was responsible for suggesting the use of the Salem Church building for pupils, and if when the building was so used and the discomforts it caused the children became known, were these made known to the Board. I knew that these discomforts existed there for I could see much of it from the windows of my drugstore.

One night Mr. Grayson invited several of us to meet with him at the school, that he could tell us about the conditions which existed there and have us seek some method through which they could be corrected. About ten of us met with him and listened while he told us of the congestion in the school. For said he, "I think you should know it."

We discussed the matter and arrived at the conclusion that there was but one thing to do. And that was to request the Board to provide us with another school building. A committee was named and delegated with that purpose. I had my doubts if that request would be granted, as I knew that there then existed a definite attitude against it. Which had been crystallized at the dedication of the Archer School when Rev. Mills, the pastor at Central Baptist Church, while making the opening invocation, had used that opportunity to refute that the school had been provided by the Charleston County Delegation to the General Assembly, but was altogether through the beneficence of Franklin Delano Roosevelt, with the members of the Delegation standing by and listening to him. And then to hear Representative Zerbst, who evidently had been provoked by the tenor of his prayer, announce that this, the Archer building, would be the last school building they would ever provide for Negroes and not to ask for more.

Which in itself carried the weight of authority as all funds required for the construction of new school buildings could only be obtained from and through the County delegation, however much the school Board may desire it. Whether the School Board could and would exercise sufficient power to overcome that attitude was the question—the answer to which, if favorable could bring us relief, but if it was not so, then would have sufficient force to further repress our schools.

I cannot avoid commenting upon Rev. Mill's action at the dedication exercises at Archer School, for it was both inadvisable and devoid of truth. True it is that the addition made to the school was in part defrayed by a federal grant. But since it was necessary to largely supplement that grant with public funds which came only from and through the County delegation, with what may be added was the most enthusiastic gesture towards Negroes that I have ever witnessed, there can be no question as to who provided us with Archer School.

Neither can I avoid a further comment—and that is, that it was only the propriety associated with the sanctity of prayer which withheld a challenge against the full truthfulness of what Rev. Mill's expressed to God. I sought to correct the impression which Rev. Mill's prayer conveyed by speaking personally with the members of the delegation and by telling them that we knew that it was altogether through their interest and action that we got the school. I doubt if I was able to convince all of them with the sincerity of my statement. Or myself, if I could ever again enlist their wholehearted support for our schools. Much of which goes to show how easy it is for one, and especially one who has but passing interest in a community, to do much harm. And which were the things which cause me to seriously doubt if our request for a new school building would be granted.

I was the spokesman who went before the Board to present the appeal for a new building. I found its personnel had had several changes since my previous appearance before it. As Miss McBee, the head of Ashley Hall, Dr. John F. Seignious and Mr. Lee Rodgers had recently been elected Commissioners. Mr. Rutledge Rivers introduced me to the Board and in doing so mentioned the appreciation he held for me because of my very "splendid cooperation" in the development of the Charleston High School.

I began my presentation by describing the overcrowded condition at the Simonton School and of the use of the Salem Church building, with the attendant danger of injury to children there, who were compelled to cross the street to reach the lavatories in the schoolyard and also the other inconveniences they suffered there and asked the board to provide sufficient addition[al] facilities so that the overcrowding in Negro schools could be corrected. I said that it was imperative that something be done at once and asked that for the purpose of giving immediate relief that the Shaw School building be put into use as it could accommodate at least 400 pupils. Mr. Rivers interrupted me at this point by saying that "under no conditions" would he allow the old Shaw School building to be used as it was a fire trap and that he would not expose any child to that risk. Dr. Seignious took the occasion to inject a comment—"why don't your people practice birth control?" I paid no attention to the latter remark but in continuing my presentation, expressed appreciation for Mr. Rivers' consideration of the danger from fire and the necessity to safeguard children from it. But said I there was an equally dangerous threat which must be considered in an overcrowed building and that threat was the danger from stampede.

For said I, I had witnessed a stampede at the Simonton School many years before and saw many children injured in it. Mr. Rivers again interrupted by asking when that happened and which I replied to by recounting what had happened while I was a pupil there when a Fiji Islander visited there. Then Mr. Rivers wanted to know had I attended Simonton School and when I said that I had and that that was one of the reasons for my interest in the school, a stillness settled over the meeting. I quickly closed for I knew that I had said enough. Mr. Rivers broke the stillness by announcing that he would appoint a committee to visit the Simonton School the following morning to investigate the conditions there and to report back to the Board at once. Mr. Johnson was named as Chairman of that committee.

The Committee visited the school the next morning and went over the situation with Principal Grayson. Perhaps had Mr. Grayson restricted himself to the conditions in his school we would have had another Negro public school in Charleston. But instead of doing that he recommended that a double daily session be inaugurate and that he could carry it on if additional teachers were provided.

I shall always believe that had the issue taken place within a white school that its solution would only have been made by providing an additional school building. But since the issue involved only a Negro school—with its correction prescribed by a Negro, and at so small a cost, an increase in the principal's salary and a few additional teachers, the Committee recommended that. As it would avoid them the necessity of going to the County delegation for funds for a Negro school and only to seek instead a slightly larger operating allowance. Which was no large amount—for the Judas Iscariots are never overpaid.

I realized that it would be futile to oppose the adoption of the double daily session at Simonton School. As I well knew how few of our group would join with me in taking a definite stand against it. For while some would join there were the many who would not. But who would sit idly by waiting for someone else to do for them what they were not willing to do for themselves. And also that in that number were the many who believed that whatever white authority decreed, that that alone made it right.

As I had anticipated, the double daily session brought hardship as well as problems to parents and pupils. And which as subsequently seen, ran the gamut from filthy classrooms down to shortened hours of daily instruction. I shall speak only of the latter. For it is in that that the greatest injustice was done to our children. Before the inauguration of the double daily session these children were given five hours of instruction each day. But with the inauguration of the new system these hours were reduced to from four to four-and-a-half hours of instruction each day. Which during a school year amounted to a loss of [a] month of instruction for each pupil.

The rank and file of the children who were subjected to these impositions came from the lower walks of life and from homes where parents could give but very little assistance to them in getting their "homework" done. And it was these who suffered most by the change. For they were the ones whose hour of supervised study had been taken away from.

And there were also the social problems which followed—which came to homes where mothers went to work as domestic servants and who when their children attended morning sessions feared more consequence but who when their children were placed in afternoon sessions were compelled to leave them alone during the morning hours, to their own resources which often resulted in delinquency.

Much more could be told about the ill effects which followed the inauguration of the double daily session at Simonton. But that would be largely but a waste of time as its consequences are too commonly known. Suffice it to say that its standards had fallen far below what they were when Higgins was its principal.

[Editor's note: End of Known Manuscript]

TIMELINE

JANUARY 1, 1863
Emancipation Proclamation signed.

APRIL 9, 1865
Robert E. Lee surrenders at Appomattox Court House.

APRIL 1877
Troops withdrawn from S.C. Reconstruction ends.

OCTOBER 8, 1878
John Allen born to Thomas and Mary Ann Hargrove McFall.

AUGUST 27, 1886
Magnitude 7.6 earthquake hits Charleston.

MARCH 5, 1888
John goes with father to hear Frederick Douglass speak.

AUGUST 26, 1893
Hurricane death toll nears 2000 in Charleston vicinity.

MAY 1896
The U.S. Supreme Court decides *Plessy v. Ferguson* legalizing "separate but equal."

APRIL 1899
John graduates with honors from the Philadelphia College of Pharmacy; a few months later he opens a pharmacy at corner of Smith and Morris Streets.

DECEMBER 1, 1901–JUNE 1, 1902
South Carolina Inter-State and West Indian Exposition opens. John is a member of the entertainment committee.

JANUARY 18, 1902
John marries Josephine Carr.

WINTER 1902
John becomes friends with poet Paul Laurence Dunbar.
John purchases first home at 70 Bogard Street.
John mediates labor troubles of building tradesmen.

1905

Separate seating installed at baseball park and auditorium. Efforts to increase voters' registration of Negroes.

BY 1907

John teaches Materia Medica and Therapeutics at Hospital and Training School for Nurses as well as serves as its financial Secretary-Treasurer.

SPRING 1907

Richard T. Greener gives his analysis of propagandizing white supremacy.

FEBRUARY 27, 1914

John purchases store property at Smith and Morris Streets.

1918

John presides at meeting to support Food Conservation and Liberty bonds; he prepares a petition and pressures for hiring Negro women at the Navy yard. Influenza Pandemic reaches Charleston.

1919

John drives a petition to allow Black teachers to teach in the city of Charleston.

1920

John charters and manages the Charleston Mutual Savings Bank until 1942.

1922

John petitions the S.C. state legislature against confiscating his home at 150 Ashley Avenue.

1925

John drives the incorporation of Avery Institute for training Negro teachers.

1942

John resigns from Board of the Colored Hospital and Nurses Training School.

JULY 23, 1954

Death of John Allen McFall. *Brown v. Board of Education* Supreme Court decision May 17, 1954.

ACKNOWLEDGEMENTS

The story of how I discovered this manuscript is for another place and time. Publishing this manuscript became more than a notion.

Thank you—

Dr. Edmund Drago of the College Charleston, who told me that "John McFall deserves a book."

John McFall's wife, Josephine Carr, and sister, Thomasina Alston McFall, who gave him the time to write one.

Edith Work, who took possession of her father's manuscripts.

Dr. Jessie Carney Smith of Fisk University, who recognized their value and preserved them.

Lynn Navarra, for the right to publish.

Family, friends, and colleagues whose ears I bent as I made this journey—which I could not have made at all without the patience and nourishment provided by my spouse, Alvertis Hollister.

And of course, to my granduncle John, for writing his own book. You were indeed a scholar and a storyteller.

Lahnice McFall Hollister
Kittawah Press

INDEX

Voice of the Negro, The (publication) 175

wages
labor conflicts and scale of
139–141, 156, 224, 226–227
of author 63, 64, 79, 91, 100
of Mason and Hanger workers
227
Wagner, F. W. 122, 127
Wainwright, Robert 69, 119, 142
Walker, Jackie 14
Wallingford Academy 315
Wallingford Church 19
Warrick, Dr. 95, 98
Warrick, Meta Vaux 98
war stamps 220
water 50
Welch and Eason Grocery Co. 16
welfare services 169–175
Wesley Church 19
Weston, Kate 120
Weston, Tony 183
Wheeler, Jack 125, 131
Wheeler, Joe 109
Whilden, Dan 141, 155
Whipper, Mr. 75, 76
White, Dr. 96
White, George 301, 319
White, Walter 274–275, 282
Wigg, Emily and William 36
Wigg, James E. 75–76
Williams, Bruce 75
Williams, Mr. 182–184
Wilson, Harvey G. 267
Wilson, Mae 98
Wilson, Woodrow 205
Wister, Owen 196
Wood, Leonard 235
Woodward, Sidney 129
Work, Edith McFall 161, 181, 257,
258
World War I 185, 195–201
W.T. Thompson & Co. 259

Y.M.C.A. 169, 198
Young, Charles B. 110
Y.W.C.A. 169

CPSIA information can be obtained
at www.ICGtesting.com
Printed in the USA
BVHW041829121121
621519BV00012B/511

9 781737 681311